The Pursuit

of

Awesome

Stellar Musings & Advice on Achieving Your Dreams

Diana Bunici

LIB
ERT
IES

For the ones who make my world sparkle, Mama, Tata & Daniel.

The Pursuit

of

Awesome

First published in 2016 by
Liberties Press
140 Terenure Road North | Terenure | Dublin 6W
T: +353 (1) 405 5701 | W: libertiespress.com | E: info@libertiespress.com

Trade enquiries to Gill
Hume Avenue | Park West | Dublin 12
T: +353 (1) 500 9534 | F: +353 (1) 500 9595 | E: sales@gillmacmillan.ie

Distributed in the United Kingdom by
Turnaround Publisher Services
Unit 3 | Olympia Trading Estate | Coburg Road | London N22 6TZ
T: +44 (0) 20 8829 3000 | E: orders@turnaround-uk.com

Distributed in the United States by
Casemate-IPM | 1950 Lawrence Road | Havertown, PA 19083
T: +1 (610) 853-9131 | E: casemate@casematepublishers.com

ISBN: 978-1-910742-31-0
2 4 6 8 10 9 7 5 3 1

A CIP record for this title is available from the British Library.

Cover design by Liberties Press
Internal design by Liberties Press

Table of Contents

Foreword

Introduction

In Print

On the Box

On Air

On the Silver Screen

On Line

Foreword

I heard about *The Pursuit of Awesome* when I was in the studio working with Kodaline. It sounded like a great idea to me and I was honoured that Diana asked me to write something for it. What it means to you does not belong to me. It is yours to ignore, to engage with, to feel, to laugh at, to get irritated by or to interpret as you will. And so it is, as it finds you, it is yours. That's awesome.

Songwriting is a craft, it is an art, it is a way of life. There is a big difference between self-expression and creativity. Screaming is self-expression. Coughing to attract attention is self-expression. Clapping your hands is self-expression. It has its place and there is a component of it in songwriting for sure.

What do you want to say? Why do you want to say it? Will you say it? How honest will you be? Are you willing to go to a vulnerable place and visit the corners of yourself that most people hide from? These are some of the questions I ask when I work with an artist to write a song.

Then there is creativity. If the destination is the thing you want to say, then the creative part is the path you beat to get there. A songwriter is doing something immeasurable. They are making meaning out of life experience. I don't believe that art is made to be understood. It is there to be felt, to be experienced. When we analyse it and run a tape-measure along the edges of it in the hope of devising a formula, we are missing the point.

Meaning comes from the recipient's own experience of receiving whatever the creator puts into the world. The 'stuff' of songs is born from the desire to say something, the chance to say it and a way to say it. Like all art, this is not static. It doesn't end once it is 'finished'. It is experienced anew every time, it is in flux, it is alive.

Coupled with the cultural backdrop that frames where and when we encounter a song, a poem, a picture, it is a living, breathing, evolving entity. Understanding is what we get from mathematics. Meaning is what we get from art.

The fashionable wave of our 'reach for the stars', self-help culture has perhaps done some good. People should believe in themselves. What else is there to believe in? We are all we've got. But the idea that anyone can be anything if they try hard enough feels like a distortion of a good idea to me. I am far more interested in exploring limitations and uncomfortable places.

Our desire to reach for the stars, the arc of where we've been and the struggle and beauty we experience on the way, whether we get there or not, feels infinitely more important than just 'getting there' or 'making it'. When we acknowledge our limitations, we know where we stand and we can decide where we want to go.

If we bathe in delusional grandeur and think we've already arrived, why would we care to go on a journey? For me, the journey is what it is all about.

Johnny McDaid, Snow Patrol

It is about ... the JOURNEY

Introduction

I remember it like it was yesterday. That moment of sheer panic; heart-beat quickening, head spinning, brain about to explode trying to process what had just happened. It's rare that I accost people at industry events but when I spotted Paul Costelloe at a London-Fashion-Week do, I just had to go over and say hello, and I had to have him in my book.

As far as first encounters go, it went beautifully. In a smooth uninterrupted monologue, I introduced myself, told him about me and The Pursuit of Awesome, *bigged up our Irish connection and invited him out for a coffee, if he so pleased. Paul listened intently, nodding appropriately, expressing delight and showing interest. When I finally stopped speaking, he broke out into a huge grin, accepting my offer.*

'I'd love to join you for a coffee, but why you'd want me in your book is another question,' he mused.

'Well because you're Paul Costelloe. You're a phenomenal fashion designer, you've just showcased at Fashion Week, you're an excellent ambassador for Ireland and it would be an honour,' I quipped.

Paul gave a hearty laugh, eyes twinkling.

'Darling, my name might be Paul but I'm certainly not a fashion designer, I'm a Swiss banker. I'm here for a few days on business. I wish I was the man you're looking for but I'm afraid it's a case of mistaken identity, although I am hugely flattered.'

I was stumped. What are the chances I'd meet Paul Costelloe's doppelgänger, also called Paul, at a fashion event in London where the real Paul resides and had just showcased?!

I apologised profusely, backing away slowly and steadily, doing everything in my power to keep cool and stop myself from bolting away in panic and pure embarrassment. Luckily, this was a one-off and the rest of my contributors to The Pursuit of Awesome *were a little more straightforward to meet.*

It's a funny process, writing a book. I've interviewed plenty of authors throughout my career and I knew the writing process wouldn't be half as glamorous as one would imagine but let me tell you, it takes a lot of sleepless nights and endless hours of staring at your computer screen. Pester-power levels were at an all-time high all time high trying to secure interviews, juggling diaries, chase up photographs – and that's before any words have been put to paper. Transcribing, researching, editing, re-editing, chasing up facts – I've done it all single-handedly, and the feeling of satisfaction when everything is ready and you can finally type those magical words 'The End' is hard to describe. It's almost euphoric.

The Presenteing as a Kid

My love for books and reading goes way back. As a child, the library was my favourite place in the world, and bookstores my haven. I devoured Enid Blyton's Mallory Towers *and* The Famous Five, *I went on nightly adventures with Nancy Drew, adopted the Baby-sitters Club crew as my sisters and dreamed of living the sparkly lives of Jessica and Elizabeth in the Sweet Valley series.*

And then there was Goosebumps, *instilling a fear of anything and everything in my tween brain. In books I found a safe place, I felt included, understood; I could escape from the real world and let my mind wander to all sorts of strange and beautiful places. Sometimes I'd have up to three or four books on the go the same week, such was my enthusiasm to gobble up the stories.*

I loved to write too. I had a special diary I called 'Kitty' and would jot down daily the trials and tribulations of my inner-city Dublin life. While my classmates groaned at the prospect of writing essays, I found myself oddly pleased. I couldn't imagine anything better than going home to my empty copybook and bringing all sorts of beautiful characters to life. I'm not ashamed I was that nerd who couldn't wait to get my corrected homework back, excited to see if my teacher enjoyed my story as much as I did conjuring it up.

I always knew I wanted to work in media, and television fascinated me. Although more of an observer than an extrovert, I loved people and listening to them speak. I loved asking questions and learning new things. Like most teenagers I daydreamed of what could be but I never really knew how to get 'in'. I didn't have any connections and on more than one occasion, ignorant adults tried to discourage me, telling me I'd never work in television because I wasn't fully Irish.

Me in Moldova

It made me sad, not because I thought they were right, but because I knew they were wrong. I knocked on every door I could. The Internet and Google became my best friends. I emailed newspapers, radio stations, magazines and production companies to get my foot in. I wanted experience and I was prepared to work my butt off to prove my worth and to show them I was an invaluable asset. At first nobody replied but I remained undeterred. I stayed positive and slowly but surely the opportunities appeared. Perseverance is key in this business. I learnt that a long time ago. If you're passionate you must never give up. Instead, work harder to become better, stronger and irreplaceable.

At fifteen I spent a week in FM104, mainly answering phones in reception and shadowing various presenters and people as they went about their daily work. A week in the Star newspaper followed where I must have photocopied half a forest of trees, did enough post office runs to rival Postman Pat and met Westlife, my teen idols, at a press conference where Brian announced his departure from the band. That summer a stint in Kiss magazine followed, where I did various bits and bobs and stalked editor

Big Smiles Xox

Susan Vasquez, completely in awe of what to me seemed like the most glamorous job in the world.

My break in TV came in my final year of college when an email from Ireland AM appeared one gloomy September afternoon. They had kept a letter I sent four months previously on file and finally a work experience position was free. I jumped at the chance to work as a guest greeter, waking up at 4.30 AM twice a week to help out on the live breakfast programme. I'd help print the presenter's scripts, make tea and coffee, bring guests to studio and other small jobs in between.

On top of Tata's car

Whenever possible I stayed back to learn the skills of research, helping put together briefs for the presenters, write suggested interview questions and brainstorm for ideas. I loved every second. Ireland AM gave me experience of a buzzing working environment. I knew from my first day that I needed to work in television, that there was absolutely no other option.

Despite my 'in', I was determined to work harder. I pestered producers in other stations and production companies left, right and centre, I scoured Google for auditions and job openings and I did every evening course goingto help pick up any bit of extra experience.

My parents were my rock. They encouraged and supported me endlessly. They reassured me that no dream was too big, that whatever I wanted was right there at my fingertips, that I just had to reach out and grab it. I firmly embraced this positive mental attitude, letting nothing stand in my way; especially not my Moldovan background.

I'll never forget the excitement of securing a job as presenter in RTÉ. I was in my final weeks of college completing my thesis on children's TV programmes, when an advertisement on the Den website caught my eye.

I applied immediately and kept my fingers crossed. By the time a phone call came, inviting me to audition, I had almost forgotten I had applied in the first place! My first audition was daunting. I was quite a shy twenty-one-year-old. I was confident in my abilities but I was aware that in a group situation I was always the quietest in the room. I had this idea in my head that all kids TV presenters were loud and zany and I knew that I was different. I managed to get through and left feeling happy with my performance.

The next day my family went on holidays to Monaco. We were just three days in when RTÉ called me back, requesting to see me again in the next round. I remember I was in the back of a rental car, munching on a baguette, when the call came. It was a stressful day of driving a few hundred kilometres to stay in a villa we had rented online only to find it was a case of false advertisement and that call lifted everyone's spirits.

A few days later I was on a plane back to Dublin. Audition two came and went, although this time I was uncertain about my performance. I left for the airport a little disheartened, hoping I had done myself justice. I was back in Monaco a few days when RTÉ called again, so I packed my suitcase one final time and returned home to a day of workshops; I was down to the final six.

It's not much of an anecdote. I got the job eventually and my life changed in ways I could never have imagined. I worked on elev8 for five seasons and it was the most rewarding, challenging, satisfying and defining years of my life to date. I can't imagine a better crash course in presenting live telly than being thrown in at the deep end, and I enjoyed every single moment.

Presenting elev8

After the first six months I began to find both my voice and my feet. I revelled in the live-studio environment, never knowing exactly what was going to happen. Every day was different: new guests, new people, new content, new games, and each one with its own challenges to navigate.

I will never take for granted the massive opportunity RTÉ gave me in kick-starting my career. Sure, I had worked hard on my studies and building up connections but it was no doubt a matter of being in the right place at the right time also. I pinch myself to this day when I look at my back catalogue of work.

Seven hundred episodes, two hundred and eighty hours of live TV, two documentaries, collaborating with so many wonderful charities, meeting all sorts of inspiring people and well-known personalities, hosting events around the country, MCing a garden party for the President of Ireland, being nominated for various awards. Even writing this book: had I not had this incredible opportunity, perhaps The Pursuit of Awesome *would never have been born.*

Strike a Pose!!

I wrote this book as much for myself as for anyone reading in search of some guidance, motivation and inspiration. One thing I've discovered is that nobody out there has the answer to everything; we are all human beings trying to work it all out. Whatever that 'it' may be, doesn't matter. We're all united in our yearning and desire, and our journey of discovery. Each of my contributors has an important lesson to share.

They were all once young boys and girls with high hopes and big ambitions, dreaming of a future that could be; from Hozier to Rob Kearney to Cecelia Ahern and Rory McIlroy. Amongst the stories to follow you'll also meet some new heroes, shining a light into industries that often seem distant and exclusive. They'll share with you their high and lows, their successes and failures, and the lessons they've learned.

From Al Pacino's producer Barry Navidi to author Derek Landy, Harry Potter actress Evanna Lynch, Markus Feehily from Westlife, CBBC's Martin Dougan and Kodaline's Steve Garrigan; each of the contributors in this book has kindly and generously spoken honestly about their rise to fame and success.

You'll learn that it's not always going to be easy. You'll learn about the importance of taking risks and embracing failure. Testing times build character. An easy life is a boring life. All the best people I know have suffered and endured hardship. Adversity is not to be feared but embraced. It's in the most testing times that you really discover who you are, what you want, where you want to go and who you want to bring along with you on that crazy journey.

Backstage with Hozier!!

Remember, you are the director of your own life movie, the author of your own autobiography, the artist in control of the paintbrush and indeed, the blank canvas. Splash those colours proudly. Life's too short to stick to a palette of black and grey. Be true to yourself and your passions and the life you dream of. Be not afraid to take a risk. Be not afraid to fail. The fear of failing is a wicked thing. It can stop you dead in your tracks, root you to the spot and make you feel like you're drowning or in quicksand. But when you face up to it? And better yet, conquer it? There is no feeling more liberating and satisfying.

Remember, go forth confidently in the direction of your dreams.

Diana Bunici

XOXO

P.S. Oh, and I did manage to finally meet the real Paul Costelloe!

In Print

'Either write something
worth reading
or do something
worth writing'

- Benjamin Franklin

The world of books is a magical place.

Carefully chosen words, beautifully constructed sentences; exquisite characters, both good and bold and somewhere in between; jaw-dropping, twisted plolines and a plethora of emotions reawakened. Whether you're reading to escape or reading to feel accepted, few can argue against the power of a good book.

To read is one thing; to write, another. No one can understand the endless hours lovingly dedicated to crafting the perfect story more than the wordsmiths themselves, the authors. Delve into the world of print over the next few pages and feel inspired as some of our most celebrated children's authors, wonderful chick-lit writers and talented illustrators share their stories of success.

Derek Landy

Award-winning author Derek Landy is a master of children's fantasy and suspense. Mind you, it's not just the little ones – big kids like Steven Spielberg adore him too. With numerous prestigious writing accolades to his name, the Dublin-born novelist has been gripping millions of readers around the globe with his charming characters and endless wit and passion, and in doing so fulfilling a lifelong dream.

As a child, I loved spending time in my own head. I was friendly; I was funny; I was outgoing; I was upbeat and optimistic. I was full of life and I had lots of friends but I really was happiest being alone. At the age of three, I developed a stammer. I was very fortunate not to be bullied about it or slagged off about it too much. Every so often there would be a kid who had never heard anyone stammer, who didn't know what it was or what it meant but overall everyone understood.

In life, each of us has our crosses to bear. It might not be as obvious as a stammer or a physical disability, but we're all messed up in some way or another. It's about the people around you. Not just your family but also the people you choose to allow into your life that will make the difference. To a certain extent it's about attitude and so long as you have the people who will support you, your attitude can help you overcome most of your problems – not all, but most.

During those early years, I wanted to be an artist, a writer or an actor. The writing was *always* there. When we'd get our home-work in primary school and it was to write a short story I was always that kid who thought, 'Oh excellent, a story,' while my classmates would groan. I'd never understand why. That was my first indication that my attitude to writing and reading books was a whole lot different to everyone else's. I was too young at that stage to think about careers. I knew I liked writing but I was also good at art. I still dreamt I would one day write and draw my own comics.

I was serious about acting. Even though I had a stammer, I was often given big parts in the school plays that we had. When I was on stage and the spotlight was on me, I knew that nobody was going to interrupt me because I knew the lines; it was all scripted. That allowed my confidence to flourish; when I was acting, I wasn't stammering.

I remember in secondary school I had to do two impromptu speeches in front of assembly. I had come second in a writing competition and everyone shouted, 'Speech, speech,' so I had to get up in front of hundreds of people. Because there was no danger of me being interrupted, because the spotlight was on *me*, I was able to relax and my confidence skyrocketed again. I delivered two funny speeches and I felt, 'Oh my God, I can finally speak.' In school, in my normal day-to-day life, I struggled to get the words out – there were so many people and the conversation was usually flowing so fast and I was always in danger of being interrupted. I would be fine for half the sentence and then the momentum would be lost and someone would speak over me and I'd fade away.

The stammer was debilitating. I went through about a year where I couldn't answer the phone; I didn't want to say the word

'Hello.' It was hard to buy tickets on the bus because I couldn't say the name of my destination.

Throughout my entire twenties, up until *Skullduggery* happened, I was very much a victim of my stammer. However, in the same way that the spotlight of the stage secured me in my own space, where I was the most important person in the room, and my confidence went up – the same thing happened with *Skullduggery*. All of a sudden, I was the most important person and everyone was listening to me. It was an astonishing revelation to realise that all it takes is just you, yourself, to say, 'Listen, I'm important, I'm awesome, and everyone else will be forced to listen to the pearls of wisdom coming out of my mouth.' That's all it takes.

Suddenly not only are you in charge of the stammer but you realise when you *do* stammer, you don't actually care too much any more, whereas in the past you'd blush and clam up.

We were all big readers in my house. That respect and love for the written word was always there and my sisters and brother and I all had this ingrained love of books. I think the stammer and the fact that I couldn't communicate as fluently as I would have wanted to in real life, made me appreciate the written word so much more – the same with all those film noir movies and the screwball comedies with everyone speaking really fast. They're a marvel of writing and performance. Everyone is so smart and so clever and so funny and so quick. I watched those movies as a kid and just stared at them and marvelled.

You could say I took a very convoluted route to being an author. One of the big questions I get asked these days is, 'How do you become a writer, what steps do you take?' or 'My parents aren't keen on me being a writer, how would you advise me?'

I'm always kind of hesitant because being a writer is a very hard thing to be. Being a successful one, who gets paid, is next to impossible. Yet it happens, and it happened to me. It's a very weird split between being realistic and pragmatic, and listening to your heart.

In secondary school I didn't know what I wanted to do. I knew I was good at writing but I didn't view college or a course as a way to be a writer. I viewed *writing* as a way to be a writer. I wasn't the best student by any means: I liked the things I liked and I hated the things I didn't like. I didn't study. I was always reading comics or drawing comics instead.

The first time I did the Leaving Cert, I failed Irish and Maths – they were always my two worst subjects. I repeated my final year, and it was a miserable year. I did my best not to make any friends but I inevitably did because people are nice. Even though I wasn't applying myself any harder than before, I did manage to pass everything the second time round. I began studying animation in Ballyfermot in Dublin. I lasted a year there before my lack of talent got me kicked out.

I was raised and brought up on a farm. I always hated working there and I promised myself I wouldn't make a career out of it. However, after school and college, I found myself living my nightmare. It was terrible. It was miserable. I worked there for approximately the next ten years and it was torture. Because I had messed up everything else, I thought, 'What do I have left?'

I realised that, one thing was writing. It was the one thing that I'd always been good at but hadn't really thought about much until now. I decided I was going to be a writer and write movies. I absolutely adored film. I taught myself how to write screenplays. I bought a few books; I examined films; I read screenplays; I learned about structure and character and I just wrote. I wrote and I wrote and I wrote. I'd be working on the farm during the day and I'd be writing every spare minute in between because I realised that was my only chance to make something of myself. I managed to get two movies made – *Dead Bodies* and *Boy Eats Girl*.

They didn't make me any money and they didn't send me to Hollywood but I didn't need that. I just needed acknowledgement that I was good enough, that I was a writer and that I could call myself a writer. Because of those movies I got a wonderful agent in London. My life changed a little bit. I was now working part-time on the farm and going to London every few months to take meetings, to try and get something else moving.

A few months after my second film came out, I was in London to take some more meetings. I was in a hotel room when I had a sort of revelation that changed my life. I didn't have much money. I was staying in the only hotel room I could afford. It didn't even have a TV; it didn't even have a bathroom – every floor had a bathroom, it was *that* cheap. I remember being in that very threadbare room, with just a bed in it. No desk, no chair, no nothing. It was just a bed and a lamp and that's it. I remember standing looking at the bed with the window behind me and two completely unconnected words popped into my head and formed a name – 'Skullduggery' and 'Pleasant'.

That's really the biggest problem I have when people ask me for advice for being a writer. 'I've got this passion and nobody understands it – but you understand it. Should I keep on trying?'

Sometimes I say yes and sometimes I say no.

The point is, if something had happened when I was standing in that hotel room – the car outside had beeped its horn or someone else had passed by the door or I was distracted in some way or other, even if the room had had a TV, 'Skullduggery Pleasant' wouldn't have popped into my head and where would I be now? Maybe I would have found success somewhere else or maybe I would have been just another struggling screenwriter.

That moment of inspiration changed my life entirely.

My life had been leading up to it, absolutely, but nothing else had. It was not the culmination of a thought process. I hadn't heard 'Skullduggery' and thought, 'Hmm, that's an interesting name, what can I do with that?' It just popped in there a propos of nothing.

I've realised over the years, when I ran it through in my head, my God, that moment that has led to my life changing in every conceivable way, that moment could just as easily never have happened and then I would not be here.

We are mere pawns in the game of life and it's astonishing what you have to rely on in order for things to work out. It's terrifying. When 'Skullduggery' appeared in my head, I instantly knew this was going to be the best character I'd ever create. This guy was different and new and yet owed so much to the stuff I loved as a kid, the detective, the private eye, all of the comic books and movies I watched. He was absolutely the result of each and every one of my obsessions over the years but he was new and unique.

I started to feel that little tingle of excitement. I didn't really know what I was doing for the first half of the book. I wrote about thirty pages and I sent them to my agent, Michelle, who had always encouraged me to try writing prose and give screen-writing a tiny break.

I told her, 'Michelle, I'm writing a book. I think it's for younger people, it's about a skeleton detective.' She asked me to send my thirty pages to her and when she got back to me, she was extremely excited. She thought it was good and so I continued writing and that tingle just grew and grew and grew. With her acknowledgement and seal of approval, I *believed* in what I was writing. Her reaction was always an honest one. If *she* felt I was onto something special and *I* felt I was onto something special, it *must* have been something special.

It took about six months to write and edit the book. It was finished by Christmas and my agent sent it out the first week of February. A week later I was driving my parents and my gran to the airport – they were catching a flight to a wedding in England. On the drive my mother was gently suggesting that maybe I start looking for a proper job – 'Hey we're all really hopeful about this writing thing but it takes time and your heart isn't really in the farm so maybe you should get another job. I've heard about this job going. You could drive a truck delivering mattresses.'

I thought, 'Wow, OK Barbara, thanks for that. I'm going to stick to writing for just a bit longer.' I told her that Michelle had sent the book out to a few publishers and that I wanted to see what would happen. I dropped them off at the airport and drove into Dublin, to my favourite comic book shop, Forbidden Planet. I was browsing through the comics when my agent called me. I moved into the book's section so I could actually hear her and she gave me good news – HarperCollins were interested. I didn't really know what that meant. Were they *mildly* interested? Does it mean they think it had potential? I didn't know that it meant they wanted to publish it and I *certainly* didn't know it meant they wanted to give me any money for it.

My agent continued, 'Also, this other publisher is also interested, oh and this other one, and another, and another – it's looking good Derek.' I called my mother as soon as I got off the phone. She was waiting to board the plane. I told her the news and she was hugely excited. Over the next week, every day my agent would call to tell me a new publisher was 'interested'. A week later after that initial call, Michelle rang again.

She asked me if I was sitting down. I said, 'No'. She said, 'Well maybe you should,' to which I replied, 'Oh I'm fine Michelle.' She told me the news: 'HarperCollins have offered a million pounds.'

For some reason I was really calm. We both were. I put down the phone and went into the kitchen where my mother and brother were yapping away. They realised I had been standing there for a minute, silently. I looked at them and said, 'HarperCollins have offered me a million pounds for my book.'

From that moment on, it all changed. I had been the black sheep of the family; the kid who messed up in school and in college. I didn't have a degree. Suddenly, from that moment on, I was a golden child. From that moment on, whenever I walked into the room my mother had a massive smile on her face that went on for months. After ten years of being on the outskirts and on the brink of failure or not quite success, I had landed on something wonderful and amazing.

Skullduggery stayed with me for eleven books. It was difficult to say goodbye to him and the rest of characters. To me, Skullduggery and Valkyrie were more than just characters. Every time I wrote a new book, it was like meeting up with old friends. However, you don't want to do the same thing over and over again unless you have a very good reason, unless this is a story that lives and thrives within you. Not every writer has a long-running series. Most writers just write individual books and then move on to the next.

I wasn't content to be just writing Skullduggery for the rest of my life. I really also wanted to do something different. As a kid, I promised myself that I'd never lead a normal life.

With my circumstances with *Skullduggery*, I was afforded the opportunity to indulge in my love of movies and comics and awesomeness. I've built up a collection of props and costumes from movies like a facehugger from *Aliens*, Michael Keaton's Batman suits and Christopher Reeves' Superman suits. I have light-sabres, a machete used in *Jaws* and Captain America's shield, which is fantastic to carry around the house feeling awesome about yourself. My house is full of toys and statues. In my office I have *Star Wars* statues everywhere. I've got paintings on the wall. I fill my house full of creativity so I never have to seek inspiration. Everywhere I look is an idea. It is that same buzz that you want to pass on to somebody else.

Writing has allowed me to meet some of my personal heroes; meeting Steven Spielberg was one hundred percent a cool moment for me. When the book was just published, my agent and I went to Hollywood to sell the rights. There's still no movie news to this day but in that week we went around the studios because everyone wanted the rights to *Skullduggery*. It was a week of being pampered by executives and meeting amazing people like J. J. Abrams who has just done the new *Star Wars* film. Meeting Steven Spielberg was the highlight. I got to meet him in a lovely studio with palm trees outside and everything looking very colonial and just gorgeous. The door opens and in walks *the* Steven Spielberg.

I just started grinning. This was the guy who pretty much shaped my childhood and the childhoods of millions of people. To meet him, to talk to him, to chat to him about *Skullduggery* was awesome. He had been reading my book to his kids and he really loved it. He was telling me about parts he loved, ideas he had, he'd get really excited and loved that he was mentioned in the first book. It was absolutely wonderful and astonishing.

I feel exceptionally lucky. There are better writers than me out there who will never even have a book deal because the right editor did not pick it up or it wasn't appreciated. Or they might even write a book and nobody will buy a copy. Not because it's not any good but because of the market or world events, which can overtake your little piece of art. It's a game of luck.

For a kid who never wanted to be normal, never wanted to be ordinary, I haven't done too badly. If I travelled back in time and met my teenage self and said, 'Dude, you're gonna have an extraordinary life,' not only would my teenage self not be surprised by the success of *Skullduggery* and my writing, I don't think he would be surprised that I had finally somehow managed to achieve time travel.

Derek's Tips for being a Better Writer

Ignore what's hot right now.

By the time you finish your book, it's not going to be hot any more.

Forget about trying to predict the next trend. *Make* the next trend. I wrote Skullduggery and I packed it with every genre I wanted to write. It was that attitude, that really carefree attitude that resulted in Skullduggery being the way it is.

Have fun.

I don't say that dismissively. I got my agent because I sent her the script for one of my movies, *Boy Eats Girls*. It's a zombie movie and it's a comedy. My agent is a literary agent – she does film and TV too. She's not a genre-specific agent but she wouldn't be the biggest fan of zombies. She said the reason she took me on is because she could see and feel the fun that I was having in the script. That has led to my absolute belief that if the writer is having fun writing, the reader will have fun reading because hey, fun is contagious.

Slice off a big piece of yourself with everything you write and put it on the page.

You have to deliver a piece of actual honesty, no matter what you're writing about, be it zombies, skeleton detectives, a love story or a thriller or science fiction or a story of Russian aristocrats in the nineteenth century. It doesn't matter the genre, the style of the type – you have to put a bit of yourself into it – a bit of your own humanity into what it is you're writing. There's a reason most writers are insane and that's because everything they write, they slice off another part of themselves and lay it on the page. You have to do that. You have to connect with an audience – no matter what you're writing. Emotional honesty is the core of all writing, and you need that.

Sarah Webb

Sarah Webb has been scribbling in her diaries ever since she can remember. With thirty-five novels to her name, she is a firm favourite on children's bookshelves, with readers from all over the world – the USA, Australia, Poland, Italy and even Indonesia.

A bookseller, festival planner, children's and adult fiction author and winner of the Children's Books Ireland Outstanding Contribution to Children's Book Award 2015, there's no stopping this passionate author.

I never 'decided' to be a writer. It's just something I've always done. As a kid, I wrote knock-off Enid Blyton stories – fan fiction, it would be called now. 'The Magic Sofa' was the first story I remember writing. I still have a copy of it, in a tiny notebook, to this day. It was about a family who owned a magic sofa that could fly, a bit like a magic carpet. They had all kinds of adventures.

As a teen, I kept diaries and I still have those too – I love reading them and finding out how I felt and what I thought about the world when I was age thirteen or fifteen or seventeen. It's fascinating. I had four major preoccupations as a teen: parties, friends (and falling out with said friends), clothes and make-up, and yes – I hate to admit it – boys. I even kept a 'boys I like' list at the back of my diary!

I've worked in children's books for over twenty years now, as a writer, festival programmer, reviewer and children's bookseller. A career highlight to date was definitely winning the Children's Books Ireland award for outstanding contribution to children's books in 2015. It was a huge honour for me and something I'm very proud of – I was thrilled to be given an award by my peers.

I've published thirty-five books to date but that first book as a writer is a massive career milestone. Thinking back, I can't help but smile. My first book was called *Kids Can Cook*. It was non-fiction, full of recipes for children – cakes, buns, and fun things like that. It was turned down by many publishers but every time it was rejected, I kept sending it back out. Eventually a small Irish publisher called Children's Press took it on.

I was gobsmacked when Reena Dardis from Children's Press rang to tell me she'd like to publish it. I was in my wee house with my young baby son and I did a little dance in my kitchen/living room: it was a pretty small house.

It was definitely one of the highlights of my life. A first book is a very special thing indeed. It was all the more special because it meant I could buy my own car with the money I got after it was published and had sold quite a few copies – an old, second-hand Honda Civic.

As a single mum with a full-time job in Waterstones bookshop, my weeks were really busy, and I spent a lot of time pushing my son to his minders and back in his buggy. Having a car made a huge difference to my life and gave me back some time – time I could spend writing. It was a real godsend.

To this day, my favourite part of the whole writing process is creating characters. I spend months thinking about my characters before I start writing a thing – who they are, what makes them tick, what they love, what they hate. Then I create their world: where they live, their family, friends, pets, school. And then I put them into an opening scene and start writing their story. For me, character drives plot, so that's what I start with – creating characters. While you're writing, you are living in a world of your own creation – that's pretty amazing. The act of creating characters and their world is what keeps me gripped.

Being an author is a truly wonderful job. You can work in your pyjamas, set your own hours, and follow your passion.

There are negatives too – the money isn't great, especially starting out. You may need another job, which is the case with a lot of people who work in the arts – artists, musicians and so on. I review children's books, I teach, I talk to children in schools and libraries. I like variety and much as I love writing, I also like getting away from the desk and meeting people.

Researching a new book or topic is one of the most enjoyable aspects of writing – it's fascinating and I learn so much. I love coming up with new ideas. I have far too many rattling around in my head. I have – touch wood – never run out of ideas.

I have lots of notebooks on the go all the time. I also use my phone to jot down ideas and thoughts. Ideas can be very particular to an individual person. I might write down 'dolphin . . . US girl . . . communication'. Now, anyone else would ask, 'What on earth is she talking about?' But I'd know. I'm not precious about my ideas. Everyone has such different passions and interests; that's what makes life interesting.

I find inspiration everywhere. I adore writers and illustrators like Judy Blume, Roald Dahl, Maurice Sendak, Judi Curtin, Oisin McGann, Alan Nolan, Martina Devlin, Marita Conlon-McKenna, John Boyne, Shaun Tan, Oliver Jeffers, Eoin Colfer, Roddy Doyle and so many more wonderful creative people. I'm a huge reader and good writing also inspires me so much.

Women like Mary Robinson and Mary McAleese have influenced me. The suffragettes – who fought for women's right to vote – have left a huge impression on me too. Malala is an amazing woman and an incredible role model.

I'm also greatly inspired by the girls and boys I meet every week when I visit libraries and schools. They are so amazing and so smart – the future of Ireland is in very good hands! I look to nature too. I enjoy travelling – train journeys, storms, the sea, good movies, good TV shows – so many things.

As a children's bookseller I've met so many wonderful writers that I admire over the years, from Jacqueline Wilson, to Jo Rowling and Michael Morpurgo. One of the highlights was meeting Judy Blume when I was a young bookseller in my twenties. She told me that writing for children was a real joy and privilege and that I should definitely do it. She was completely right – it really is a joy and a privilege.

Going to college isn't essential to becoming an author; reading is.

I just happened to study English, but if you want to write, *write*. Start now and never give up. Write your heart out. The more practice you get as a child or teenager, the better.

Sarah's Advice:

My diaries are forevermore reminding my how difficult the teenage years can be. With the luxury of hindsight I say:

Don't worry too much about what other people think.

Hang out with your grandparents and godparents more. They won't be around forever and they are cooler than you know.

You may be young, but you can do whatever you set your mind to. Don't let anyone put you off, or say you can't do something – you can.

Believe in yourself.

Will Sliney

Illustrator Will Sliney has loved cartoons and comic books all his life. His wildest childhood dream came true when Marvel Comics came knocking on his door with a job offer.

This Cork-man spends his time drawing Spiderman and conjuring up his own series about Irish folk legend Cú Chulainn.

Ever since I can remember, I was always mad about cartoons. Watching cartoons and playing video games took up a lot of my early years, but so did drawing. If I was playing a video game, I would be coming up with my own video game concepts, drawing the stories for them, and it was the same with my favourite cartoons. I used to create my own characters and even write out the backstories for them – what kind of powers they'd have, and so on.

Like most kids, I wanted to do everything. I wanted to play football and I wanted to be a Formula One driver but I never really knew that you could go out there and do these kinds of jobs in real life. I always thought it would have been cool to work in these kinds of professions but it was only when I got to college that I realised that there were actually those kinds of jobs out there and that I could actively work towards getting there.

As a youngster I certainly drew more than other kids but I definitely don't believe a talent for drawing is something that you're born with. I think the more you draw, the better you get. When I was in school, I used to draw a lot more than other people and that's how I improved my talent and skill. I kept at it all the way through my teenage years, which has definitely helped improve my skill and style.

The road to Marvel started when I was studying multimedia. It was a mixture of everything. There was a small bit of illustration and I realised that's what I really, enjoyed doing. I wanted to work as an illustrator so much. I did my research and figured out a way to reach out to these companies that would give me the opportunity to make drawing my lifestyle. One of the most important things in getting a job with these people is to actually get your work in front of them.

When I finished college I put together a portfolio of five or six pages of my drawings in the comic-book style. I optimistically flew over to San Diego to try and show it off to all the publishers at ComicCon. I quickly realised that probably wasn't the best way of doing things. It's like turning up at a football stadium with your football boots saying, 'Will you have a look at me playing?'

It took some time before I realised that instead of trucking halfway around the world, the best route was to start a little smaller and look for a more achievable job in comic books.

The rejection is all part of it, you have to learn that you're not going to be good enough straight away – you can learn from failure all the time.

I wasn't too deterred after my trip to San Diego. I knew I was on the right track so I just kept working. I started out in a really small job in Dublin and it all went upwards from here. At the time, a publisher called Atomic Diner hired me to do a superhero book called *Atomic Rotten, Route 66*. It was the first time I had ever been paid to do comic books – although looking back, it wasn't much. It was amazing to finally have some of my work published; seeing my work put together into an actual comic book that was sold in shops was invaluable experience.

Holding that first copy of *Atomic Rotten* was fantastic. I can still remember that new book smell. It was a really nice achievement and it gave me the confidence to move forward.

My parents were always extremely supportive. They didn't bug me to do a 'real job', or anything like that. They knew how much I loved drawing and how passionate I was, how hard I was working and how serious I was about pursuing a career in my chosen field. They allowed me to chase my dream. When I came out of college I was working in an e-learning job and any moment I had I'd be drawing, working on my sketches, always trying to get better. Seeing me do that proved my genuine interest to my parents and showed them how serious I was about it. I was so dedicated: I'd draw at lunchtime: I'd draw before work: I'd draw into the evenings.

About five years before I got my job with Marvel, a talent scout came to Ireland. He had an early look at my work and he was very encouraging, telling me to keep at it and that I was getting closer to being able to work for them one day. From that first meeting, I stayed in regular contact with Marvel, sending on my drawings by email over the years – so they were always casting an eye over my work. I knew I had to get a better understanding of anatomy and work on my storytelling and all that. I suppose they also needed me to be able to prove that I had plenty of work published. Marvel wanted to see that I had a track record working for companies and that I was employable.

At another show in Dublin a few years later I met with the same talent scout once again. He told me that I was finally ready and that they'd have some sort of contract for me the following week. Hearing those words was brilliant. I'd been dreaming of this for so long, hoping that one day I would actually get the chance to work for this dream-company. After putting in thousands and thousands of hours of drawing, it was a nice realisation and a funny moment.

Sure enough, a day after the convention, I got a phone call from Marvel asking me to do a test-page. I had just signed up to do another convention in Belfast the following day. I knew I was under pressure to get this tester done up and sent to Marvel before I got on the train to Belfast the next morning. I stayed up all night and got the work in and made the train as planned. Unfortunately, as soon as I crossed the border, I had no Internet. I sat there anxiously praying to hear back from them but with no way of checking my emails. When I got to the hotel I plugged my laptop in but of course, the cable wasn't working so I had to go about fixing it.

Eventually I managed to get online and an email was there telling me I had the job. It was surreal. I was in this random hotel room jumping about the place with joy.

My first assignment with Marvel was a series about an all-female superhero troupe called the Fearless Defenders. Usually, for someone starting out, you're assigned single issues. Needless to say, I felt very lucky to be offered the opportunity to work on an entire series. You could say I started with a bang! It was a new issue, a new book. It was very exciting.

I worked on that series for a full year before they began to consider me for one of the *Spiderman* books. I started out with single issues before eventually working full-time on the *Spiderman* series. Funnily enough, I felt more pressure on *The Fearless Defenders* that I did working on *Spiderman*. That first page on *The Fearless Defenders* was the toughest page that I ever worked on. I worried about it so much.

There were so many more eyes on my work, and the standard was super-high. Those pages definitely took me a lot longer than anything else I'd done before. I wanted to impress and do Marvel justice.

Spiderman is my ultimate character to work on. That's what I was always aiming for. I've been working on him for almost two years and I still love him. With Marvel we work at a pace of a page a day. They release a new issue every month and a comic book is about twenty-pages long. It varies from artist to artist, but I'm quite fast, so I aim for a page and a quarter each day. Every artist's day is different because you have to work during the hours when you're most productive. I work my best in the morning so I start then and keep going well into the afternoon.

I draw directly onto my computer screen via a tablet called a Cintiq. It's the same process as drawing with pen and paper; the only difference is that you can zoom in. When I started working, I travelled a lot, and having A3 pages on the go made it a little difficult in terms of things like scanning. By going down the digital route, I was able to carry my work in a laptop bag.

If I told you, you'd never believe how many times you have to draw the laces on a boot or a buckle on a belt. There's always a challenge in every issue or series – something new that you might not have drawn before – and you have to figure out how to do it in an effective way. You do have to study and practise quite a bit before you can apply it to the proper comic strip. The challenges change every month, but you kind of have a set process as to how to approach these new challenges and difficulties.

One of my favourite things about the job is that you're constantly improving and always focusing on improving yourself. You might look at work that's a month old and cringe at something small that you've improved on in that short period of time. In this job, I'll be learning until I can't learn any more, which is the best thing.

To this day, I still collect comic books so I can study the different illustrators that are out there. My favourite at the moment is a guy called Stuart Immonen. He works on the new *Star Wars* books and I really admire him. To be honest, my favourites change all the time. I learn different things from different artists.

A few years before I began working with Marvel, there was an animated series called *Star Wars, The Clone Wars*. I was lucky to work on the comic-book adaptation of that. As a huge *Star Wars* fan, that was particularly cool for me. I get a lot of nostalgia on a lot of the comics I get to work on.

My favourite thing is when someone comes up to me with a comic I've worked on to be signed. It'll have dog ears and it makes me smile because it means they've read it twenty times over, back to front.

They'll always bring their own drawings to show me, which I find very interesting.

Four or five years ago at a book launch there might have been one or two people with a portfolio but now you might get a couple of hundred people with portfolios – which is amazing.

My biggest highlight so far has been going to the Marvel offices in New York. When I was going in to sign my contract and I was walking through those doors for the first time – that was magic.

The whole place is set up to impress – it's where they bring in the actors for the first time too. There's a Thor room and an Iron Man room and a Hulk room, amazing artwork and these huge sculptures . . . that moment was a real 'pinch me' moment for me. I was over the moon and delighted to be there. It was a huge dream come true for me.

Marvel aside, I'm also extremely proud of a comic book I released a couple of years back focusing on *Cú Chulainn*. I've always loved his story but I realised you could never find a full story of him anywhere. I thought he really suited the superhero style so I decided to write and illustrate my own comic book dedicated to him. I wanted to get my stamp on him out there.

After working in comic books for a few years, it was nice to have a book that launched in Ireland that people could connect to. It really kicked things off for me here. It was really cool. To this day it holds the record for being Ireland's fastest-selling graphic novel. I hope to go back some day and make more Celtic warriors come alive in comic-book form.

My advice if you're interested in drawing is to just keep drawing. The deal is, the more you draw, the better you get. If you're getting frustrated with drawing certain things that you don't feel are working, just remember that the more you practise, the more you'll improve. Keep going.

To get spotted, attend the relevant conventions and get face-to-face time with the necessary scouts. The one thing the guys at Marvel always say is don't just blindly send off fifty images in an email for somebody to look at. Each company has different submission guidelines.

Find the relevant emails of the talent managers and email them politely asking if you can send some of your work. They'll get back to you and say 'yes', and it kind of goes from there. They'll look at your work and give you a few pointers, or they might give you a sample script of their own work so you can see how they handle their own characters.

These companies do want to see new talent and it's all about being nice and professional and asking for permission to send your stuff off.

Remember, practice makes perfect.

Paige Toon

A former Heat *magazine editor and author of over a dozen novels, Paige Toon grew up between England, Australia and America, or wherever her Formula 1 racing-driver dad took her! Passionate about books, magazines and films, Paige is a firm favourite with chick-lit readers around the world. And yes, Paige is her real name.*

I know it sounds clichéd, but I've wanted to write ever since I could remember. As a little girl, I used to escape to the back of the garden to write poems and songs. The first job I ever wanted to do was to work in a magazine. I wanted to be an author before that, but when I started reading magazines as a teenager – I quite fancied it as a fun job. I remember writing sad stories in my childhood years.

I used to think that my parents and relatives thought I was just a kid who would always write happy endings, and so I would make them as sad as possible for the shock factor. I've always liked surprising my audience.

By the time I got to university, I decided to study philosophy. I was worried that doing English would put me off writing. When

I wrote my novel, *One Perfect Summer*, I created this heroine called Alice who goes to study English literature. I remember thinking, 'I wish I had done that, that would have been really lovely.' Philosophy still allowed me to open up my mind, though. It allowed me to be creative in my own way, without forcing literature down my throat.

Post-college, I took a year out before finding work experience at a small magazine. I really wanted to write film reviews and so off I went to work for a film magazine called *Neon*. I did one week's work experience. They were only too happy to have someone come in and offer to help. They weren't a massive publication by any means. For bigger magazines like *Heat*, there was up to a year's wait, but I quite liked working in this smaller office. I used it as an opportunity to shine and make an impact.

Being quite determined and passionate, I didn't think a week was long enough – so I nicely asked if I could stick around a little longer. I promised to clear out *Neon*'s entire video cabinet if they kept me on. I think they thought I was a little crazy but they obliged. I was just really, really, really enthusiastic.

At the end of my placement, the editorial assistant, who had the most junior position in a magazine, asked me if I wanted to cover for her because she was going away for a couple of weeks. I jumped at the chance and by the end of that, I'd had a whole month in this office. I really tried to make an impact where I could. I did my best to be enthusiastic and helpful and ask the right questions. When I left I gave my CV to the editor and said, 'Please, please, please think of me if you need anything.'

Three months later, I got a phone call from the editor of *Big* magazine, a teenage title. She needed an editorial assistant. After working there for about three months or so, I got the job. I was about twenty-three at this stage, which was actually quite old for a newbie. A lot of people go into the magazine industry straight from school. I felt like quite an old editorial assistant. I was sort of the magazine's secretary. I would do everything from changing the photocopy paper to replying to the millions of readers' letters.

They'd write in all the time, wanting to know what it was like meeting Leonardo DiCaprio and all of these other famous people. They'd sort of just expect bands to pop in for tea and hang out. That never happened during my time but I do remember Westlife coming into the office before they became absolutely huge.

I got to interview a young Jake Gyllenhaal before he became really famous. I got to do film reviews too, which was what I had always wanted to do. I also used to handle the work-experience students, who they call 'workies' in the industry. The one thing I really noticed, considering how much I never took it for granted that I got a job there, was that it was quite amazing how few work-experience people stood out throughout the time that I was looking after them. I felt very few made the most of such a great opportunity. Over the course of a year, only two or three would stand out.

It just goes to show you can make a difference if you try really hard.

I worked at *Big* for about a year and a half. Just before I applied for a job at *Heat*, my editor said to me, 'Don't wait until you feel ready to move on': their last editorial assistant had been there for two and a half years and she had got a bit fed up with the job. My editor said, 'Jump before you feel ready', that was the best advice she could have given me because I had been thinking, 'I can't move on from here until I've been here for at least a couple of years.' I just assumed that was what people expected.

I did eventually go for a job at *Heat* magazine as the editor and reviews assistant, and I got it. Oddly, a week later *Big* closed down; I was lucky I jumped in time. Five months after joining *Heat*, my boss, the reviews editor left and they were a bit disorganised to say the least. I was covering both the absent editor's role along with my own and when I finally asked for it, I ended up getting her job. It was a very quick progression going from the lowest position to editor of a magazine.

When I began working at *Heat*, the magazine was on the verge of closing down. It was selling less than 30,000 copies a week. Over the next couple of years it rose to selling 600,000 copies a week. It was an exciting time to be an editor at one of the biggest magazines in the world. It was pretty incredible.

I liked interviewing people like Sir Alan Sugar. I remember asking him what he thought of Jordan and Peter Andre – because there was some sort of scandal going on between them at the time. Or maybe it was the Beckhams . . . And he was like, 'I don't bloody know.' I was asking him stuff I knew he wouldn't care about, and my editor loved the technique. I remember him saying he wanted more of that. I had to ask the slightly silly questions sometimes to get an amusing response.

The dragons from *Dragons' Den* were also really fun to interview. I remember going in once and pitching ideas to them. They were supposed to be jokey ideas but they all took them very, very seriously. One of my colleagues said, 'Suggest making candles out of your pets,' and that's what I went in with. I had a good laugh during my time with *Heat*, that's for sure.

To get a good interview, being quite succinct is important. When you interview people who aren't used to television, they can go on and on forever. Getting to the point and being interesting is important too. Don't avoid controversy all the time. Fair enough, you don't want to put yourself out there too much personally,but have an opinion about things, otherwise it's boring. And you should-n't be afraid to be cheeky. I remember one time my editor couldn't believe I had asked one particular question. I was interviewing a woman who had just been kicked out of *The Apprentice* who wasn't very well liked. I asked her how it felt to be the most hated woman in Britain. I said it with a twinkle in my eye and she laughed and went along with it but it could definitely have gone wrong!

In the magazine industry, every day is different and your duties depends very much on the title of the publication and your role. As an editor of a weekly, you usually have copy coming in on a Monday. You've got to edit all the work and put it through to the sub-editors. I'd get the pages laid out and sent to print, or I could be out viewing a film or at the video or book cabinet seeing what had come in, and making sure we had the right dates. You would also be speaking to lots of people to find out what's happening or double-checking facts and then commissioning things for the following week.

We'd usually have a weekly TV meeting and sometimes you'd have to nip off into the TV room and watch a TV programme and then sit down and write a review. It used to take me about three hours to write a review when I first started because I was so picky and scared of getting it wrong. I got a bit quicker as time went on. The work was always very varied.

The way into magazines is with experience and it's worth your time when you're starting out to save for a little while so you can afford to work for free for those initial two or three months. Even when you get employment, it's not the best-paid job in the world.

As you can imagine, I was terrified making the transition from editing magazines to becoming an author. I'd wanted a book deal for years and years and for me it was the absolute pinnacle. If I didn't make the transition to author, I still believe it would have been my biggest regret.

I was extremely lucky to get my deal and I definitely didn't follow the typical route. What happened to me was very unusual. I had this book idea while working at *Heat* as reviews editor. Because I used to get lots of books sent to me by lots of people wanting their books to be featured, I had a good relationship with many publishers and publicity people.

One of them at Simon & Schuster, Nigel Stoneman, had become a friend of mine. I loved his no-nonsense attitude. He's say, 'This book isn't very *Heat* but the author's *loooovely*, if you could squeeze her in the chart then put her in.'

We became friends because I just liked him being straight to the point. We went out for lunch one day and he said to me, 'You should write a book. You'd get a book deal easy.' And so I told him about my idea. I think he was just speaking off-hand but he was surprised by my sudden enthusiasm. I told him about the idea for *Lucy in the Sky*, about a girl who gets on a flight to Australia and gets a text message from her boyfriend's phone saying, 'I've slept with your boyfriend four times this month.'

And he said, 'I love it, I'm going to go back and tell my publisher.' I got very, very nervous, almost sick with nerves.

About five minutes after I got back to the office, I had an email from Nigel saying his publisher loved my idea and wanted to meet me. Not only that, but I also had an email from said publisher asking *when* we could meet.

I met with Suzanne, the publisher, a week later. In that space of time, I wrote the first three chapters of my debut novel, bearing in mind I had only written a page and a half of this story previously. My brother came up with the title *Lucy in the Sky* and I quickly changed the heroine's name from Meg to Lucy and wrote a five-thousand-word synopsis. I sent the synopsis through to Suzanne ahead of our meeting but held onto the first three chapters. We met, she told me how much she loved it and asked to see some written material and I obliged. I sent the first three chapters and two days later she offered me a two-book deal.

Around the time I came up with the idea for *Lucy in the Sky*, my mam, dad and brother had moved back to Australia and I stayed behind in university in England. Born in England but growing up in Australia to an Australian family, I felt incredibly homesick. I was going out with a boy, who ended up being my husband, who had no interest in going to live in Australia, and I was very torn between the two countries. I have an overactive mind and I'm always coming up with weird ideas, so I can't recall exactly how the initial idea came to me but I decided to write a story about this girl called Lucy who was – like me, caught between two countries – and unlike me, two men.

When it came down to it, the book practically wrote itself. I had my initial ideas, but it just took on a life of its own. It was an absolute joy to write. Even to this day, nothing else competes with it.

You couldn't keep me away from my computer. I kept on the full-time job in *Heat* at the time, and if I had a quiet moment in work, occasionally I might have been doing a little bit of writing. I remember my editor looking over at me a couple of times, giving me a knowing look. I'd write before work, at lunchtime, after work and at weekends. I didn't go out or socialise that much during that time, but I was just in the happiest place, to have this book deal and to lose myself inside these characters lives. It was so much fun to be in their heads.

After I completed the book, we sent it to Marian Keyes, who is absolutely my favourite author. I'd reviewed her books at *Heat* and met her a couple of times and asked if she would give me a quote for it. I felt absolutely sick with fear. That's when it first started sinking in that all of my friends and family would be reading this book – my mother-in-law, my husband's granny. I'd written a few swearwords in there and a couple of steamy scenes. I thought of my colleagues at *Heat* reading it and judging me.

Because I wrote *Lucy in the Sky* in two and half months, I thought I'd be able to write my second novel, *Johnny Be Good,* in as speedy a time as well. It turns out I can only write in the winter and that I'm completely unproductive any other time of year. I also fell pregnant right after I delivered my first book. I tried to write *Johnny Be Good* before my baby came and it was really, really stressful. I managed to get fifty thousand words into it and after I had the baby, my mind just cleared, and I wrote the book very, very quickly again. I ended up rewriting those first fifty thousand words. I remember thinking, 'Please, please, please let some of my readers love this almost as much as they love *Lucy in the Sky*,' and a massive, massive, massive chunk of them loved it even more.

It was just amazing, and such a relief. I've thought that every time I've delivered a book, and every book I've ever written has had a big chunk of people tell me it's their favourite. That's pretty nuts.

With most of my ideas, I tend to write from experience. My dad was a racing driver and my book *Chasing Daisy* was definitely  inspired by him and the racing scene I grew up around. My dad had raced in Formula 1 and won Le Mans in 1983. I remember him taking me to the Australian Grand Prix as a teenager and introducing me to Senna and people like that. It was pretty nuts.

A friend or a friend of a friend had worked in hospitality for the Formula One-scene and after talking to her about being, as she put it, 'a waitress in a car park' – getting to fly all around the world with the Formula 1 team and staying in amazing hotels and dealing with these racing drivers who are doing one of the most dangerous jobs that you can do, that was where inspiration came from. There was a crash in one of the chapters and that's based on a crash my dad had when he was racing in America.

My dad said there have been two points in his life where he was absolutely certain that he was going to die and this crash was one of them. His steering locked, brakes locked, he was going straight towards a concrete wall at crazy speeds. He said he was absolutely certain he was going to die. I thought, 'What must that have been like?' and channeled it into my book.

Most of the time when an idea takes hold, if it's the right one, it sticks. I've always come up with the idea for my next book while I'm writing the one before. You find inspiration from anywhere. For me it happens to come from other books and movies and songs and things. Sometimes I'll be walking down the road and an idea will pop into my head, and it will be pretty nuts.

The best thing about being an author is being able to create your own little movie inside your head. You're living vicariously through your characters and it's just really fun. I think writing is a lot like acting. You really have to put yourself in your characters' position and that's the biggest compliment a reader can pay me is that they really have felt the emotions. I love knowing that they cried and laughed because I'm sitting there crying when I'm writing a sad scene. I really connect to the characters and that enables my readers to connect with them too. Sometimes I read other books and I don't connect so much because I don't feel like the author has connected.

Writing commercial women's fiction is a great genre to be in. You have to write what you're passionate about and I love reading chick lit and young adult fantasy stuff too. I love *The Hunger Games* and I've got an idea for a book from it, which at some point I will write.

You have to write about things you believe in. As long as you're connected to your characters, there will be readers out there who will connect. If you don't love what you're writing or there's something wrong with the scene, then stop. Go for a walk, take a break, try to skip past that scene and come back to it later or just try to move the story onto another scene – so that you're excited about what you're writing about once again. I would never deliver a book that I'm not one hundred percent happy with or almost one hundred percent happy with.

I've learned from experience that when writer's block strikes, the best thing to do is take a break. There's no point sitting in front of a computer screen, staring at blank pages and feeling rubbish about yourself. It's better that you take yourself out of the situation, go for a walk, listen to some music, go and see a movie and just let the world inspire you so that you can get writing again. That's what I do. More often than not, my characters start speaking to me again. If my characters are keeping me awake when I'm trying to fall asleep, that's a really good sign.

I still can't quite believe what I've achieved as an author. It feels very surreal. Sometimes I realise that there are hundreds of

thousands of people reading my books and w'
makes my brains explode a bit. I just feel so l

My proudest moment was getting that firs.
an absolute dream come true. As far back as I can rem.
wanted to write and the first job I ever wanted to do was to be a
author. In the future I want to continue writing and never take it
for granted. I get too much enjoyment from it. Oh! And Marian
Keyes did give me a quote for that very first novel.

She said, 'I loved it, I couldn't put it down.'

Paige's Tips for Rocking Work Experience

You can impress your supervisors by being really eager, really keen,
asking the right questions and not getting grumpy if you're asked
to sit there for hours on end cutting out newspapers. With work
experience, it's all about attitude and enthusiasm and pleasantness.
Being friendly and keen is so important. I really believe if you are
passionate about getting into the magazine industry and you *really*
want it then you will absolutely succeed because you'll try that bit
harder.

Cecelia Ahern

Author and screenwriter Cecelia wrote her first book PS I Love You *aged just twenty-one. Fast-forward twelve years and twelve books, and she has been published in over forty-seven countries, and has sold well over twenty million copies worldwide. With screenplays including* Samantha Who *and Hollywood movie adaptations of her novels under her belt, the Dublin-born writer has put in hard work to follow her childhood passion . . . well, one of them!*

I'm privileged to say that I've achieved my childhood dreams. My twelve-year-old self would think I am *the* coolest person on the planet, *ever*. Well, I'd like to think she would be happy. My goals were split between being a writer or Beyoncé. I suppose one out of two ain't bad!

All I ever wanted to do in my early days was become a pop star. I loved singing and dancing and that's where my priorities lay. Even back then, I loved to write. I used to pen songs with my friends and record them onto cassettes. I loved writing poems and short stories, but mostly I used to write in my diary every day.

I was an absolute bookworm too and reading was a passion. I loved Enid Blyton's *Famous Five* series and the *Sweet Valley Twins* and *Sweet Valley High* series; and of course, the whole *Baby-sitters Club* series. The funny thing is, I've recently started writing young adult fiction and my editor is the person who created the *Baby-sitters Club*. It's such an honour for me to work with her every day.

Those books were brilliant and I learned so much from them but the real stand-out book from my childhood was *Under the Hawthorn Tree* by Marita Conlon-McKenna. It was about children growing up during the Famine and it was the first really serious historical book that taught me something about the world at a very young age. There's another book called *The Best Little Girl in the World* – about anorexia, that I adored. They were the first of the big issue-driven books that I read at the ages of eight, nine, ten and eleven.

At the age of twelve, I somehow came across a course in DCU that really caught my attention. It was a course in communications and I remember thinking, 'That's what I want to do.' I loved the media side of things in school. In transition year we learned about advertising, marketing, writing articles and things like that, and I really, really enjoyed it. To me it didn't feel like work and I knew then that was the side I wanted to get into.

My college years were spent studying journalism and media communications in Griffith College. It wasn't just creative writing – there was radio, broadcasting, TV and film production, and the whole practical side of it really appealed to me. I didn't think I wanted to be a writer because I didn't want to be a straightforward feature writer. I only liked writing fiction for myself or about myself, for myself. After graduation, I signed up to do a masters in film production – I was accepted into the course but only stuck at it for two days before deciding to drop out to go and write *PS I Love You*.

I was twenty-one and going through a time of searching for myself. I was thinking about how devastating it would be to lose the people I love – that's when I thought about how beautiful it would be if they left letters behind.

I love the written word and to me it feels as though people give a part of themselves when they write. The idea for the book was born from the fact that I would have liked somebody that I love to have left letters for me.

It was a massive decision leaving my masters course, and the writing required a lot of dedication. It really took over my life.

People say things like, 'What made you want to be a writer?' or 'Who inspired you to be a writer?' – and the answer is Nobody. I think writing is in you.

It's the way that I've been ever since I was a child. If I had a busy head, I would write things down and then I'd feel better about it, almost immediately. It was my way of working things out; to understand the world and myself.

As soon as I started writing *PS I Love You*, I knew that it was stronger than anything else I'd ever written. It became my *everything*. I was writing all night – I'd start working at about 10PM and I'd write until about four in the morning. Then I'd sleep for most of the morning and day, get up, type up what I had handwritten the night before, and then start working again. I didn't leave my house for three months. I really hibernated and just wrote this story. I was laughing along and I was crying along, and it was a very intense time. I completely immersed myself in the world of my characters.

When I first sent the book to my agent, Marianne Gunn O'Connor, I was just looking for advice. I didn't know I was actually going to get a deal! We went back and forth for a long time; I had to keep sending her more chapters to make sure that she was being held by the book. I didn't send her the full book from the get-go, obviously! I only sent three chapters and then she'd ask for another and another and another. It was about two weeks later that she called me and said she wanted to represent me. I fell off my chair because that was a very big deal! It's only then that I began thinking about publishers. We sent out ten chapters to a bunch of publishing houses, and a week or two later, I got my first deal, with HarperCollins in the UK. I'll never forget that day. Marianne asked to meet me. I knew I was going to hear something good, but I didn't know exactly what. It was just so exciting!

It was Christmas time and I remember meeting Marianne in the Merrion Hotel in Dublin. I thought to myself, 'Well my life is changing, here I am, twenty-one, fresh out of college, living at home with my mam, no job.' I was prepping my CV to send out to the world and then, all of a sudden – boom, I got a career. Everything changed. Every day there was something new which was incredible.

My coping mechanism during that mad time was to get back to work. I felt really encouraged by the feedback I had gotten and of course, getting such an exciting book deal. It was overwhelming in lots of ways. My way of coping was to think, 'Well, I got to this stage and this success because I love writing, so I'd better go back and write some more'. I began writing my second novel before *PS I Love You* had even been hit bookshelves. There was a whole year for me to write a new book without any kind of feedback or criticism or anything like that. That was important.

I remember it so well the first time I saw my book in physical form. It arrived to the apartment where I was living and I literally carried it into every single room. Every time I moved room, it was with me and I'd prop it up somewhere I could see it. I remember washing the dishes in the sink and it was propped up beside me on the draining board. I just couldn't take my eyes of it. I'd get a thrill seeing it in bookshops but a part of me was almost too embarrassed to stand near it in case people thought I was showing off. I didn't want to go too close to them in case somebody standing beside me would be holding a copy of the book. It was a real buzz, and it still is a real buzz.

Then things got even madder. *PS I Love You* was going to be turned into a movie! The phone call came the same week as the American book deal. It was one thing after another, and I was extremely excited. First of all, here I was writing a book for my own enjoyment, and then all of a sudden, here I am with a publishing deal. It was all so new to me; I wouldn't even have thought that would be something that would happen. I was buzzing every single step along the way.

Samantha Who came along thanks to *PS I Love You*. The producer of comedy development at ABC contacted me. She'd read *PS I Love You* and loved the book. She wanted me to create something original for them for their half-hour comedy slot. That was another thing I wasn't planning on – or ever thought about. I came up with two ideas for them and they flew me over to L.A.

I had to pitch it to all the studios and meet with a lot of writers. I was twenty-four then and it was very overwhelming and terrifying. I was literally up all night and wouldn't have slept at all before any of those meetings. But you go in and it's a cozier environment than what you would imagine. I was mostly meeting young women in high positions who made amazing things happen and that was a very comfortable atmosphere – a very 'can do' atmosphere. I'd go in and simply tell them my story and I felt confident because that's what I do; that's what I'm good at. I had to try to get my world across to them and it worked – thankfully!

We agreed at that stage that I was not going to be giving up writing as a novelist and moving to L.A. to work as a TV writer. That's a totally different career and one that I couldn't have done.

I still write screenplays to this day. I have so many ideas that aren't always very 'novel', so it's a nice way to tell the story through a different medium. I feel more comfortable in these TV meetings now. I'm finding my feet and I'm able to run them a bit more. You know, the older you get, the wiser you get, and all that. I'm finding my voice a lot more; I'm learning every day.

What happened to me is unique and I think we were all in awe over the years. Every day a new opportunity would pop up and we'd all just giggle about it: 'Can you believe this is happening?' My mam is funny; she wouldn't be blown away by a lot of things. She'd say, 'Well of course that happened, you're good enough for that to happen.' She really believed in my potential.

There are three elements when it comes to my story ideas: experience, imagination and observation. They're the three elements I always use. Obviously imagination is incredibly important as an author. They're not my personal experiences but there are elements of my life in there. And observation? Well, I think that's the role of an author – to observe the world, absorb everything around you and let it work its way onto the page.

Ideas come about in bizarre and different ways. *The Marble*

Collector came from the simple phrase, 'I've lost my marbles.' I thought, 'I want to write about a woman who actually, physically *does* lose *actual*, marbles, and wants to go on a journey to find them'. It was supposed to be a short story and then I got thinking about who owned the marbles, and what the importance of them was? Then this whole other story developed – the father/daughter story. It's a completely different thing to anything I've ever written before. That's an example how a story can come from just one phrase and the analysis of the true meaning of phrases. I'm always asking questions, and always trying to get to the root of things. I'm curious.

PS I Love You is the book that changed my life and set me out on the course and career that I'm on now and the that book touched a lot of people's lives. I'm kind of remembered for that one the most and it's an incredibly special book to me. I wouldn't have the others if I didn't have that. If I'm recommending my books to anybody new, I always recommend the latest. My most recent, in my opinion, is the best one I've ever written, and hopefully I'm always improving. I would say *The Marble Collector* is the book I'm the most proud of at the moment. I wrote *PS I Love You* twelve years ago so the change between my writing now and then is very obvious.

There's always a part in the books where it gets quite tricky. With *The Marble Collector,* I had written the whole book – it's two stories – and I knew that the book publishers would love one story and be unsure about the other. I was saying it to my husband the whole way through the writing process, 'They're not gonna like this bit, but I love it and I'm writing it anyway!' Of course I sent it off and all the feedback I got was, 'We *love* this story, are not so sure about the other one,' so I had to write half the book again and I'd never had to do that before. The only other time I've had to do that was in *How to Fall in Love.* I decided, very close to the end, that I wanted to change my character's profession and change from third person to first person. That was quite intense.

I love doing the research for my novels. Working on *The Marble Collector* was really interesting. I got to go to a glassmaker, where she showed me how to make marbles. I went into studio and got to make some for myself. There's the side of the research process that's practical and you go and do things. And then the other side is where you're always reading and looking things up. I bought a lot of books on marbles as well as marbles themselves, just to have on my desk while I'm writing – to be able to pick them up and feel them and touch them and know what you're writing about. There's a lot of googling!

After months and months of working on a book, once I type 'The End', I go to the pub, on my own. It doesn't matter what time of day it is. I have a glass of champagne, by myself, and I celebrate, by myself. You don't realise how stressful writing a new book is until you're finished. You feel such a release when you write 'The End' and I'm usually crying my eyes out because I'm saying goodbye to the characters, and I've wrapped up a whole story and it's very emotional. I don't want to talk to anybody for that glass of champagne. I don't want anyone to join me. I just want to go and have my glass of champagne and kind of toast my characters.

What really attracts me to writing is ideas; I get really excited by ideas. I'll often think, 'Ah, I wish I had thought about that one!' It's very important, obviously, to have ideas when you're writing, or it makes things very stressful.

Taking a step back and looking at my career, I feel very lucky. I've been published in forty-seven countries. I have twelve novels, that's a lot of books! It's overwhelming knowing that over twenty million people have read my stories and connected with my characters. It's very difficult to wrap my head around that, but if anything, it's encouraging. What's incredible is that I write these things because they come from my mind, and I'm writing them for me because I'm in the mood to write them or because I'm curious about them. What I've learned from *PS I Love You* is that, no matter what's going on in your own mind, there are other people that you've never even met – from across the other side of the globe – that have connected and are feeling what you feel. People who are worrying about things you worry about; people who are afraid of things you're afraid of, and who love the things you love. It has made me realise how connected we all are, without us even knowing.

For me, the perk of being an author is getting to do what you love every single day. Life is stressful enough without having to go to work every day and not being happy with what you're doing. Writing is a happy moment, a moment of clarity. Finding something that you feel passionate about is a really important thing to do. You don't have to do it as a career; as long as you find something that you enjoy doing, something that really makes your life happier. when I was younger that was my dancing, that was my dance class, I used to take classes a couple of days every week and I lived for that dance class. It's important to find something.

There are two very different worlds of being an author. There's the one where you're sitting in a room all by yourself, writing, which is the one I love; and the other is where you're out travelling the world, doing big events, TV and promotion and all that kind of thing which is nerve-racking for me. I find it stressful. Ever since I was in school, I've hated reading out loud – that was my number-one fear. If anyone asked me to read, I'd go to the toilet and disappear until the class was over. Funnily, I've literally taken on a job where I read out loud every day! If you don't face your fears when you're younger, they come back to bite you.

For the future, I want to try to maintain what I have. Doing things once is great. If you can do them twice; it's kind of miraculous. My dream is to continue writing novels, all the while surrounded by my beautiful, precious family. Whatever else comes after that is a bonus. Writing is my passion, my love.

On the Box

'Don't bend; don't water it down;
don't try to make it logical;
don't edit your own soul according to the
fashion. Rather, follow your most intense
obsessions mercilessly.'
-Franz Kafka

Television is a powerful medium. Think about it: how many TVs do you have in your home? Multiply that by how many homes there are in Ireland, Europe and the globe.

Daily, hourly and by the minute, we turn to television for entertainment, escapism and information. The whole world is accessible to us through the remote in the palm of our hands. At the helm are our favourite presenters and anchors, smoothly guiding us through our daily indulgence, whatever it is we choose to watch on the box.

In this chapter, step behind the camera with some of our favourite telly-faces. Get an insight into their lives as they share their highs, lows and everything in between.

Laura Whitmore

ITV 2 Jungle girl Laura Whitmore is living the dream, presenting prime-time television in the UK. A regular face on MTV, her transition to network television marked a monumental step in her ever-blossoming career. A regular on red carpets, with invites to the hottest showbiz parties, the Wicklow native hasn't done too badly for herself since her DCU days.

It might seem like it all happened overnight, but I've put in my hours of hard work to get to where I am today. Winning *Pick Me! MTV* kick-started my career but I had been working hard in the background for a long time to earn my stripes. I always knew a career in media was for me but I didn't quite know how I'd get there. I had big dreams and big ambitions and I hoped and prayed that my hard work would one day pay off.

Once I finished school, I thought long and hard about my options and I settled on studying journalism in DCU. I threw myself into things from the get-go. I even got to live in Boston for a semester. There, I studied broadcast journalism for six months and got a completely different perspective on TV. I loved the freedom of college life.

My journalism course required about twelve hours of class a week – you could either do just that, and go to the bar, or you could try and fill up your free time with extra-curricular activities and doing bits and pieces and that's exactly what I did.

One of the best things about my time in DCU was setting up a fashion magazine. I was also on the student's union and I was in the drama club. It was all those extra things that I was able to do that probably helped me to succeed in the long run. Growing up, I wasn't the most extrovert kid by any means, so all those extra-curricular activities helped build up my confidence and brought me out of my shell.

During my college summers, I worked for East Coast Radio, a station based in Bray, County Wicklow, where I'm from. It gave me a taste of what working in media was really like. As part of my degree in my final year, I did an internship. I decided to do my internship with Newstalk radio. I was there for about two months before was made permanent.

In Newstalk I was a researcher. I did do some bits and pieces on air which was fun but also nerve-racking. I still think nothing will ever be as hard as Newstalk was because it was quite an intimidating atmosphere in there. Working in current affairs definitely built my character. Two months into my job, I saw an ad about auditions for a new MTV presenter – they were taking in videos from all over Europe, and the position would require moving to London. Of course I jumped at the chance to enter.

A friend from DCU borrowed a camera and we filmed a short two minutes. It was awful. I mean it was *terrible*. It wasn't anything fancy, just me speaking to camera. I always say to people putting together a show-reel, it should be about *you*, not who you're inter- viewing. It doesn't have to be fancy or high-quality. I think your personality always shines through if it's just you on camera. My reel was just me, on camera, talking about nothing in particular.

I got a call to say I was in the final one hundred and fifty, whittled down from three thousand applications. I remember it was Valentine's Day when I got the call to invite me over for a screentest. I had just broken up with my first boyfriend, and that phone call really turned my mood around! The whole audition process was a whirlwind and very surreal. There was a massive queue outside – boys and girls, people from all over Europe and models who were six-foot tall. I thought, 'I'm so out of my depth, the best I can do is just go for it.' I always say fake it till you make it – no one knew I didn't know what I was doing. After that first day, I made it to the final fifty.

I remember being really intimidated because there were so many beautiful models. I can specifically remember seeing someone completely freeze in front of the camera and thinking, 'Oh, I can do that way better.' Sometimes you forget that the people you're intimidated by are just people too. I thought, 'Whatever happens, I need to keep talking, even if I mess up.' From watching TV, I knew everyone fluffs up from time to time. It's about how you handle that situation; nobody's perfect.

My radio and journalism background and my drama classes from when I was a kid really helped me get through that part of the audition. So much so, I can say I was really enjoying it towards the end. When I got through to the next stage, *Pick Me! MTV* sent me to the Empire Film Awards to do a report. I was still travelling back and forth to Ireland. I kept everything a secret the entire time.

The first time I went over I took the day off work. I think I told them I had a hen party or something. I just didn't want anyone to know. When I got down to the final ten, I thought, maybe I should say something, just in case it makes the papers.

I never really thought I had a chance of winning because there were a lot of people I recognised when I got to the auditions. I remember recognising Eoghan McDermott. There were some actresses I'd seen in *Hollyoaks* and people I'd seen on Nickelodeon too. I thought, 'No chance I'm gonna get this.'

Regardless of the outcome, I knew it would be a great opportunity to meet producers. I thought at least I'll get someone's card and they'll definitely give me work experience and that might be a good foot in the door. That was what my hope was – to just get my foot in the door.

I got on really well with everyone, all the producers and crew, and I developed a good relationship with them all in a short space of time. The final was held at the Soho Hotel. There were three judges, Emma Willis, Trevor Nelson and Alesha Dixon, and I was announced as the winner. One of the first people I called was my dad. He said, 'Oh Jesus, I thought that thing was fixed, it mustn't be if you won.'

I knew winning would mean some big changes in my life. I moved to London. I think I knew one person there at the time. I got a houseshare with two English guys who were complete strangers. The whole thing was so weird because I didn't really have time to think about it. I remember starting two weeks after I moved, and I still hadn't found a place to live. I remember feeling so incredibly lucky because I had always planned to move to London. London's scary at first; it's a big city and it can eat you up, especially if you don't know anyone. I calmed myself by thinking about my job and about how I'd make friends and meet people through that. Having a job was some form of security. I felt really lucky to be given this opportunity, so I had to make the most of it.

I was still in Ireland, packing up my life, when I found out about my first official assignment for MTV. I got a call from our executive producer telling me my start-dates. She also let slip that I would be going to L.A. to cover the MTV Movie Awards. I had never been to L.A. in my life. I tried to play it cool but I was a little bit scared and apprehensive because it's such a big, glamorous event. I did my own hair and makeup and there weren't big budgets for fancy dresses. I borrowed my friend's dress from Topshop for the trip. My first gig was to interview Coldplay. I remember it being such an amazing and memorable first day. I'm a big fan of Coldplay so interviewing Chris Martin did have my heart racing a little bit. I wanted to get a good interview. I wanted to prove myself. I was psyching myself up in my head, 'Come on Laura, just pretend you know what you're doing. He doesn't need to know that you don't know what you're doing . . .' While that's going through my head, my producer said, 'Oh Chris, this is Laura's first day.' I was like, '*Duuuuuuude.*' Chris was lovely. He started asking me loads of questions to put me at ease. I was really lucky that I had really lovely people, both on my team and on the interviewee side.

I've realised in time, the people I'm interviewing are often way more nervous than I am. At the end of the day, I'm the one in control. I've got the power.

To this day, the people I've met in MTV are my best mates. I was so emotional on my last day in *MTV News*. I'd been doing news bulletins for seven years and I wanted to move onto other projects. It was a big decision for me to leave and when I told the bosses, they asked what to make you stay.

It was great leaving on my own terms and being able to decide to do all of the awards, Ibiza and all the *MTV Asks* shows. I'll forever be part of MTV history and family alongside people like Cat Deeley, Davina, Donna Air, Edith Bowman, Zane Lowe and Trevor Nelson, Dermot O'Leary and Russell Brand.

MTV is amazing but doing something for ITV or any of those networks is different because it's a different audience. People's grannies and aunties see what I'm doing on there. In hindsight, hiring me was such a risk for ITV. I had only been working in MTV for two years at that stage and I had auditioned for the Jungle role alongside everyone else.

I actually auditioned for the role in the *This Morning* studios, sitting on the couch. They had Joe Swash there and a few other people too. Talk about an intimidating situation! I do think Joe helped me get the job in that he was really helpful and made it easy for me. There were so many people there with a lot of experience. I had experience with MTV which really throws you in the deep end, but I had never hosted a big live show like that. The fact that they took a risk and picked me, that meant a lot. I didn't tell a lot of people I was going for the job because I didn't want anyone to know, just in case it didn't work out. Never tell anyone anything, is what I say to myself.

I always think it's nice to challenge yourself and take yourself out of your comfort zone. I love *I'm a Celeb*. I remember how nervous I was that first year. I felt physically sick. I think nerves are good because they give you those butterflies and you get that adrenalin rush. It's such a tiring show because it's every day and you're sleeping weird hours because it's broadcast live in the UK. I remember it being quite draining. You're kind of the ringmaster on that show. I'm so lucky that I work with the best team in TV. With TV, the presenter is just one part of it. You need a good team around you. If you don't have a good team, you're the one who looks stupid.

I've made so many mistakes on air, from saying the wrong thing to missing my chair. When I first started *I'm a Celeb*, I'd watch Ant and Dec beforehand and I'd see them making mistakes and it made me realise that the best presenters are the ones who are real. Dec's always making mistakes and then doing a cute little laugh to cover it up.

I don't want to be a slick presenter because that's boring to watch. I think the most important thing is to be natural and to be yourself because you can't keep up the façade.

I remember hearing a great piece of advice from Trevor Nelson when I first started out in TV, and that's to talk to the camera like it's a person you fancy. Talk to the camera as if it's just one person, always keep people at home part of the action, and never exclude them. Don't have in-jokes. Sometimes Joe will say something stupid and I'll look at the camera and make a face – it's about keeping the audience involved and intrigued. You have to keep the camera as your friend. I remember doing a photo-shoot with Davina and being super-nervous because I adore her so much. I remember she grabbed my hand and squeezed it and said, 'Just have fun.' That was a great piece of advice.

My mom always said to me, 'If you have a voice and you're given an opportunity to use it, don't be selfish with it.' I think it's really important that I work with charities like PLAN's 'Because I Am a Girl' campaign, sponsoring little girls, or that I went over to Africa to work with girls in schools there. Sometimes you can get caught up in this fun world you're living in but if I have a large following on social media and I can tweet something or say something that makes someone else aware about an issue, I think it's important to use that voice.

I'm quite lucky that I started this job when I was twenty-two or twenty-three and I had those four years in college to grow up privately and out of the limelight. The tough thing about this industry is the intrusiveness. A lot of times what's printed is so wrong and all you want to do is say something. I learned a long time ago to stay quiet because there's no point in being vocal. I remember the papers speculating that I was going out with Niall Horan and I said, 'No, he's like my little brother.' They then wrote another article saying I was denying it. I realised I was fuelling it and that there was no point. It's both funny and odd when you're dating someone new and pictures appear everywhere and you think, 'Oh great, now even my dad has seen it!'

Dad will then call and ask, 'So, who is this guy?' Anyone else wouldn't have to tell their parents until they were sure about it.

It's a small price to pay and it's not the worst in the world. I remember once being chased, by myself, in Soho by a bunch of photographers. I was really scared because they were quite big guys. I remember trying to get into a cab and whacking my head in the madness of it all as the camera tried to push at me. I was really upset and rang my mam, feeling scared by the situation. If I go to an event, I know I'm going to be pictured; that's just the way it is. It's when it happens unexpectedly and you're out doing your own private thing that it's a bit scary. It was just the one time and I'm so grateful it hasn't happened since.

There's a Wilson Philips song called 'Hold On.' It's on the first album I ever got. I was about three. The lyric is, 'Nobody can change your life except for you'. I always think that's really important. If you're doing a job that you don't like or if you're in a situation you're not happy with, I do think you're in control of your life, despite obstacles – so go and do something about it and change it if you're unhappy. If want to be a presenter or do something, *anything*, it's important to remember that you're the only one who can control your life.

If you believe in yourself and you push it, there's no reason why you can't do it. There's always a way to get yourself out there. I don't come from a rich background. I didn't know anyone involved in TV – I was lucky that I found this opportunity and went for it. If I'd never entered that competition, I don't know where I would be now.

My advice to anyone hoping to enter the industry is to just go for it. If you want something badly, just go for it and believe in yourself. Nobody else will believe in you, unless you believe in you. Know what it is you want to do. Be sure that it's what you want and realise that nothing is as good as it looks from the outside. There are always opportunities to work in your local radio station or newspaper, where you'll get the chance to work your way up. You don't have to be on MTV straight away. Take your time, gain experience, learn. It's what I had to do too. There are a lot of ways in.

How to Work a Red Carpet Interview

Be comfortable in what you're wearing.

I was working on the BAFTAs and I was really happy with what I was wearing but it was snowing, so I had two pairs of tights and thermal underwear on too. You want to feel good, you want to feel pretty, you want to feel fashionable but you need to be comfortable too. Dress for yourself. Your clothes, or lack of, shouldn't get in the way of you doing a good job.

Do your research.

Be as prepared as you can. I don't mean having sheets of things, just read stuff. I don't like working off scripted questions, I like having a conversation. If you've read stuff about whoever you're interviewing, it's in your head anyway. You don't have to know everything one hundred percent. If they mention a new project, you can say, 'Oh yeah, I've read about it.' Have as much prep as possible done.

Have a good relationship with your team.

They have everything you need on standby and they will save your life. I've had situations before where people turn up on red carpets who you didn't expect, or they might be a new artist and you don't know who they are. If you've got a good researcher, they'll whisper in your ear and give you some guidance – two facts can be all you need. I've had situations where I've interviewed people and I've had no idea who they were. It can be a fun game. 'Sooo, are you having a good time? What's next for you?'

Martin Dougan

CBBC Newsround *presenter and Channel 4's 2012 Paralympics reporter, Martin Dougan was thrown into the limelight upon winning a nationwide presenter search. A former carpenter and Scottish wheelchair basketball captain, the broadcaster has seen his career go from strength to strength, anchoring the BBC's live childrens'news programme.*

You could say I was a bit like Forrest Gump as a child. I had these big casters on my legs, along with disability boots that enabled me to get about. I walked a bit like a duck listening to rap music. Despite my disability, I always loved my football – both playing and spectating. I liked hanging out with my mates, and like most young boys, I dreamed of being a footballer. I grew up in Glasgow, which was quite a rough city, and I learned to stick up for myself really fast. I always knew I wanted to be different. As well as football, I was obsessed with TV and movies.

In school they asked me what I wanted to be when I grew up. All the other kids said they wanted to be firemen, policemen, doctors. I said I wanted to be Batman.

When I was really young, I didn't notice my disability. I grew up in a strong Glaswegian family. My mam wouldn't allow me to mope or feel in any way that I was different to everybody else. In primary school I was bullied for having cerebral palsy but it didn't bother me or discourage me too much. I could walk but some things definitely proved a challenge, my balance wasn't great.

Sometimes my school wouldn't let me play football for the team and I wasn't allowed to do PE with the class. It made me feel terrible. I knew I was good and I knew that I had it in me. When you're young, even if you're not good at something and you want to do it but somebody doesn't let you, it's really frustrating. As a young person, you don't understand why not.

Apart from the restrictions imposed in school, there was no point where I felt like I couldn't do anything. When young kids would pick on me, I kind of understood why, even at a young age. Mind you, I always made sure to stick up for myself. I was never in a position where I felt ashamed or put down by my disability, and I don't think anybody should either, because being different is pretty good. I always knew that I was good at stuff and that I had the ability to make people laugh, so I was happy.

As a kid, I always knew that I would end up having an operation that would benefit me. I also always knew there was a chance one day I could end up in a wheelchair. I was thirteen when that happened and I was in hospital for three months. Leaving your friends being able to play football and coming back and you're seeing the world differently – it's very, very hard.

What affected me most was girls – I was a boy who liked the girls growing up, like most young guys. When I was thirteen, the world was very different to what it is now. I used to feel that the wheelchair put me at a disadvantage. My mates would still let me play football and if I had to jump over a wall, they'd throw me over, but with girls it was a different story. Growing up, I understood the complexities of my disability, and emotionally, I had been ready for the life-changing operation. It was more the social barriers that resulted that were the toughest thing of all. One day a woman I had known for years started speaking to me differently because I was in the wheelchair. She spoke to me as if I was a child. People also began to stare. I had to get past those social situations where people looked at you and stared and spoke to you differently, or felt sorry for you without even knowing you. There are lots of frustrations but you learn through time that it's other people's problem, not yours. I'm pretty capable of doing anything I want.

There was one moment when I was in my bed after the operation – I had casts on my legs while I was in recovery. I remember one morning, rolling over and falling out of the bed. My dad ran to pick me up straight away but my mum stopped him. She basically said, 'You've got an option, you either get up yourself, because the breakfast is in the other room, or you can lie here all day, but nobody's going to help you.'

I was not a happy bunn. I was swearing, I was screaming and I was really angry, like the typical stroppy teenager, but I think that was the moment where I realised that the people closest to me weren't going to be able to help me all the time; that I needed to do it for myself. If there was one defining moment, that was it.

When I could walk I played football despite not being very good. Mostly I was the goalkeeper but I used to play out-field at times too. After the wheelchair, I continued to play until the opportunity to play basketball came up when I was sixteen. I went for a local team in Glasgow before moving to a team in Edinburgh. I managed to do well enough to train with the Great Britain team and play for Scotland. I did that right up until I was twenty-three or twenty-four.

Playing wheelchair basketball made me feel good. I was sixteen and new to being in a wheelchair. I was still trying to figure out who I was back then. I went from not knowing many boys in wheelchairs to meeting this bunch of guys who played basketball really, really well. They had friends, they had girlfriends, they had partners and they were funny and used to tell jokes with a really dark humour. All of a sudden I fitted in and I saw that the wheelchair wouldn't stop me from having a future.

We had a player who had no legs and he was really small. We used to put him in the lockers and we used to get the medical women to go to the lockers and he used to jump out. We used to travel all over the UK and all over Europe together and we're still good friends now. That's the one thing I'll always take away from those years.

I have my younger brother John to thank for my Channel 4 adventure. He's the one who decided I should go for it when he saw the advertisement on the telly announcing that Channel 4 were looking to find the next Paralympics presenter for London 2012. I wasn't convinced. It wasn't something I had ever considered. I wasn't bothered about being famous or being on TV. I always thought it was a cool job but not something I would ever do.

Anyhow, my arm was twisted and we made a short three-minute video. I introduced myself and where I was from, and why I thought I should present the Paralympics 2012.

My brother filmed it and I edited it together, really badly. As a result, Channel 4 sent me to a boot camp for five days. During boot camp, they caught us off guard a little bit. We had to read news stories to camera; we had to learn how to structure our writing, writing reports to time – ninety words to fill thirty seconds. We were taught basic journalistic skills and how to be good in front of camera. At the end of the boot camp, they asked us to do a five-minute piece explaining why we should be the next Paralympics presenter. I can't remember what I said but it obviously worked.

I was in the Channel 4 building when I found out I'd got the gig. Channel 4 had broken us down and built us back up again, so when the production member came in and told us we were in, there was a happy feeling at the end of it but there was also a feeling of being ready because we'd worked so hard.

It wasn't a surprise to anyone, I don't think. The final eight were all people from everyday life who were taken and put into this whirlwind situation. I think that once we had passed a certain point, it would have been more of a surprise if we didn't get it. I've always had that confidence, I don't think anyone's better than me. I was delighted to be a part of it.

The happiness was overcshadowed by the realisation that something big was going to happen and I'd better be ready for it. I moved to London where I did all sorts of placements to pick up the necessary skills. I started from the bottom. I knew nothing about TV and had to build up that reputation and trust.

In the build-up to Channel 4's Paralympics coverage, I appeared on a music show called *Freshly Squeezed* with Rick Edwards. That was really daunting because it was the first time the Paralympics 2012 reporters were going to be revealed. After the show, things spiralled and I reported online at lots of events in the months that followed. The execs were slowly building us up, with proper on-screen experience.

I can remember doing my first live broadcast at GB House during the Paralympics. I was nervous but not terrified. I had butterflies rather than that sickly feeling you get. I was in GB House, where all the athletes go after they've raced and it's where the families go too. We were doing reports when Johnny Peacock won his race; we were sitting at GB House watching them, so we got all the reaction. I remember it clearly but the funny thing is whenever you do your first live report or bit of presenting, you never fully remember – you just wing it. It goes so fast, you wonder, 'What did I say? What did I do?'

A personal highlight for me from that time was when I was covering the weightlifting. There was a man from Iran who weighed four hundred pounds. Channel 4 got the first interview with him because we were the rights holders to that particular event. And this man was huge. I'm in a wheelchair and so was he, but when he sat in his, his arms were the size of my head.

He'd just lifted the weight of an elephant – he was pumped and in the zone. He came into the interview pen, grabbed my shoulders and picked me up. He had this massive beard and he was sweating and I felt my face getting closer to his face and he gave me a sweaty, beardy kiss. We were live on TV and it completely took me off focus. I was like, 'I don't know whether we should talk about the kiss first or the fact that you've just won a gold medal.' That was my stand out moment. I'd never experienced someone so strong. It was just one of those nice moments you take away for yourself. You can't script that kind of stuff.

My *Newsround* story begins while I was still training for the Paralympics. At the time Channel 4 put us in different placements and *Newsround* was my very first stint. I got to know the team over those three months in London. After the Paralympics I was out of work for about six months. One evening I met a *Newsround* editor at an awards ceremony where the Paralympics had won an award. He said he was looking to do a special on the legacy of the games and asked me if I wanted to present it. It was supposed to be a one-off but I did that one report and never left. It just kind of happened from there.

When I first started at *Newsround*, I presented live from studio from the get-go. It was the first time I presented live from any studio and it was the first time I'd done anything of that scale or of that type. They just threw me in which was great. To be the first disabled presenter on *Newsround* is always something I'll hold dear. I can remember doing well for a couple of months and then for some reason, my confidence took a bit of a knock. I just couldn't present live. I froze live on air. I was in studio and for some reason my bottle went. I was reading quite a long piece of autocue and it was quite long and detailed. I had a couple of stumbles and then my body started shaking uncontrollably, I couldn't get my breathing in order. People could see that I was quite uncomfortable but they didn't know why. For a man who's so confident all the time, who's never really felt that before, it was scary. My team were in shock too because they'd never seen me like that before.

I don't know why it happened but for a good six months after, there was a sort of mental block in my mind. To overcome it, I thought about how I used to prepare myself for a game when I did the athlete stuff, playing basketball. When I used to play basketball,

I used to visualise myself doing my job well because I didn't want to be caught up in the moment; I just wanted to do my job. I did the same with *Newsround*. I began listening to music before going on air – music that makes me feel as if I can't be stopped, Public Enemy, Kings of Leon, Mumford and Sons, stuff that really gets you going.

It's all about preparation for me. If someone gives me a story or a bulletin to do, I will know everything about it. I'll write my own scripts and I'll make sure that even if something does go wrong, at least I know what I'm talking about. Research is number one. Always know your stuff and put the time to know what you're talking about. It will save you and when you go live – you're the person people are going to want to hear because they know what you're talking about. I think the worst thing is if you go on live television and something goes wrong and you don't know what you're talking about. The autocues have gone down for me a couple of times and you just get on with it. I've learned you can't rely on it. You shouldn't look like you're reading anyway, you should sort of know what you're going to say next and be able to put your personality into it.

On *Newsround*, you learn everything there is to learn at such an early stage of your career. Not only do I present and report, but I'm also an assistant producer. I'll write my scripts, I'll edit stuff. It gives you a great knowledge of how to write for six-to-twelve-year olds. I feel that if you can talk about the conflict in Syria with a six-to-twelve-year-old and help them understand that in thirty seconds, you can write for anywhere. You also get a really broad knowledge of how things are put together. You're kind of like a cool teacher when you're presenting *Newsround*; or a cool older brother or sister. You're not only covering news stories, you also get to have fun with it. Our audience love One Direction and movies and all sorts of stuff. Variety is wonderful. For example when the Rugby World Cup was on, I was covering that but then I also did the Brits and the refugee crisis in Calais. You never know what you're going to do from one day to the next.

The kids really appreciate it. You think nobody's watching but when you meet the kids and they tell you they loved your report on Syria or whatnot and that's really special. That's the part I love. I didn't have presenters like that to look up to when I was young. *Newsround* is unique in what it delivers for that age group.

Meeting David Beckham was another awesome moment. He's one of the last true celebrities in my eyes. Not only from the footballing point of view but the way he's handled himself in life and the way that he comes across. As you can imagine, interview-wise it was quite restricted, but David is a huge basketball fan like me so we found common ground there. We were only supposed to have a five-minute interview but he stopped his PR team from interrupting and we sat for twenty minutes speaking about what him and his family get up to when he's not busy. It didn't feel like work, meeting him. With most celebrity interviews it's very, very strict. In my eyes Beckham is the biggest star I've interviewed. David understands kids so I felt that he felt safe knowing we weren't trying to trick him into saying something, we were just trying to find out what he gets up to.

The hardest job I've done so far was going to the refugee camp in Calais. We spoke to the children there. As reporters, we have to protect children a wee bit more than we have to protect adults. Some of the children there were alone, and you can't film a child without consent. You've also got to be careful in the way you phrase things and the way you report, so for those reasons, that's been my toughest assignment. Everything had to be done right but also in a way that was engaging and not scary or sad. To get that balance was pretty hard. It took about two weeks from when we started the report to it going out on TV. We knew the refugee crisis wasn't going to go away and we took our time. It was best that way, to get it right rather than to rush it out.

There is no typical day in the life of a broadcaster. For me it's about getting to know who is working with me; the cameraman, the floor manager, and the person controlling the autocue. I know them all on first name terms; I know their wives' names and their kids' names. At that point everyone's there to work together, so it's important to spend time getting to know your team so that everyone's comfortable.

Newsround goes out live at 4.20PM. When it comes to four o'clock I change a little bit and sometimes I have to apologise to people. I become more focused and if I don't like something, I'll change it. If I say something in rehearsal and it doesn't quite feel right, I'll make people change it. Ultimately, you've got to do what is comfortable for you, especially wording-wise. The stories must always remain accurate but you can work with how you tell that story so that it rolls off your tongue better and sits well with you as a presenter when the red light comes on.

I'm not interested in fame or being a celebrity; for me it's about being good at what you do. I'm a broadcaster at the moment but I'll never be the finished article. I'll always be learning all the time, because things constantly change. I think it's important to remember that you're always going to make mistakes but as long as you stick by your decisions, you needn't worry about what other people think as long as you believe it's right.

Be happy being yourself. I'm going to make mistakes and I'm going to say things wrong sometimes but as long as I truly believe in myself and willing to say sorry when it goes wrong, that's all that matters.

Martin's Top Tips for Budding Broadcasters

Don't give up.

It's such a tough industry that at an early stage you'd be inclined to think that there's no space for you. That nobody's going to give you the time of day because there are so many chasing the same dream. What you've got to remember is that you can always bring something unique to the party. What can you bring that makes you different from the rest? Identify that and embrace it.

Be knowledgeable about what you're doing.

Don't just become a presenter because you want to be on TV. You're wasting your time if that's the case. Go into broadcasting thinking you can be the best because it's your genuine passion and you know everything about it – or are at least hungry to learn. TV isn't as easy as you think it is. You might watch TV, people talking and telling jokes and having a laugh, but there's been a lot of work put into that to make it come across that way. The good presenters are good because not only are they great at their job but they know what they're talking about. They are the best at what they do because of that.

You're goning to take a lot of knocks.

You might have to start on the lower end of the ladder. Keep focused. You might get sidetracked every now and again, but try and get that focus back as much as you can. Keep reminding people that that's what you want to do. Don't compare yourself to anyone else. Take it in your own style, run with it and enjoy it.

Miriam O'Callaghan

*Entertainment and current affairs go hand in hand for talented
broadcaster Miriam O'Callaghan. A TV and radio host with a background in Law, Miriam's successful broadcasting career spans over two
decades across the UK and Ireland. Miriam is the face of* Primetime *and*
Saturday Night With Miriam *on RTÉ One.*

You wouldn't think it to see me now, but I was a very shy child. I
was extremely quiet and I lacked confidence. I didn't think I was
ever going to go on to achieve very much for that reason. I worked
hard on myself to gain confidence and to stand strongly on my own
two feet. I definitely had to push myself at times to come out of my
shell, especially during my college years. Having come out the other
end, I'd like to think that I am an example of how somebody can
go on and achieve quite good things without being the star of
everything during adolescence.

I suppose my confidence began to flourish when I began my
studies in UCD. I was quite young starting there; just sixteen. Going

to university young meant you had to come out of yourself a bit or you wouldn't survive. I think it's just like everything in life; if you've very young, you just have to force yourself sometimes to do uncomfortable things and test your own limits and prove to yourself you are capable in those times when you are doubtful.

I remember going to debating societies and I would absolutely hate it but I'd just get on with it. I'd also go along to the Law Society because I was studying law. I'd make myself meet people even though I was very shy. Putting myself in those sometimes uncomfortable situations was definitely worth doing; it stood me well.

Young people coming out of school should realise that there are lots of different degrees you can do, or maybe no degree at all and still end up in broadcasting. Upon graduating from UCD, I began working as a lawyer in Dublin. My TV break happened when the BBC came to town to do a film. They really needed young lawyers and someone suggested they approach me. I suppose I fitted the brief because after an interview, I got the job. Upon completing filming, the producer sent me a nice thank-you note and said, 'You know you should think about broadcasting, you look good on camera!' That's the first time I really gave it any thought.

I think it's vitally important for anyone who wants to be front-of-camera to work behind camera too, at least for a little while. That's where the power is. I've always believed that.

I began my TV career as a researcher in the BBC and then moved on to becoming a producer. I had the privilege of working on a show called *This Is Your Life*. It was super.

It was a programme a bit like *Piers Morgan's Life Stories*, presented by an Irish man called Eamonn Andrews, who was similar to Terry Wogan. He was very nice and he used to mind me because I was the Irish girl on the team. I remember going to America where we were doing big Hollywood movie star shows and I thought, 'This is so exciting'– bright lights, Hollywood – and

Eamonn used to ring me up on Sunday mornings and say, 'Miriam, we're going to mass up the road now.' Eamonn made me realise, very young, that you should never ever lose sight of where you come from.

Coming from a law background, I was learning as I was going along in my early TV years. Sometimes I felt out of my depth but I think you kind of feel out of your depth all the time in life. The difference is when you get older, you just get better at acting like you know what you're doing.

It's quite good to doubt yourself sometimes. I always think the most interesting people and most successful people, and the people that I respect, are people who do doubt themselves.

I think when you're young it's about faking it till you make it. It's a bit of an acting game really; you just have to fake it till you make it, even if you're really nervous about doing something, even small things like picking up the phone to ring up somebody.

I remember doing Bob Geldof's *This is Your Life* and having to phone up his first wife, Paula Yates and I was really nervous thinking, 'She's going to think I'm an idiot', but it was fine - most people are very nice. If you're not too confident or unsure about something all you have to do is ask. People are there to help. A lot of the time we're all worrying about the same things anyway.

The transition to front-of-camera happened when I was working as a producer. The head of youth programmes in the BBC saw me and asked me if I would like to work on a documentary about young people in Hungary. I of course obliged and I quite enjoyed it. I was initially reluctant to go on screen because I think it's a very fickle role, people can just decide I want a blonde today and I don't tomorrow.

Interestingly, the man who was the editor of *Newsnight*, saw my report and rang me up and said, 'Would you like a job on *Newsnight*?' So that was my next gig. I was very lucky; it doesn't always work out that way. I was about twenty-nine at the time, I remember being slightly nervous about the position because I had only worked as a producer and researcher for eight or nine years. After some thought, I decided to dip my toes in the water and it went OK.

I think when you're very young you tend to gravitate to entertainment a lot. Certainly, I know I did when I was in school or I was a teenager. However, I think as a female presenter or broadcast journalist, doing serious material gives you longevity. It gives you a longer career. People are less able to dispose of you.

Personally, although I like fun as much as the next person, I'm more serious at heart. I love being able to ask questions on behalf of the public. I think that's what my job is to do – always ask the really difficult question. The kind of question that before you ask, you have to stop and think, 'Am I actually going to ask this politician this question?' I don't bottle it, or at least I try not to, and just ask go for it.

I'm known for sometimes asking very tough questions on big presidential debates, or even of the Taoiseach. I've probably made a lot of enemies along the way but I know my position is important and I want to represent the public well. I want to get the answers to their issues and concerns. It doesn't mean that I'm not afraid though. At times I do feel that tiny bit of fear, but you have to get on with it.

You always have to think, 'What's the worst thing that can happen?' We're all doing a job.

I feel privileged to do what I do. It's just such an honour to be in people's living rooms in the evening time. It's a privilege to interview and meet the people I've met.

In particular, the people who have done really courageous things in their lives, or even parents who on a daily basis are dealing with children with special needs or people who are looking after their mum or dad with Alzheimer's . When people give you their stories and speak to you, that is such a privilege, and I never, ever stop respecting that.

Even after all these years, my job continues to excite me every day. In a few minutes, I'm about to do live TV! And believe me, you never forget it's live. As my mother always says, 'You know it's live TV. You could ruin yourself every time you go on.' You just have to be a bit careful. I'm a bit of a messer but I enjoy live TV. It's fun.

If anything goes wrong on air, I think, 'Don't panic.' It's important to keep your cool; after all, as the anchor, you are the person people see in their living rooms. Somebody gave me a great tip once – if you're ever on air and something falls down and you've time to fill, explain to the viewers at home how it works – explain about the people in the gallery and how it's like the cockpit of an aieroplane. I actually rehearsed that in front of the mirror a couple of years ago and then one night I actually had to do it! People loved it. I introduced them to the floor manager, who nearly died.

My proudest career moment to date is probably a programme I did on John Hume, who a key figure in the Irish peace process. There was a big RTÉ programme where people had to vote for Ireland's greatest person and he won it. I feel proud knowing I championed him. Other people championed Bono, Michael Collins, but I championed John Hume.

Also a very important and special day was a few months ago when the marriage referendum vote happened in Ireland. I was up in Dublin Castle for the day presenting the results and the sun was shining and people were so happy. It was a very emotional day.

For anyone wanting to work in broadcasting, I can't be more encouraging about radio or print. Go out and work for your local station or your local newspaper or your local online site. Or even do a blog yourself. The great thing about online is you can do whatever you want. You can write something up and if it's good and luck is on your side, you can go viral, with hundreds of thousands of people seeing your work.

> **Don't ever accept people saying, 'Oh it's very hard to get into the business,' – ignore them. If you really want to get in, you'll get in and keep going.**

I'll share an insider secret I discovered many years ago in my early twenties in those BBC meetings where people sounded really intelligent. All these guys would be spouting theories and I'd be sitting there thinking, 'How do you know all of this?' I discovered they all read the *Economist*. My advice to anyone who wants to go into current affairs journalism is to buy the *Economist* or read it online, and you will be the most knowledgeable bore at the meeting! You will out-bore everybody else. You will know everything in the world if you read the *Economist*. I jest, but it is a great publication and I do recommend you pick up a copy. Remember to follow your dreams. You are in control at all times, even when it doesn't seem like it's not quite going your way. It is. Trust fate.

Eoghan McDermott

Radio host and Voice of Ireland *presenter Eoghan McDermott is a regular face on TV screens. With a cheeky demeanor and his trademark locks, there aren't too many things he can't tackle. Quiz shows, music documentaries, prime time entertainment and drive time radio,; he knows the sky is the limit.*

The road to my broadcasting career has been a series of fortunate twists and turns. You could say I chose to take the alternative route to get here, but I wouldn't have it any other way!

The rollercoaster began for me as a teen. I explored a million-and-one interests and hobbies, everything from magic to rollerblading and ice hockey. Not many people know this but I was once a practising magician. I took it so seriously I became a member of the Society of Irish Magicians, and my ice-hockey adventures even took me to the World Ice Hockey Championships.

I was one of the first members of the Irish ice hockey team – yes, that's a real thing! I'd train weekly with the Dublin Flyers on the North Circular Road in a space about a fifth the size of a real ice rink. Our determination paid off and we got to the World Championships. We were a dedicated team but it wasn't to be. There are usually five or six goals scored in an ice-hockey game and we lost 43-0 in our first game to the Netherlands!

I played for Ireland until I was about nineteen. I was in college at that stage, studying politics and Irish in UCD. That's when I started taking an interest in dance; soon realised that ice hockey and dancing aren't really companions. The dancing came about because of a charity fashion show I had auditioned for. There were dancers involved and they were having a way better time than the models, so I felt inspired to take some classes in order to be able to join them the following year. I auditioned and really got into the dancing thing . . . more than I ever thought I would! I was taking as many classes as I could find and I even went over to London and L.A. for weekends to take classes with people.

When I finished college I ended up dancing in New York. I mentored with a guy called Jermaine Brown. He was choreographing Christina Aguilera at the time, and was doing stuff for Britney and JLO and all these people who are massive. He was quite the dude. For a full year I did the dancing thing. It was amazing but I was flat broke. I hadn't a bean.

After about six months, I asked my parents for money but I ran out of that about three months later. For the last three months I was working illegally as a waiter in a restaurant off Times Square. Because the portions were so big, any time steak was ordered. It would invariably never be finished. I used to get the half-eaten steaks, trim off the sides and bring them home. I lived with four other people in this tiny two-bedroom apartment and all we used to eat was steak. It was the best time of my life, just being absolutely flat broke in America.

I moved back to Ireland not long after and choreographed a couple of singers. I choreographed this one girl who unfortunately didn't go on to make it as a singer but she got asked to support Chris Brown, pre-Rihanna, when he was huge. We did six dates supporting him.

I suppose fate had a part to play in all of this because at one of those Chris Brown shows, there was a producer from TG4. They were doing a new drama series called *Seacht* and were in the process of casting. It was supposed to be like an Irish *Skins*, set in a performing-arts school. He got in touch asking me to audition, which I did. My character was DJ Pete. He was supposed to be well cool. I managed to get the part and filmed that series for three summers in a row in Belfast.

It was off the back of that, that TG4 offered me a music show called *Pop 4*. I hadn't done any presenting before but I was keen to try. There was hardly any budget and it was my first real foray into presenting and it was amazing. I had a boss who was a little eccentric and never took no for an answer – so we ended up at the World Music Awards.

It was the first time we did a big glitzy global awards show. Jennifer Lopez was there and it was exceptionally cool. I remember wearing my debs suit. We weren't really supposed to be there but my producer had lied and said we were RTÉ when really we were TG4. He lied his way in and we got amazing access. We had a chat with Jennifer Lopez, the Pussycat Dolls and even Tom Cruise for about eleven seconds. The buzz of 'we're not even supposed to be here' overrode any nerves. Tom was walking down the red carpet and I just remember screaming at him, 'Tom, come say hello to Ireland.' And he did, he ran over! We speed-talked. He high-fived me and then – boom – he was gone. I think I was delirious for about two hours afterwards.

Before that night, my heart was probably still more with dancing but after the buzz of the event, I realised TV was something I wanted to pursue more. I worked hard to get to know people and try to get more gigs. I put together a little show-reel. I was trying to get into RTÉ for years and never heard back from them – ever. But that didn't stop me. I thought, 'If there's nothing going on in RTÉ, I'll look further afield!'

I entered a competition called *Pick Me! MTV*. Laura Whitmore ended up winning it. Going in, I knew they were looking for a girl, but they were accepting boys. I did well, getting down to the last five. Off the back of that, I put together a new show-reel online. One day Channel 4 rang me to say they had seen my reel. They invited me to London to screen test for *T4*, which was on at the time with Steve Jones. That was the first time I ever flunked a screentest. They gave me a couple of links to write which I then had to deliver to camera. I also had to have an on-camera chat with one of their reporters. For some reason I got really nervous: I was trying too hard to be funny and stumbled over words. I left feeling absolutely devastated, thinking, 'I'm not good enough. I'll never do anything ever again.' I ended up not getting a call back, surprise-surprise.

In the meantime, I cracked away with *Pop 4* on TG4. Spin 103.3 got in touch. They liked that I could speak Irish and they had a new weekend show they wanted me to do. It was called *Pop Raidio*. It was two hours on a Saturday and mostly tunes with little links in Irish in between. I tried to make the most of that pulling in bands and guests and finding anyone who could speak a little bit of Irish. I tried to make my own mark on what the show was already. The boss liked what I was doing and it wasn't long before I was offered the chance to work on a show in English. When we started it had very low ratings but by the time we finished, about a year and a half later, the ratings were more than five times higher than they had been

In the meantime Spin had got a new boss who worked for a station in London called XFM. It was one of those serendipity things. He had been headhunted by the parent company of Spin to set up a pop-music station in Jordan in the Middle East. He went to Jordan, set up the station and returned to Spin for a few months to oversee the schedule. He then returned to the UK to look after the entire XFM station, managing the London, Manchester and Scottish offices. He approached me with an offer to move to London with him. I had got to know him during his few months on Spin and I suppose he saw potential in me.

At first, I thought he'd forget about it but a few months later he got in touch. I was on a three-month part-time contract, with nothing guaranteed. I wasn't sure how well it was going, if it was working for me or if I was a bit try-hard, if London was even the place for me, whether my accent was welcome or not.

It was when the boss called me into the office and offered me the drive-time show that I could relax. It was a lovely two-year contract, the money was really nice and that was the first time I thought, 'I'm a proper presenter now, this is my actual job.'

Up until that point I was still a little wishy-washy about what I wanted to do. I had tried so hard after the World Music Awards to break into the industry, with not much success. I lost the faith a little bit. I wasn't making a whole lot of money and a couple of years had passed and I felt a little stagnant.

My first big interview on XFM was with the Red Hot Chili Peppers and it went terribly. The whole thing was a little surreal. The band had just released a new album called *I'm With You*. The boss at XFM asked me to go to L.A. for a one-hour interview with the Chilis – it was a big deal. They brought over three radio stations and we were one of them.

We flew over first-class to L.A. Not the norm at all. I was reading Anthony Kiedis's autobiography. The band started out in L.A. as kids; they formed this punk band and they just exploded and were making all this money. They went off the rails, he got into drugs and he lost his way for ages, and the whole band staged an intervention. They have an amazing story.

My first night in L.A., one of the most random things that has ever happened in my life, happened. I'm sitting in the lobby of the hotel in Santa Barbara, chatting to the other radio guys and the girl from the record label, and who walks in only one of the guys who used to be in *Seacht* with me on TG4.

His name is Diarmuid Murtagh and he's been in *Vikings* and has had good bits and pieces in good dramas. He was auditioning for stuff in L.A. and when he walked into the lobby and saw me, we were both in awe. What were the chances? We had big hugs, chats and then, of course, went to get a drink at the bar. We stayed up far too late and I woke up the next morning feeling not great at all, a terrible headache, the room spinning – the whole lot.

I listened to the album as planned but I just felt like I needed to go outside and lay down in the air for hours. We went to interview the band and I could hardly remember any of my questions. It was awful. I was concentrating so hard on not throwing up and being a mess that the interview itself was terrible. That was the first time I really felt like I had let myself down. I learnt a massive, lesson that day. I genuinely think about it all the time. Any time I'm asked to socialise when there's an important work-gig on, I have flashbacks about how I felt that time going back to my boss. I remember being really disappointed in myself.

I'd been on XFM about six months when *The Voice of Ireland* came around and I was asked to audition. I do think XFM helped get me noticed. XFM has launched a lot of TV presenters like Russell Brand, Dermot O'Leary, Ricky Gervais, Simon Amstell, Jimmy Carr and other cool people.

The Voice of Ireland producers only saw a couple of boys. The audition went well and I remember thinking I had done myself proud. I was walking down Tottenham Court Road in London on the way to XFM one afternoon when a random number called my phone. I answered and it was the head of RTÉ Entertainment at the time, Bill Malone. I'd never met him but he introduced himself and said, 'I saw your audition for *The Voice* and I really liked it. You've got the gig.' I remember fist pumping the air, feeling like Will Smith at the end of *The Pursuit of Happyness*. I went into XFM, gloating to my producer, 'I'm going to present *The Voice of Ireland*' and he turned around and said, 'Now that's not very cool, it is?'

As the series has progressed, I do all the auditions and have all the people crying and snotting on my shoulder but that first year, I just did the live shows as the backstage presenter. My first live show was a little scary. I hadn't done live TV before but having the radio background gave me a little security. I was really excited. I lived abroad; nobody really knew me and I felt like I had nothing to lose. I had no reputation to tarnish. I was able to start from scratch and build up. TG4 was amazing but nobody really watched it – it was quite a small audience. Being new was brilliant because it gave me the space to make mistakes and learn, without those mistakes having consequences.

The Voice UK and all the other Voices I'd seen were a bit boring; everyone played it very straight. I decided I wanted to make my own mark and do things a little bit differently and show off my personality. We'd be a little big slaggy with the contestants, always in a nice way but never afraid to poke some gentle fun. We did a few skits. Whenever you're doing something with a bit of humour – some people will find it funny and others will absolutely hate it. I prefer that. The worst thing you can do is be beige.

I wasn't afraid to try stuff and have it not work. I think that's something everyone starting out should do. Be brave and don't be afraid to try stuff.

The more established you get, the harder it will be to try stuff because you'll be on a bigger platform and more people will see you and it's more of a risk. If it doesn't quite work out, everyone will let you know – they won't be shy about it.

On the finale of season two, we recreated a bit from *Dirty Dancing*. I had my own little studio backstage and Kathryn, my co-presenter was on the main stage. I was doing a big thank-you to Kathryn and said something along the lines of, 'It was amazing to work with you, I've had the time of my life,' and then 'Time of My Life' kicked on, and we got up and danced down the corridor, all the way to the stage where I caught her off guard. I've got the dancing background – so I choreographed that section. When I pitched it to the producers they didn't love the idea, but once I got the choreographer of the show on board and she choreographed her dance troupe as my backing dancers, coming up onto the main stage, where I danced with Kathryn ending in a smooch, *Gone with the Wind* style, it went down really well.

For a couple of weeks after that, random people in the street would come up to me and say how much they loved it. That was the first time people stopped me on the street and said, 'I love that thing you did', and it was a great feeling to have someone acknowledge something I'd created. The fact that producers were initially against it, and I fought for it and it turned out to be a success, made me feel even better. It pays to be brave sometimes.

I always think people in media take themselves too seriously sometimes, getting caught up in their own little world.

It hasn't all been a breeze, this media game. I've done many screentests and auditions over the years and they haven't all gone my way. I got very close to taking over *The Xtra Factor* with Caroline Flack when Olly Murs left. They thought I was really good but a bit too much like Olly. They wanted to try something completely different. I was really disappointed. Not in myself, but just not to get it.

That's the nature of the business though. If I'm going for a gig it's because I think I could get it and if I don't get it it's because they're looking for something different, not because I'm awful. Apart from the *T4* thing, where I was disappointed I didn't do a good interview or screentest, I don't think I've ever gone away from an audition feeling bad about myself.

Being in the media is a job and you have to work hard. Sometimes the hours are long but it's never boring. You're always going somewhere different and meeting new people. In that sense, it's a dream job. A lot of those people are exciting and talented people. Who doesn't want to chat to musicians and actors and authors? Media keeps you young and on your toes; it keeps your mind sharp and keeps you ambitious, I think.

The horizon is always moving and the possibilities are endless. There are the obvious perks of getting to meet famous people and travel and getting free stuff too. I get invited to things I sometimes can't go to but I'll send my mam. Introducing your friends and parents to cool people occasionally is fun. My mam loves

One Direction. I brought her to see 1D in Cardiff, where my sister lives and I introduced her to Harry Styles. She got her photo taken and her friends thought she was just the coolest.

If you dream about a career in media, remember to be very patient. It takes a lot of hard work and knocking on doors to get your face or voice on air. It's really important to know what you're good at and equally important to know what you're not good at.

If you want to be like Russell Brand but you're not naturally funny, you probably won't make it. If you want to be the next E! presenter and you love the glamour but not entertainment gossip, that's not going to work for you. Realising what you don't like is just as important as realising what you do like.

When you find what you're good at, just annoy people. You can't be too persistent. If you're not persistent enough, you'll never make it. You have to keep trying. Most people will say no but one day someone will say yes and then you're laughing.

Once you get your foot in the door, say yes to everything that's legal!

Ian O'Reilly

He may have found fame in Chris O'Dowd's Moone Boy, *but Mayo actor Ian O'Reilly is still pinching himself. Swept from obscurity and thrown into the limelight, the young comedic actor has been making waves in the industry, embracing both his newfound star status and love for the world of drama.*

I kind of fell into acting; I had tried a lot of things, from horse riding to football to gaelic, and I wasn't any good at any of them. I went to a very small primary school with only twenty-five people in the entire school at the time. There were seven people in my class and we were the biggest class in the entire school – we were very proud of that. I discovered that two of the lads in my class did drama classes and I couldn't believe that I hadn't known about it before because we were really, really good friends for about six years. They encouraged me to go along and try a class and I loved it!

It's really nice to make people smile, and when you can do that with something that you're doing, it makes it even better. It just so happens that acting allowed me to do just that! We did a lot of things like improvisation, where we had the freedom to do what we wanted; there were no real rules. It was more, 'You do what you want to do, and do it in the way that you want,' more so than, 'Run this length of the pitch and come back,' which I wasn't very good at. The creativity really appealed to me.

Moone Boy was my first ever audition. I'd only been doing drama classes for three or four months when I heard about the opportunity. The casting director had sent out an open call to a lot of places around the country – everyone was free to go along. My drama teacher rang my dad and she said, 'Listen, there's this thing happening and there's this part that I think Ian would be very good for. I think he should go and chance it.' Dad told me about it and I went for it, and the rest is history!

The audition involved reading lines from a script to camera. As the auditions went on, we'd be in the room for longer and longer. For other auditions on different productions they might make you improvise on the spot. They might say, 'You're a turtle; Mary over here is a banana. Now, make a story out of it.' I've never been in an audition like that myself, but I've heard that they can make you improvise to see how you think on your feet.

There were three auditions in total for *Moone Boy* and I know it's very clichéd and cheesy, but I honestly didn't expect to get the part. I don't think I even fully understood what was going on; I was only twelve. It was a very surreal experience because I never ever expected to go for an audition for something like that.

I remember even when I was going for the audition and they explained to me what it was. I still didn't fully comprehend it. When we actually started filming, it was a completely different thing to what I thought it was going to be. The characters looked completely different; the house they lived in was completely different.

It was a Thursday evening when the phone call about the part came. I was at home, in the sitting room, watching *The Simpsons*, when the house phone rang. I picked it up, said, 'Hello,' and it was the casting director on the line. She said, 'Ian, this is Amy. You have the part if you want it.' I was so excited; I hung up the phone and went to tell my dad. He made the good point that we should maybe call Amy back and I was like 'Oh yeah!' I was so delighted I ran up to my nanny, who lived next door screaming, 'I got the part! I got the part!' She didn't really know what was going on either.

My first day on set was in Boyle. On a shoot that's seven or eight weeks long, we usually film on location in Boyle for two weeks and then the rest in Wicklow, in Ardmore Studios. The very first day, David's scene with me was the first one to be shot. It was the one where David or Martin has just got the bike and he's cycling down the road and Padraig is running after him, asking for a go on the bike. I remember it feeling so strange. There I was running in the middle of the road with a camera on the back of a golf cart following me. Not only that, but I was running after a fella I didn't really know who was cycling this bike. I remember thinking, 'This is strange, but I like it.'

Because I hadn't done anything in the acting world before, I didn't know what it was like to be on set. I remember being so delighted that we got lunch for free – I genuinely couldn't believe it! I thought, 'Wow, we get free lunch, what a fantastic day.' With each passing day on set, I got more and more used to it and I started to get my wits about me. I remember realising for the first time just how much work goes into a production behind the scenes that you don't even see or hear, and which is are so important. It's changed the way I watch TV. I'm always thinking about cameras and angles and what it must have taken to get a particular shot.

As newbies, we were so lucky with the crew that we had. Chris and Nick and the directors that we had were all so accommodating with myself and David and Sarah who had never done any acting before. They always took the time to stop, and explain everything to us to make sure that we knew what was going on. Looking back, that was really important. If they hadn't been so patient, I know I would have made a million more mistakes than I already did.

Small things like helping to explain a scene or even saying things like, 'You know what Ian, let's try the scene like this.' I really appreciate that they were always looking out for us.

Chris O'Dowd is a really nice guy. There's not much bad to say about him, really. He's someone I look up to. Coming from Mayo, in the middle of the countryside, where my house is surrounded by bogs, you'd think, 'Well how am I supposed to ever do things and achieve my greatest ambitions?' But then I met Chris who comes from an equally small place – Boyle, County Roscommon – who has gone on to do great things, and it showed me – wow, I *can* go on to achieve big things too.

The toughest day I've ever had on set was when we were filming the second series. I was very comfortable in my surroundings at that stage. We were filming out in a hilly golf course in County Wickow. I was at the top of this hill with three other lads who were also in the scene. I had to get this glove and run down the hill and hand it to this fella who was putting a ball into the hole. Now I usually have bad hearing as it is, but at the time I had a cold, which made my hearing even worse. For some reason, I couldn't really hear what the director wanted me to do and each time I did it, I kept getting it wrong – over and over and over again. I didn't realise what it was I was doing so wrong. Looking back at it now, I know it was my fault for not asking what they wanted me to do while I was with them at the bottom of the hill. I was too shy to ask and I ended up getting really worked up and upset, wasting everyone's time. It was the only day where I felt, 'Oh, I want to go home.'

I never usually felt that. I used to stay back late just for the craic; we never wanted to go home. I suppose I'm not a great person with making mistakes. It's something I need to work on, to accept that they happen. Hindsight is a great thing but I was young and silly and I should have asked. It might not appear very challenging on paper, but it was a really tough day for me.

An awesome day was when Paul Rudd did a bit of filming with us. He had a part in *Moone Boy* and I remember being so excited to meet him. You might recognise him from *Friends* and a bunch of other films. We had to keep it a secret that he was involved with the show, even on the call-sheets we created fake names for him. I think we called him 'Stephen Bentley' or something; absolutely nobody outside the crew was allowed to know that he was in the programme.

There was a real air of 'Oh my God, Paul is coming' about the whole thing. The first day he came into the dining bus and sat down beside David and me, and started talking to us like any other person. It was just so cool because we never expected him to be like that. He spent ninety percent of the time there with us and he'd speak to anybody and everybody who came up to him. He was exceptionally nice. There'd been such a build-up to his appearance on set, that when he actually came and sat down and said hello casually, I was blown away. We were asking him questions about America and the dollar. He gave me and David a dollar each. He was a really normal guy and we were able to have really normal conversations.

The best thing about this whole acting thing is that I've gotten a lot of life experience from it. I've kind of learned what it's like to live away from home for a while, which was different. I grew up very quickly in that short space of time. I kind of very quickly went from being child Ian to being a more mature Ian. That can be a pro and a con depending on how you look at it.

Sometimes I do miss just being a kid and getting away with things, but growing up quickly has served me well. I'll pick up on things much quicker than friends my own age. I wouldn't trade the life experience I gained through *Moone Boy* for anything. Getting to meet so many cool people is also a perk the job. Fantastic people from all walks of life that I never thought I'd meet. Even David from Leitrim, if I'd never done the show I probably would never have met him in my life purely because he's from Leitrim and I'd have no reason to go there.

Moone Boy has created lots of special memories for me. Going to the British Comedy Awards during the first season was really, really exciting. I'd never even been to an airport before, never mind being on a plane. They treated us like royalty. They gave us tickets to see *Lion King: The Musical* and tickets to Winter Wonderland which is a big winter theme park in the middle of London. It was all so cool.

For my first time out of the country and to have an experience like that, it was really special. I feel so lucky. Even if I never do a piece of acting again in my life, at least I know that I've always had those three summers of 'wow'. Summers that were just completely random, completely out of the ordinary and things that a lot of people don't usually do. It's an experience I will cherish forever. There's so many amazing people that I met and I've made so many friends. It's very cool.

For anyone wanting to make it into acting my biggest piece of advice is to just keep trying. Sometimes you'll 'um and aah' about going for things and think, 'What if it goes wrong?' but the best thing is just to say, 'Yes'. If you say no, you'll never know what could have happened. Say yes to a lot of things – sensible ones, of course!

One opportunity often leads to another and another. *Moone Boy* has given so many cool opportunities, which would never have happened if I hadn't put myself out there by auditioning. If you don't put yourself forward for things, you're never going to get there and you're never going to be able to experience cool new things. Just go for it!

I hope to keep acting; I like making people laugh when I can. My dream character would be funny and witty but at the same time not doing it at someone else's expense, but also someone who has more depth and meaning to them than the stereotypical funny guy. It's a strange industry, this acting game. Rejection is hard to deal with at first but once you get used to it, you learn to bat it off because you know it's not personal. All going well, I'll have a massive acting career and I'll go to Hollywood. Whatever way things work out though, I know a nine-to-five job isn't for me. If I can't act, I'd love to work as a TV presenter. That seems like the coolest job ever and I reckon I'd do a pretty good job at it!'

On Record

'Music gives a soul to the universe,
Wings to the mind
Flight to the imagination
And life to everything'
-Plato

Music is unique in its ability to bring people together – whether through laughter or through tears. It speaks to us in ways no other medium can, reaching out to touch our hearts directly. We've all got a favourite song, a favourite lyric, a favourite melody; be it from the movies, television, record, or burrowed deeply in our digital sound libraries. A song can have a million different meanings depending on the listener, and a single note can either fill hearts with joy or make them crumble.

Music is a gift for everyone to enjoy but not for everyone to produce. Only a select few are gifted enough to pen the songs of generations and the soundtrack to our lives.

Thumb through the pages that follow and meet some talented creatives who are lucky enough to call music not only passion but also their life.

Steve Garrigan

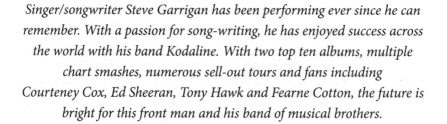

Singer/songwriter Steve Garrigan has been performing ever since he can remember. With a passion for song-writing, he has enjoyed success across the world with his band Kodaline. With two top ten albums, multiple chart smashes, numerous sell-out tours and fans including Courteney Cox, Ed Sheeran, Tony Hawk and Fearne Cotton, the future is bright for this front man and his band of musical brothers.

Songwriting for me is a form of escapism. There's nothing I love more than being lost in a song. When I sit down and write, all of my troubles and worries disappear. Music has and always will be my passion in life.

One of the best and most indescribable feelings I've ever had is hearing people sing back our songs – songs I wrote in my bedroom. Never in a million years did I imagine that one day thousands of people would be singing them back to us in unison. It's been a mad few years, but experiencing that, night after night, gig after gig, all over the world, that's what really makes it all worthwhile. It's the best feeling in the world.

From a young age, music came naturally to me, and singing and performing has always been in my blood. I come from a musical family; in fact, the first time I ever sang was when my dad bought me a karaoke machine. We used to sing our hearts out every night; my two sisters, my brother, my dad and me. Celine Dion was a popular choice at the time. *Titanic* was just out and 'My Heart Will Go On' was everywhere.

I think every artist can remember the first time they stood up to sing in front of a crowd. I have vivid memories being eight years old and getting up to I sing the Bee Gees' version of 'Words' in a bar. I won a Casio watch for my efforts that night and even at that young age, I loved every second of being in front of a crowd. I felt comfortable on stage and I remember getting such a buzz off it. There's a video in my parents' house from that night and they play it occasionally, much to my embarrassment.

My family has always really supported my passion. My grand-dad dropped in a video of me performing at a talent show in Mosney to his neighbour who happened to be Alan Hughes. Alan thought I was a good singer and gave me a part in his pantomime. We were a Boyzone tribute band and I was Ronan Keating. My mam bought me a live Boyzone concert video and I watched it over and over to help me get into the part.

I've been writing songs since I was thirteen. The subject matter varied but I mostly wrote about things that I was going through or that affected me. My first ever song was inspired by my brother's friend who passed away. I suppose it was my way of dealing with what had happened. I sat down and it was the first thing I wrote about. Looking back, it was a terrible song but the lyrics were pretty deep and in a way, quite strange for a thirteen-year-old.

Like my family, my school Colaiste Choilm in Swords was unbelievably supportive of my love for music. I was a bit of a nerd up until third year – a complete study freak, who was all about exams. I wanted to be a lawyer and I put in all the work back then. Transition year is when it all changed for me and I really opened up my eyes to music. That's when I formed my first band, which grew to be Kodaline. I started to think outside the box, that it might actually be possible to have a career in the industry. Of course, I had no idea where to start or who to turn to, or who to ask for advice. I certainly didn't know anything about how to get a record deal but I think that's when the seed was planted.

I was about fifteen when myself, Mark, Vinny and another local friend decided to form 21 Demands. We were united through our love of skateboarding. People first started to hear about us when we won the Battle of the Bands in school but we came to nationwide recognition when a classmate who played bass for us at the time entered us into a televised music competition called *You're A Star* on RTÉ. We were all very young and had to get time off school. It was a big deal for our parents, our school and the local area. I suppose that's when people first started paying proper attention to us. We toured around the country and we released a song called 'Give Me a Minute' which we wrote ourselves.

It was the first ever number one in Ireland by an unsigned band and the first ever song in Ireland to go to number one through downloads alone. We were runners-up on the show, and following on from our weekends spent on live TV, we gigged in pubs all around the country and pretty much played anywhere that would have us. We were fiercely dedicated. I remember it was around the time of my Leaving Cert. I did an exam, half an hour later rushed out to catch a flight to Cork, played a gig and then flew back and did another exam the next morning. We did anything and everything we could to make music happen.

Although we were slowly gaining credibility, we knew the gigs we were doing back then were only happening because of *You're a Star* and we knew that we needed to go away to find our own identity. We really wanted to become better songwriters so we made the decision to completely stop gigging. We went off and got real jobs and I repeated my Leaving Cert. Unfortunately, I'd let school slip when *You're A Star* and music kicked off and I wanted to have a back-up. It went much better the second time and I did Economics, Politics and Law in DCU for a year. I loved DCU but as soon as I was there I knew it wasn't what I wanted to do. I knew that I wanted and *needed* to do music, I just hadn't quite figured out how I was going to do it.

All the time I was at school, I wrote songs all day, every day. I was writing songs on the way into school, in lessons, on the way back, looking out the window of the bus and seeing people walking down the street; I'd write about anything and everything. I did the same when I was at home. Any time I had free I'd go into a local studio with Mark and Vinny and our friend Phil. Phil Magee is an engineer and producer who grew up around the corner. He was extremely kind to us. We had no money to our names but Phil was generous with his time; any cash we did make, we'd give to him. We worked really, really, really hard on our songs and we still do to this day; we're just very fortunate that we get to do it for a living now.

Like everyone else, I had doubts along the way and it wasn't plain sailing. The wonderful thing is, when you start to have doubts and when everything seems to be going wrong, those are the times that really test your belief in yourself and those times will ultimately define you.

I've had loads of rejections from people, but it didn't deter me. I remember sending demos to everybody and anybody and pretty much everyone turned us down. We never got any reasoning either. Most people didn't reply and if they did, they'd just say, 'We're not interested at this point.' But it's funny; the people who rejected us the first time are the people who ended up signing us two years later.

Everyone deals with rejection differently but we didn't take it as not being good enough, we took it as, 'What can we do to be even better?' We were very mature in that sense. We'd examine our songs and our playing and we'd try to improve ourselves constantly. I think that without those rejections we wouldn't be where we are today. We learned so much from those times.

The Kodaline story began when Mark and I were sent to Brighton to work with a songwriter. The label interested in us was testing the water to see what we were like working with different producers. We did everything they asked of us and I had a feeling coming back from that trip that we definitely had something in the bag. It took a few months to come through but I had a gut feeling that we'd get a publishing deal; it took us a little while longer to get a record deal. There were only three of us in the band at this stage. We hadn't even met Jay yet.

Vinny was working in Curry's at the time; Mark was doing lights in the Button Factory and I was gigging in pubs – sometimes to nobody at all. I spent a good two years gigging in local bars in Swords. I didn't want to do a job that I didn't enjoy, and for me, music was everything. Sometimes I didn't enjoy playing to drunken people who'd just shout at me and tell me I was terrible, but I think for any musician, they really have do that at some point. Get into a pub where nobody knows you and just sing and play, because it's the hardest thing to do, especially if you're playing your own songs. It's a really, really big confidence-builder. After that, when you start pulling in your own crowd and start building a fan base, you appreciate it so much more.

I moved to Brighton as soon as we got our publishing deal. Brighton is a great musical city: lots of bands, loads of clubs and open mics, producers, songwriters. We lived there briefly, myself, Mark and Vinny, before heading to a studio in the middle of nowhere with our producer Stephen Harris. He's produced bits for U2 and the Kaiser Chiefs, and he's become a dear friend of ours over the years.

The first time I met Steve, I was super-nervous. The first thing I saw in his house was a massive plaque on his wall; it was Santana and it said 'in recognition of ten million sales', or something silly like that. I'd never even met anyone like Steve before: a world-class producer. I was so nervous that I wouldn't even sing for him that first time. We were supposed to record a song and I couldn't sing. He was so frustrated that he stormed out of the studio and shouted at me, basically telling me to go home. I came back from that trip thinking the label weren't interested in us any more. I remember being a bit heart-broken; sure that I had ruined our chances. But at the same time, I remember thinking I had to get over my nerves. I buried my head in the studio in writing songs all the time and playing as much music as I possibly could.

The next time I met Steve, I had a record deal. By that time, Kodaline had become complete with Jay coming on board. We had crossed paths with him a few times in Dublin but we didn't know he was a bass player until a friend recommended him. We had a jam with him and the rest is history. Kodaline was formed.

It was an extremely exciting time, and things kind of kicked off unexpectedly. A week after we released our EP that had 'All I Want' on it, we got a call inviting us to Holland to play a show. When we got there, there was a massive crowd waiting to see us. It was bizarre but amazing. We played a small festival for about three of four hundred people and at that time it was a really big deal because we'd never played to so many people in Ireland, never mind in Holland! There were people trying to get in the door, and they couldn't.

That whole experience came off the back of our video for 'All I Want', which went viral. It just goes to show the important of a good music video. It had gone viral overnight on YouTube and it took off in Holland first. We shot it for almost nothing in Dublin with Stevie Russell and we had all our friends in it – we didn't expect it to do as well as it did. The video got onto a TV show in Holland that mentioned our name and it all spiralled from there and it's still spiralling today; all over the world.

When we first started out as a band, we didn't really know much about the music industry. It's always been just about the music for us, but with the runaway success of our first album, *In a Perfect World*, we had to learn fast.

The music industry can be a very tough industry to work in; it's full of false promises, shattered dreams and sob stories. I never anticipated how exhausting touring could be either, which is another thing. You know the saying, 'Be nice to those you meet on the way up, as they're the people you'll meet on the way down.' I think one of the most important things in the music industry is to be nice to everyone you meet. It's a very fickle industry but I would not want to be doing anything else. Every industry has its ins and outs and down points and there's no such thing as a perfect job. We're incredibly privileged to be doing our dream job. It's only been a short few years – believe me, they've gone by in the blink of an eye – but there have been a lot of highlights and career milestones. We've been exceptionally lucky and we'll never take it for granted.

Not many people get the opportunity to live out their dream and all four of us are so appreciative of everything that has come our way.

Playing a gig in the Sugar Club in Dublin was special. It was a sold out show and it was the first time people ever sang back one of our songs. It came as a surprise because we really weren't expecting it. 'All I Want' was the only song we had released but the crowd sang along and it was amazing.

Getting invited to join Ed Sheeran on stage in Croke Park to play our song to 80,000 people, all singing back to us was pretty special too. Glen Hansard joined us for a song and that was incredible. I'm a huge fan. I almost got sick with nerves that night. My whole body was shaking before I went out on that stage; I had the words of 'The Auld Triangle' scribbled on my hand, just in case.

It was quite surreal. It took about three days for events to actually hit me; three days until I thought, 'Wow, that actually happened!'

From the outside looking in, it might look like we're doing incredibly well, travelling all around the world, living it up, living the dream, but from the day we signed the record deal, that's when the work started. We gig every single day, we travel to a different city every day, and it can be exhausting. I think because music is our passion, the tiredness doesn't matter. We work as hard as we possibly can and we enjoy it. I think it's important to find what you are passionate about in life and to pursue it.

I think the most important thing if you want to be a song-writer is to do just that – write. Write as much as you can. Try to meet up with like-minded people like other songwriters and compare ideas. If you know any studio engineers or producers, look them up and hook up with them; knock on studio doors and see if you can go in and watch a session. Do anything in your power to get in to a studio or just to hang out with songwriters; anything that can help you learn more.

Remember that the most important thing of all is your songs. If your songs are good enough and you're sending them around, they will eventually get to the right people. Sometimes all it takes is to be in the right place at the right time. Your main focus should be on the your writing and getting as many opinions on your songs as you can. I like to think that writing about things that you genuinely believe in and genuinely feel, is the best route to go. It's hard to fake real emotion; it comes across in the recording and per-formance. You want your music to give you the same feeling that you get when you listen to one of your favourite tunes. If they don't do that, keep writing until you find a song that does do that to you.

You must never lose faith. Keep at it; it's not going to happen overnight. There's a saying I heard, 'It takes a lot of long nights to make an overnight success,' and it couldn't be truer. We worked hard for many years to get to where we are today. Personally, I don't think I've written my best song yet, and I'm excited to keep learning and growing and seeing what the future has in store for us as a band personally, professionally and collectively. I'm extremely ambitious and I love pushing my own limits. There's nothing wrong with aiming to be the best version of yourself; being the best you can be. We should all aim for that.

Emin

Billionaire Azerbaijani-born pop phenomenon Emin is a hugely successful recording artist in Eastern Europe. Smashing charts and winning prestigious music awards since 2006, the singer's star is on the rise on western shores. Having worked with Nile Rodgers and done guest performances at Miss Universe, the Sochi Olympics and Eurovision, this face is one to watch.

As long as I can remember, I have always dreamed of being a musician. Music has always been my passion, although I was always equally interested in business too. One of my first ambitions in life was to learn how to earn my own cash. Both have stuck with me to this day!

I decided in my early twenties that I wanted to make music my life. I had lots of songs written. I decided I would go and record and produce an album. It gave me my first taste of musical success. I've continued to write and record since that day. I released my first album, *Still*, in 2006 and I'm pleased to say it was a huge success in Russia.

I love what I call my 'double career.' To this day my Russian songs are very different from my English ones. I love being able to sing in two languages; it gives me the ability to have more angles to my music.

I'll never forget hearing my song for the first time on British radio. It was the first play-listing I got with BBC Radio 2, with a song called 'Obvious'. The song was co-written by Jamie Scott and me. I received Record of the Week for that one. I was in the car with my manager who has since passed away listening to BBC and then Ken Bruce introduced my song on his morning show. It was mind-blowing, unbelievable! Five years later, we premiered another song on *The Ken Bruce show*. The song was called 'Boomerang' featuring Nile Rodgers.

The inspiration for my music comes from pretty much anywhere. I'm a moody guy, so when I'm happy I can write a song, when I'm sad I can write a song. My typical day starts, hopefully, in the gym, a lot of the time it starts in the office as I have a day job – I manage a lot of businesses. The second half of the day is everything to do with music, rehearsals, recordings, performances – you name it.

I get slightly nervous before any performance because it's always live and I want it to be perfect. In order for it to be perfect, you have to have some nervous energy. My first every performance was at the age of seventeen or eighteen in New Jersey at an open-mic night at a bar. Once I got on stage I was so fazed by my surroundings that I couldn't hit any notes, or be in key or keep the rhythm as I was singing.

Recovering from that show took some time but it gave me the understanding that everything I do musically in my life, I have to be brutally prepared for.

It might sound funny, but I haven't had a career highlight yet. I think I'm still on my way towards that highlight but there are definitely some moments that I'll remember forever. Opening for JLO in front of 25,000 fans was special. Performing during Eurovision as a special guest in front of a live audience of one hundred and fifty million, doing the Olympics in Sochi, Miss Universe in Moscow – those were moments to remember. But really, so is every live show.

There's so much that I love about being a recording artist. The freedom of expressing your feelings and thoughts, and sharing them with people that share your musical taste is definitely the best thing. It's a privilege to be a musician and it's a privilege to share your music with an audience.

To be successful I think it's important to be honest in what you do. You will always win over your own audience that way. Honesty is the one thing you cannot fake and people really sense it on some underground, unknown level.

It's important not to waste any time. Learn as much as you can, about the industry, about the world – never stop learning. It's also necessary to pursue your dreams without being concerned if you will succeed or not. You should be doing it out of pure love and passion. And never be fearful as an artist to express yourself. Don't hold back: if you feel something, go for it.

My secret to success is pure hard work. Ten to fifteen percent could be talent, sixty percent is daily hard work and another twenty-five percent is luck. You can only be super-successful when all three are in place. Some people are massively talented and their success comes mostly from talent, but for normal people like myself, I compensate for not being a genius with hard work in order to be successful. Just work, work, work and you will reach your goals.

Ruth-Anne Cunningham

L.A. based singer, songwriter and producer Ruth-Anne Cunningham knows pop music inside out. Writing with global superstars since her teens, her exceptional talent earned her a global hit with Jojo's 'Too Little Too Late' in 2006. Pixie Lott, Katherine McPhee, Britney Spears and even One Direction are fans and have featured her songs on their albums. About to embark on a solo career, Dublin born 'Rooty' feels more than ready to take her spot in the limelight.

The first time I ever sang in front of an audience was on holidays in Portugal with my family. I was seven years old and I begged my mum to let me go up and sing, 'Hopelessly Devoted to You' from *Grease* on the karaoke machine. My parents had never really heard me sing before so my mum said 'Yes' and I got up and sang my heart out. I can still remember the whole loud bar becoming completely quiet, my parents shocked at my secret talent. The crowd was taking videos of me, and after my performance everyone come up to me to tell me what a great job I had done. I knew in that moment that performing was what I wanted to do for the rest of my life.

It was around that age that I wrote my first song, called 'Baby I Need You.' It was an R'n'B/pop tune. I was obsessed with Mariah Carey back then and she definitely influenced me. I didn't play an instrument then, so the melody and lyrics came from my head. It was a bad song but thinking back, it's interesting to me how I knew song structure; I had a verse, pre-chorus and chorus. I'm not really sure how I knew to do that, as I was never taught it.

From then on, singing and songwriting became everything to me; I was obsessed. I had a little two-track tape recorder with a microphone and at the age of ten, I would record myself singing Mariah Carey songs over and over until I got every note perfect. I wrote songs all the time and taught myself how to play the piano at twelve. I just wrote, wrote, and wrote. It was my number-one passion all the time. I was so determined to make something out of music; I went and got myself a manager.

Around the time of my Jojo co-write, my manager put me in a writing session with a big writer called Billy Steinberg. He and his partner Josh had started a song called, 'Too Little Too Late'. We wrote it and I said to my manager, 'This song should be a Jojo song.' While we didn't have the relevant contacts ourselves, Billy did. We had written the song two years before it was released and it was actually going to be a Pussycat Dolls' song initially. But then, as often happens in the music industry, it didn't work out and the song was floating around for a while before Jojo's people heard it and wanted it. Once it was released – bam, my life changed!

I'll always remember the first time I heard that song on the radio. I was in New York in a cab, having just arrived for a writing trip from Ireland. 'Too Little Too Late' came on the radio and I screamed with excitement.

The cab driver must have thought I was crazy. I still get really excited when I hear any of my songs on the radio because it can be so hard in this industry sometimes. Hearing what you've created on the radio and knowing that it's going out to millions – that makes the hard work and the politics behind the scenes worth it.

My highlight to date is Jojo's 'Too Little Too Late', just because it was my first big hit with proper global success. It caught me completely by surprise and because I was so young, it was a special one! Going to see One Direction in a huge stadium with 80,000 people singing our songs was also very special. One Direction are a massive phenomenon and it's a nice feeling to be part of that music history.

I love everything about creating music, listening to music,

dancing to music. It's the one thing in life that never lets me down. No matter how sad or angry or tired I am once I put on a tune and I'm up dancing, laughing or just feeling it.

Getting to write music helps keep me sane. I write about what I'm feeling and in a way it's my therapy. I'm lucky that I can make music anywhere but L.A. has definitely become a huge hub for great producers and writers and I moved here to challenge myself, to become better at my craft.

Everything inspires me – stories and life experiences, travelling, meeting new people and learning new things, heartbreaks. A good song to me is something that feels authentic and real and makes you feel something. If it's not believable and too clever or robotic, I don't like it. The best thing about my job is being able to make music everyday for a living and getting to meet other writers, producers and artists that love music as much as I do, all the while creating music and having fun while doing so. There are negatives too, of course.

The worst thing is the business and politics that comes with it, as in every job. This industry is not designed in a way that supports and appreciates songwriters enough, and that can get frustrating.

These days, because of streaming services, songs are making a lot less money and a lot of songwriters out there are struggling to pay rent. For my future, I want to keep writing. I am embarking on a solo career, and while I'm nervous, I'm also very excited. It's been a long time coming and I just want to get my music out there! My sound is a mixture of Lauryn Hill and Alicia Keys. There's no one artist in particular whose success I want to emulate. I just want my music to connect with people. That's the magic of it.

Markus Feehily

For former Westlife band member Markus Feehily, music is everything. Thrown into the limelight in his late teens, the Sligo-man grew up in front of an audience of millions, travelling the globe playing music to legions of dedicated fans. Living the ultimate music dream, life was a rollercoaster of multiple number-one singles and albums, countless international gongs and endless red-carpet events.

Music to me is incredibly powerful. I feel my most comfortable when I have a microphone a couple of inches away from my face, my eyes are closed and I'm lost in song. I've never been the biggest extrovert, and singing has always been my way of letting it all out. I tend to keep it all inside and then let it all out in those two and half minutes – whether in studio, where it's more intimate, or on stage. When I sing, I'm so relaxed. I'm just singing my heart out, completely lost in the moment. It's the only time I forget about everything else.

Thinking back, music has been in my life for a very long time. I have memories of singing from the age of three or four in playschool and then, in primary school, where my first few teachers were quite musical. I played the tin whistle too and I can still get the odd tune out of it to this day!

Music was very much in the family too. My dad and aunties were into music and were always playing something. Where I grew up in Sligo, there wasn't a whole lot for young kids to do and so I seized every opportunity to get involved in the local and school choirs, school plays and then, later in secondary school, the talent competitions and musicals.

The earliest memory I have of performing is singing lead in a school play when I was about ten. I sang the theme song to the *Ghostbusters* movie by Ray Parker Jr. Even at that age, I went for the more soulful song choices. I remember there were only about thirty people in the audience, but that moment stands out in my head, to this day. It's funny; all shyness went away when I sang and I was completely comfortable singing my heart out.

I always knew I would do something musical. As much as people think Westlife were put together, the idea came from Shane and me. We always said we wanted to sing together and when we met Kian in a local musical, along with some other friends from school, we put the band together and wrote and recorded a single that was released by a small local record store. That's how Louis first heard about us; we were causing a stir down in Sligo and he was impressed.

Everything happened really fast after that. With Louis's help we found Nicky and Bryan and Westlife was born. Those first few years were momentous. My life changed so rapidly. I was very naïve. I had never even been on a plane before and then all of a sudden, there we were staying in fancy hotels, being chauffeur driven and preened by a group of stylists.

The first real crazy, out-of-this-world experience I had among all that madness was working with my teen-idol Mariah Carey. One minute, she was a poster on my wall; the next, there she was ringing my house in Sligo to go through backing vocals for a song we were performing together at an awards show. We were literally singing down the phone to each other. I was pinching myself for days!

For any band, getting that first number one is a pretty special moment. I'll never forget that day. We were all sitting round a table on a shabby old leather sofa in this old warehouse style south east London studio that belonged to Pete Waterman. We had all left our phones in the middle of the table and finally someone, I think it was Simon Cowell, called and told us the good news. We all erupted and jumped into a big scrum-type huddle, screaming into each other's faces with delight and excitement.

A couple of minutes later we were all on the phone to our families and friends and it just sort of kicked off from there! But in true military style we were probably back recording vocals half an hour later. I can't remember exactly what celebrations took place that night but one things for sure, we absolutely would have celebrated in style – celebrating was something we were very good at!

Over the years we were blessed with wickedly awesome experiences and opportunities; one of them was meeting the Pope, being in a tiny chapel deep inside the inner, inner sanctum of the Vatican along with our five mothers and a handful of people, sitting with the Pope listening to him pray. That was surreal. We went up individually to meet him and received a blessing. I remember kissing his ring – to this day I'm not exactly sure why! I'm sure there's a good reason behind it.

The highlights reel is never-ending. Meeting Donna Summer and spending a couple of days with her rehearsing and performing on a show called 'Discomania,' was very cool. She was the most professional and friendly woman I have ever worked with and sang live, like the record, every time. We sung a song called 'No More Tears (Enough is Enough)', which she normally sang with Barbra Streisand. I got to sing a lot of the song because my range was closer to that of Ms Streisand's, so I really got to sing up close and personal with Donna Summer – something I will never forget.

Deciding to close the Westlife chapter of our careers was a tough choice. Our farewell gig in Croke Park was amazing. I remember feeling like it all went by in a weird slow motion. I tried to focus on doing the show, singing the songs, not getting too caught up in the fact that it was the last show. It was my way of coping with it. Crying in front of people is not something I feel comfortable with and there were about 90,000 people looking at me that night. I had to try very hard to hold the tears in!

As a band, we were extremely very lucky. We had the album sales and the success but we didn't quite have that mega-famous, individually at least, thing that 1D have – which made dealing with fame easier. We could play Croke Park one night, the next sit in the corner of a pub with our friends, and all without much bother. We had fame for sure, especially in the earlier days, before I knew how to blend in and not stand out, but I learnt how to go to pubs and clubs and stay relatively unnoticed, because it meant a lot to me to be able to do normal things.

It hasn't always come easy. To this day, I constantly doubt myself on certain levels. For some reason while singing I am not shy or worried but put me in front of a camera or make me do a photo-shoot and that's a different story – I get slightly uncomfortable. I have never felt like I look like a pop star but then over the years certain people told me that I look unique, and not just another stereotypical pop star and that this was a good thing!

Even when it came to my vocal abilities, it took me many years to begin to master the art of singing live in arenas and gigs where the audience is screaming so loud that you can't hear yourself and therefore, it's hard to find the pitch exactly. You'd get people saying, 'Oh he can't sing live' but actually I could sing the song perfectly in the dressing room or studio. I had to work at it for months and years with the in-ear monitor engineer to find the right 'mix' for me, to find the mix that cancelled out the crowd noise. It's all a learning process. Finally, I'm in a much more comfortable place – sometimes in life there are obstacles and you have to be willing to overcome them by just working hard and not giving up. That's an important lesson.

Now that I'm a solo artist, I get asked a lot if it's better or worse, easier or harder, without the security of the other guys. The honest answer is, it's just different. I've enjoyed my solo journey so far. I've had so much enjoyment making music and learning about recording, production and mixing and arranging vocals. I enjoyed my time with Westlife immensely but for slightly different reasons. At the end of the day the common thing between both, and the best part, is just getting in front of the mic and singing!

These days there's not much room for error in the industry; you have to turn up and be ready, be rehearsed. You have to get a grip and forget about nerves, because unfortunately you might get overlooked if you are too shy.

For anyone hoping to make it in the industry, I would say practise every day, record yourself singing or playing, and find your flaws and try to improve and fix them. It's not about being perfect; it's about being fit and ready like a solider. These days there are so many people to compete with and so many managers and so many labels and if you're not sharp, you just won't stand out.

Also don't chisel yourself into the same shape as everyone else; don't scrub away your imperfections, take them and make them bigger and make them the reason you are different and stand out. Otherwise you could be at risk of being a clone. Be yourself and find your own personal identity and practice every day to make yourself fighting fit.

Don't wait for it to come to you. Get out there and find it, and show it what you're made of!

It's so easy to look back and advise myself now but it's so much harder to see things from the right perspective while you're going through it at the time. Growing up as a gay teenager in nineties Ireland was very difficult and it's still difficult today for some people, depending on the family and friends they're surrounded by.

Certainly it's getting better and better and we now live in a country where the people have spoken and they are behind LGBT kids. The public has told us that the majority of our country loves and accepts LGBT kids and wants them to be themselves and to be happy and equal. I still think of the people that live in homes where the atmosphere is not one of acceptance, and know that there's still work to be done.

If I could meet my younger self and offer advice, I'd tell myself, 'Although you don't feel like it now, this *big* problem that you feel you have will seem like a distant memory in ten years time and you're going to be so surprised, in fact underwhelmed, at how little people care and how people actually love you more since you came out.'

I'd also tell myself not to waste any more time worrying. I'd encourage myself to get some counselling, get on the track to being happy with myself, and tell the world that I'm proud to be who I am. They will love me even more for it.

Philip Magee

Sound engineer and music producer Philip Magee always knew that music would be his life one way or another. Dropping out of school at the age of fifteen, he embarked on the journey of learning and discovery that has led him to living his ultimate dream today, working with Ireland's newest and most exciting talented musicians.

I remember listening to Buddy Holly as a child; 'Wake Up Little Suzie,' was the song and it just got me. Whatever it was, it just got me. I remember listening to the big-rhythm guitar and electric guitar, and the voice and even though it was recorded fifty years before I was born, it was still so exciting.

Music has drawn me in ever since I can remember. I always wanted to be a lead guitarist in a big rock back. From a young age I had a deep passion for recording and wanting to know how to record. It was always a dream. I had a Dictaphone on which I was able to record myself playing guitar and then I figured out how to record myself on my cassette player to layer the sounds and make it sound even cooler. That's where my interest in how albums are made began. It was a combination of that pure passion for music, wanting to be a big lead guitarist and also a desire to make albums and records.

It's that love of music that spurred me to quit school after my Junior Certificate. I must have been about fourteen or fifteen. I enjoyed school because I loved my teachers and fellow students but academically I just wasn't feeling it. I'm lucky to have had such great, supportive parents.

Leaving school became a realistic option when I was offered a place in the training centre in Temple Bar. I'd sort of earned my right to be there, even as a teen. During school summers I had been teaching music appreciation and songwriting to kids, and in my spare time I was a guitar teacher too. I was delighted when I was offered the place; it was a dream come true.

My principal was a guitarist himself and he was extremely encouraging. He said, 'You're going into education, so just go for it.' There was no messing about; I went straight into college and did sound engineering and music production.

I was just sixteen at the time and a lot younger than my peers. I worked incredibly hard. My young age actually stood to me. Because it was a private college, a lot of the students were five to ten years older than me and in most cases it was their second course. They were all in party mode, living in the city, whereas I was getting off the bus with my school bag and packed lunch straight out the Junior Cert.

I was there to learn. It was a really good mind set. I was able to hone in and study really hard. I *wanted* to learn. While I never liked studying in school, this was something that truly interested me. I was passionate about it. I was hungry to learn and I couldn't get enough.

While I was in college, I started doing a lot of recording. I used to get paid at recording sessions for helping clean up the lecture hall and other small tasks like that. I'd often be found recording dodgy EPs and singles. I suppose that's where I really learned the craft.

Becoming a producer is more of a continuous thing. You're learning from when you're a child, right up until the day you die. It's evolving; it's how music sounds and feels to you as a producer and the people you work with. I don't know when I became a fully fledged producer – I never got a name tag!

You don't call yourself a producer when you're younger and engineering but certainly working with great producers helps as you're learning from them. You can only learn a certain amount though. Because producing is a very instinctual job, once you get more confident with that and you see success, then you can kind of call yourself a producer.

In my early days, the more I researched, the more I realised there were no opportunities anywhere for doing what I wanted to do. You had to make your opportunities; I found that out pretty quickly. I remember trying every studio and ringing up every broadcaster to see if there were any jobs –with no reply. You have to make your own luck and your own opportunities. I suppose I began creating my luck back in my Temple Bar days. I used to go and listen to all the bands in the rehearsal room and if I thought someone sounded good, I'd knock on the door and offer to record them. Through college I used to get a super rate in studio for the 10PM to 10AM overnight slot. I'd go and offer to record these bands for free. As I was getting better, I'd offer them €50 to record, and that's where I began to get a lot of work; finding bands and dragging them up to the studio from 10PM to 10AM and then going to college from 10AM to 5PM.

One of my first big breaks was through my mam. She saw a job advertised in the newspaper saying that Brian McFadden, ex-Westlife, was setting up a recording studio in Phibsborough. There were 'auditions' for engineers. When she rang up, the interview day was pretty much full, but being a Corkwoman with a gift for talking, she was able to speak to Declan, the manager, and I went in for an interview. There was a panel of three studio owners,

Brian McFadden, two other owners and of course, the manager who was going to look after the studio. I had to go in and play them my demo tape of stuff I'd written and recorded and show off what I could do. It was a bit daunting because there were a lot of people outside the room.

Luckily it went well for me and they offered me the job on the spot and I started working as head engineer in Chilli Studios. It was brilliant. I learned a lot of chops. I was working with Sisqó and Samantha Mumba and a lot of other pop stars and pop singers.

I managed to learn how to do the pop thing pretty well; it's a technical craft in itself. I was really thrown at the deep end in that job. I'd be called up at 4AM to hear that someone was flying in from Milan. It was exciting. I also had free rein. I was able to bring in bands that I loved and it was really, really great. It's where I met the Script. It's also as a result of that job that I got to judge a local talent competition, where I got to meet a band called 21 Demands, now Kodaline. I was able to bring them into my studio and work with them for a few days and create a bond.

In time, I became busier than the studio. A lot of people wanted to bring me to bigger studios; Chilli Studio was a nice size but it wasn't big enough to do a live album. I'd often be asked to go to studios like Grouse Lodge and I'd have to take leave of absence a couple of times a year. Eventually it becomes a money thing. I was being paid more doing work outside of Chilli. In the studio I'd be getting a salary, whereas when I worked for myself I was getting better rates.

After a few years, I was able to quit and go self-employed. I started working with exciting young bands, getting a better name and being a bit more choosy who I worked with. It evolved in a really nice way and slowly but surely and it's continuing now. There are lots of funny moments in studio, most unbroadcastable and publishable.

Recording with Sisqó was special. In the middle of a session he did a backflip, forgetting he was wearing wired headphones. He got caught up midair with the cable and fell on the ground. To keep his coolness intact, I pretended I didn't see it. I was pretending to patch up cables on the ground when really, I was on the floor laughing my head off. I had to talk through the talkback and say, 'Gimme two minutes, Mr Sisqó, I just need to fix something,' and then continue with my laughing out loud.

I met the Script through Delta Goodrem, before they even started as the Script. At the time they were phenomenal songwriters in America, writing songs for Delta at the same time I was recording her in Dublin. We communicated a lot through email.

Having just moved back to Dublin, Danny, Mark and Glenn were looking for an engineer. I happened to be the only person they knew; they tried a few studios but weren't happy with them. We eventually met up and started recording the first album in Mark's concrete shed, in his back garden. The minute I first heard their songs, my 'Spidey-sense' went off. I was getting tingles. It was the best songwriting I had ever heard. The band self-produce and it was just phenomenal. I heard 'We Cry' out the back garden over a cup of tea and it was phenomenal.

That 'Spidey-sense' has only gone off as few times in my career. With 21 Demands, that 'Spidey-sense' went off like crazy – the songwriting, the attitude. The songwriting was better than any band that age I'd ever heard. And it still is to this day. Even though they're Kodaline now and they would never want anyone to hear those songs, back then they were amazing. They had a lot of energy, great voices, and great instrumentation. What made them stand out was that they weren't thinking about themselves. They were thinking collectively and they were thinking for the songs. You'll often get bands where the guitarist will be thinking about his solo and how good that will look or sound. In a band like Kodaline, the guitar or keyboard will think, 'How does this justify the song? What will this do to enhance the message?' That's how you tell a really good band. A lot of bands mature into that but for a band to start off like that, that was very unique.

When you're a producer and engineer working on a song, sometimes you feel like a band member for that period. You help create the sound and you remember the little things you did on that particular record. You feel a huge sense of achievement and also that you've done something that's tangible. Even though music is invisible and you can't touch it, it's almost a physical thing; it's there forever. When you know you've done something that's gone into the commercial ether, you get a lovely warm feeling, knowing you helped create that.

You'll sometimes overhear people saying, 'Oh I love this song,' and get a real sense of pride. It's a really good buzz. It's what makes you work. Sometimes it takes months to do a project and it can be very tough but all it takes is that one little thing where you see the band playing it live or you hear it on radio or you see them do a performance, and it all makes sense then. You get a sense of achievement and a mini ego-boost as well.

A sound engineer's job is to capture the audio. It's a technical, engineering job. Your job is to record audio at the highest fidelity and the highest quality while capturing the right energy. If you're recording a trad band, a rock band, an orchestra, you need to know how to capture them using microphones and so on. You need to understand acoustics and how air works and faze/haze and electronics and current. It's a proper geeky, nerdy job.

A music producer's job is more about the song itself and where you want it to go – the emotional content the song needs to have, how you're going to capture that along with the engineer to make it come across to the audience. There's a different energy you get from a live performance compared to a recorded performance.

You can see someone standing in front of you on a stage with just an acoustic guitar. Their presence adds forty percent more energy. You need to portray that energy through tiny, little cheap white earphones, nestled inside your ear canals. You need to add more sonic energy to that. You need to know how to portray this song or piece of art that you think the audience will love.

As a producer you're on the artistic front, you're with the band and then as an engineer you're taking care of the technical stuff. How to capture the technical spects of music, the best way without interfering with the artist is to make it quick, almost like muscle memory. You need to know in a millisecond what to use, how to cable it up, what to do. They're two very different jobs, one's more technical, specific, and one is more arty-farty.

I combine those two worlds. If I was just a producer working with another engineer and I was telling them, 'Oh I want the guitar to sound airy and bright and a bit lush,' it could get tricky. Because I'm an engineer, I know how to turn that into specifics. I know what microphone to use and what distance to have it and what equalisation and compression to have to portray that feeling I have. They go hand in hand for me so it makes things go by a lot quicker.

I get a huge amount of pride from every artist I work with. It's just that overall sense of happiness when you finish an album. It's kind of like a family business. It's not just me. Even though I'm in the studio, I've got a wife and child, and they feel part of it. Every decision that I make, my wife listens to.

The best thing about it all is that with every album or record, there's something physically done; you're actually leaving something behind; a sort of legacy. It would drive me nuts to work in an office inputting data. With my job I'm completing a task with a resolution and a definite end. In the studio you're being creative and you're self employed and you're leaving something behind. This is scary because there's no stability but then you've also got the complete freedom to be yourself, and do what you want.

Everyone has his or her own route into the industry. With any job in a creative industry, people will only look at the work you've done to know how good you are. For anyone considering it, going to college is a great route. Ultimately it's about finding a unique artist that people want to latch on to. You could be doing that in your bedroom or recording them on your iPhone, creating new sounds; you can put that up on YouTube and let people find you.

You have to be optimistic in the music game and remember that the harder you work, the luckier you get. You have to work very hard to get more luck. It's very rare that opportunities will be handed to you but if you work hard to create your own, you're winning.

If your wish is to make money and have stability, that's not good enough reasoning to get into the industry. Your reasoning should be that you want to be creative and create stuff with other people to make good music. Then you've got a better chance of making it and making an living from it because that's what the artist wants, and that's what the public want. Always go with your gut. You can never second-guess what cool is. If you're second-guessing what cool is – it ain't cool. If it's something that floats your boat and it gets you off and you love it, then hopefully that will appeal to other people like you.

You need to have the quality and substance as well as the desire. The desire can't be more than the ability. You need to make sure that your abilities and what you're doing are good. Hound everyone – the worst you're going to do is annoy someone.

Hozier

Few artists are setting the music world on fire like Andrew Hozier Byrne. Since the release of his global smash 'Take Me to Church', the Wicklow native has gone on to win numerous prestigious awards, including an Ivor Novello and a Billboard Music award.

Nabbing himself a Grammy nomination along the way, the former Trinity College student is the name on everyone's lips and the future looks brighter than ever for the ambitious musician.

My earliest memory of music is being a toddler with not much vocabulary. My dad was a drummer at the time, and if my foggy memory serves me right, I was at a daytime blues festival somewhere in Dublin where he was drumming for a blues band when I half-toddled, crawled up the steps to him during a break in the set.

The first time I ever sang on stage was at St David's Hall in Greystones. I was singing *'Pie Jesu'* and I must have been seven or eight years old. It was an absolute disaster. All I remember is going for the high note and my voice breaking, probably a dark omen of puberty to come, as I hit this horrendous note. I just froze and buried my head in my hands in front of a few hundred people. I didn't really know anybody in the crowd except my family but it was terribly embarrassing. Not knowing what to do, I stood there mortified as this midi-backing track of *'Pie Jesu'* played out sadly, head in hands, until some old woman came up on stage and told me to get off!

That put me off performing for a long time. I had to do the same thing the following night and somehow I messed it up again. As a result, I didn't like performing for a long time. It wasn't until I became a teenager, and I had a deeper voice, closer to the voice I have now, that I started singing again. It was more for the love of music, because back then I definitely didn't enjoy being in front of a crowd.

I think a lot of the work you do trying to become a musician, you do in a private space, in your bedroom, or away from everyone else; certainly while you're finding your own voice or your own music, or your own way of playing an instrument. It's something you don't want to share with people until you're ready. It's good that I had those opportunities throughout school to do that – be it in talent shows or music events or whereever else.

Music was always one of the few things that I could do. As a teen, I was very interested in Delta blues music. I'd usually get up and do a cover of something, like a Robert Johnson song. I suppose it came naturally as it was certainly one of the few things I was good at. I wasn't athletic and I wasn't winning prizes at sports but I was winning music competitions, which was great. Having the opportunity to showcase something that I'd been working on and practising was fantastic but it wasn't until much later that I started performing my own music.

I could go on forever about music and still not get to the crux of why I love it so much. Music was introduced to me at an early age. I formed a love for it before I could actually articulate what that love was. I was very close to blues music, and rhythm and blues, and soul music. Certainly the first time I listened to soul music or heard something that was definitively soul, was Sam and Dave singing 'Soul Man'. It was like the first time I tasted chocolate. It was amazing. It was explosive. It was just this uncontainable energy put to music, this fantastic fire put to sound.

At first I was coaxed into singing. You know, your parents find out that you have a voice and that you can sing. Initially I sang in churches while at school, singing the hymns at Christmas Mass.

Funnily enough, I always hated it. I never wanted to sing in front of people. I was always being asked to sing and I really disliked it until I found something that was very much my own, that I actually wanted to sing.

I think that's a big part of being a teenager. You find something that gets you through, that's very much your own thing that nobody else has, that nobody else can take away from you.

I remember being a teenager and it's a really shit time. I wouldn't be a teenager again for the world. It was awful and nobody tells you that either, nobody gives you a heads-up or a warning. As you're going in to it, nobody says, 'You're in for an odd time. It's going to be awful and the social hierarchy is going to be at its most harsh, and wherever you are in the social hierarchy of your own community, you're always going to feel like shit, whether you're at the top of it or at the bottom of it. You're going to feel alone, you're never going to feel like you're enough, and you're going to feel insecure.' It's a funny stage in life. Everyone's lashing out at each other in some awful way to make sense of themselves but of course, ultimately, it all works out and it's *fine*. You'll come out the other end a stronger person.

Even during those days, I wasn't all that interested in the music that my peers were listening to. I loved classic rock' n 'roll and blues music. Tom Waits was someone I looked up to. Music was something that I just loved, something I had a greater passion for than anything else and I think that's stayed with me. My first musical education was dad's record collection and all of his tastes. The mix cassette tapes that he had put together for rehearsals of his own band as a young man – I loved those right up to the point when I was learning to drive in an old banger of a car, with an old tape machine and throwing in one of those blues tapes that I listened to in my teens.

I feel exceptionally lucky I had the opportunity to follow the dream I wanted to follow with the support of my parents. My parents didn't have that choice. My dad was drumming and supporting himself and my mam before they had kids, but they didn't have the support of their parents in the same way, and they didn't have the opportunities that I had. For him, he wasn't able to continue drumming as a career. He had to get a career in a more traditional nine-to-five sphere when children came along. It makes me think how lucky I am to follow my dreams and have my opportunity to do so and how glad I am that I did and that my parents were very supportive.

Mind you, it hasn't been easy. Every step of the way as a teen I doubted myself but I kept going. In this industry, you have to have a blind passion or belief or faith. Faith and belief are funny things because you have to maintain them; the whole idea of having faith in something is that you have a belief in it regardless, without evidence of it.

After finishing school, I went to Trinity College to study music and I got through maybe six months of it. I knew in my heart that if I had done four years of it, I wouldn't have been happy. Also theoretically, I wasn't strong. I don't know how they even let me in, to be honest! I knew that I wanted to write contemporary music – music that would be played on the radio that people could enjoy. I knew going in there that I didn't want to end up as an academic, so that kind of helped my decision to leave.

I dropped out of college without having written any of the material that ended up on my debut album two or three years later. It's funny, nothing was really happening for me at the time. If I was to go back and look at my work now – and I often do, I go back and look at my old demos and stuff I was writing – I would look at it with deep scorn and think it's absolute crap.

When I dropped out of Trinity, I knew it was going to be a while before I was going to get anywhere, and I knew there were lots of skills I still had to learn, but I had this iron belief it would work out somehow. I knew that if I didn't at least try to walk that path and see how it went, I would never forgive myself and never be completely happy. I would never have told my parents this at the time, but I felt like if it took me ten years or twenty years before I had my debut album and be able to live as a musician, I would still have to do it because I had to be true to myself.

Looking back, in those three years, I was completely lost and I didn't really know what I was doing. I was learning by trial and error. It's the best type of schooling. Every failure, you fail and do it again and you fail a little bit better the next time. The things I am best at today, are the things I have failed at most through trial and error.

I remember at the time my friends were going to college doing business courses or something that made sense; gaining an applicable skill that would work for an associated job. Whereas I felt like I had to build this dream and not have any blueprints. I had nobody to tell me or advise me and nobody I could really ask so, it was just a case of trying, blindly failing and then trying again. To this day I still question myself and I still doubt myself, and that's something I think is important, you should never feel like you've arrived or achieved what you wanted to achieve.

That's the funny little punchline in life, it seems that we're never happy. You're always looking forward to the next thing or always questioning what you could have done better, and you always want to work better and more.

I appreciate everything I have today so much. I never expected for it all to happen so quickly. It's an odd one. Making my debut album, I had no idea it could ever go this big. In my teens, late teens and early twenties I thought was going down the safe route, writing stuff that was soul pop or folk soul pop or something like that; stuff that I thought was palatable. I think with the album and a lot of the songs that ended up on the first EP, I made a conscious decision to write music that felt more honest to my influences and therefore I felt they would have been a little more left-field and obscure than just doing stuff that was stronger on the folk side or had a rhythm and blues feel. I made a decision to write stuff that wasn't palatable for the mainstream, so I was very surprised with the success of 'Take Me to Church'.

At the time of us finishing it and with everything that was in the top 10 at the time, 'Take Me to Church' was not an obvious hit – I didn't think people would get it. Certainly, I was very proud of the song and so excited about it, but I felt that only a very small audience would appreciate it. I saw my career go in a slow trajectory. I saw it as a slow grower, a slow build, and I was very comfortable with that. Things took off for that song in ways that I never would have expected. Things have gone at a pace that I never would have imagined.

It's funny, sometimes you arrive at the point of this lucid moment of 'WTF, how did this happen, what am I doing here, this is surreal'. A lot of the time I never get a chance to actually sit and  think about everything that's happened and the experiences I've had. It's only when you're forced to talk about it that it hits you. Usually you're concentrating on what you're doing that day or trying to stop yourself from freaking out or having a panic attack and just focusing on the job you have to do that day, whatever TV show it might be or whatever gig you're doing. You're more concerned about that, and life in this busy industry. I didn't know that I could physically be as busy as I've been the last year. I didn't think it was physically possible to squeeze so much in. I have to rethink my whole idea of physics!

I've been very, very fortunate and very, very lucky. There have been a lot of fantastic events and TV shows but on a personal level, the Grammys was a huge honour and there was an Ivor Novello award, which was very special to me. You tick every box, and I suppose because you're freaking out at the time, you don't grasp it in yourself and in your own heart that you're ticking dream that you've had for years. You don't actually register when it happens because you're very busy.

One of the biggest highlights has been meeting other musicians who have inspired me along the way, whose music has shaped me; people like Paul Weller, for example. I was also very honoured to sing with Bono and the Edge at an event in New York.

Meeting Lisa Hannigan for the first time was a special moment too. I remember seeing Lisa perform on *Other Voices* for the first time. Because my head was buried in early-twentieth-century blues music, I wasn't listening to Damien Rice or Lisa so when I saw her performing 'Lille' on her own, it was really special. She had her own brand of folk music and what she was doing was so much her own, there was such worth and value to it, and so many ears for it and such love – that really encouraged and inspired me. It made me feel like it was something I could do.

To actually get to meet that person and hopefully get to tell them that that's a big thing. It's music and other musicians that make you love music as an art and as a way of life and getting to meet these people is hugely inspiring and fulfilling.

For anyone hoping to make it in this industry, my advice is to do it yourself and don't wait on somebody else. It's easy to wait and fill in the gaps with what you think you might need before you can start going. You can give yourself a thousand reasons to delay or to stop.

I procrastinated for a long time and I know what it's like. I think the way our secondary school system works, you fall out of it burnt out and you don't know what to do with yourself, you don't know who you are. The education system does nothing to help figure out who you are as a person; you just learn facts and recite them, which I think is a crying shame. It takes time to figure that out and figure that part of yourself out, but a lot of it you just have to do yourself, and that's all I ever did.

Also remember that ultimately you have to stand over your music and your choices but that you will get there. Whether you believe you can or you can't, you are correct.

If you believe you can do it, you're correct; if you believe you can't, you're correct. You have to have faith. That was a big thing for me, this iron belief which stood up somehow in the face of absolute mediocrity when I was shit and making music that I wouldn't rate now or then. I knew at the time when I was learning to write that it wasn't good enough. Also, in this game there's no harm in keeping your cards close to your chest until you're ready to show them; there's no harm in working on your craft until you're ready to show it to others. Have a high standard for yourself.

In Training

I hated every minute of training, but I said 'Don't quit. Suffer now and live the rest of your life as a champion.'
-Muhammad Ali

Sport is the glue that binds us all together; entire nations unite to support their heroes on the field, in the ring and on the court. There are few people on this planet who understand commitment more than our favourite sporting stars.

As fans, we revel with them in their victories and our hearts crumble with theirs in their losses. It takes strength, perseverance, passion, fierce dedication and buckets of blood, sweat and tears to achieve a momentous win or an unfortunate fail.

Flick through the next few pages and get into the psyche of some of our most respected athletes and performers with a unique insight behind the scenes.

Rory McIlroy

Born in Holywood, Northern Ireland, MBE and professional golfer Rory McIlroy was always set for international sporting stardom. Picking up a golf club at the tender age of two fuelled a passion and desire within him to become one of the world's greatest golfing heroes. On the professional scene since 2007, he has taken the golfing world by storm gaining the respect of peers and fans alike. A big philanthropist, Rory founded the Rory Foundation to help give a helping hand to children's charities around the world.

I've no real memories of the first time I lifted a golf club. There are, however, some very embarrassing family photos of me on holiday in Spain swinging a plastic club on a beach. I doubt there was anything natural-looking about those early attempts – I was just trying, as a two-year-old, to copy my dad. I started to play golf as a toddler – so my dreams and ambitions were probably always golf related.

I think I did dream of being the world's number one, even though I was far too young to know what it really meant. That dream came in the first couple of years in primary school.

I was bitten by the golf bug from the moment I began playing and by the time I was about five I was determined that playing and practising golf was what I wanted to do every day. Beginning to witness my game improving made me want to improve all the more. I spent every moment I could on the golf course – and every moment my mum and dad could spare!

I set myself targets to aim for, such as getting my handicap lower, and tried to become as good as the best golfers at the club. I also studied the game and how clubs were made, spending time in the professionals' shop watching clubs being gripped, and broken ones repaired. By the age of seven, I was being coached by Michael Bannon, our club pro, who's still my coach to this day.

Thinking back, it was a little weird when I first turned professional to be playing in the same tournaments as the likes of Tiger Woods and Phil Mickelson. I had, of course, played in a number of professional events as an amateur against the world's best but it was a little more intense, with a lot more to play for, when it was a level playing field.

Growing up, I had the greatest respect for a lot of golfers – the first I really remember was Sir Nick Faldo. It was definitely a little strange meeting him for the first time when I was selected for the Faldo Series as a fourteen-year-old. It was when I was about ten that Tiger Woods came onto the scene and utterly transformed the game of golf. I was mesmerised.

His aggressive style of play, fearlessness against any competitor, and mental strength really took me, and the rest of the world, by storm. I followed every tournament he played and read every word written about him for many years.

I've been extremely fortunate in my career, and my highlights reel is an exciting one! My first golfing highlight was winning, as a nine-year-old, the under-ten world championship in Doral, Florida. That win really gave me the belief that I could go a long way in golf. Second has to be my first European Tour win in Dubai in 2009.

I'd turned pro about eighteen months before, and it was a real confidence-builder to win against Europe's best at the age of nineteen. Most recently, my Open Championship win in 2014 was a highlight of my career to date. I had dreamed for years of winning what I always called my home Major, so to get it done, with my mum coming to give me a hug on the eighteenth green, was truly special.

My parents have been so committed and supportive over the years. After my first Major win, I remember them saying, 'You owe us, big time!' I'm joking, of course. Their belief in me, encouragement and support was utterly selfless. I can't remember their exact words after my first win but I know they were delighted for me, proud of what we'd all achieved and the journey we'd been on. I still feel that encouragement every time I step out on to the course.

It's not always easy, though and there have definitely been testing times. I think my ability to dig that bit deeper comes from having experienced both success and disappointment.

I have won tournaments against the odds and let tournaments slip away when they were mine for the taking. During the last round of the PGA in 2014 at Valhalla, I had the lead at the start of the last day, lost it on the front nine and then had to fight very hard through the closing holes to win the tournament. I was able to convince myself on that occasion to find the motivation and focus that I couldn't find in the early part of the round.

I don't like to lose!

As a rule, I don't count my trophies but I do have a few trophy cabinets between my home in Northern Ireland and my place in Florida. I've quite often sent my trophies up to my local club in Holywood to be put on display there for the members or visitors to see. I have to admit, I'm very fond of the trophies that came with my Major wins, especially the Open Championship's Claret Jug.

Young people, boys and girls, wishing to pursue a future in sport need to be told that it can be an incredibly rewarding career. But, like everything else, the hours are long, difficult and you have to be prepared for a lot of sacrifice and be willing to endure more disappointment than success.

Just look at my own stats: I play up to twenty-four events a year in the hope of winning four or five of them – and that would be seen as an excellent return.

While there were no guarantees that I would enjoy success as a professional golfer, the journey up to that point would still have been worth it. I always felt that the discipline and dedication required to take sport as far as possible could be applied to almost any challenge in life. As I've sort of got the hang of this golf thing, I'm probably as well sticking with it.

Seriously, though, golf's my life and I still have a lot I want to achieve in the long career that lies ahead of me. I can't put a figure on the number of tournaments I'd like to win but I am still highly motivated to keep improving, in my golf and fitness, and will always aim to be the best I can. And what also keeps me interested is the great balance I've always enjoyed between golf and time away from the Tour spent at home with friends and family.

Padraic Moyles

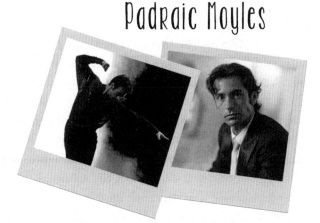

Few dancers know Riverdance *better than Padraic Moyles. A member of the prestigious* Riverdance *family for over eighteen years, the Irish-American trod the boards as both lead dancer and dance captain during his performing days. A keen and gifted dancer since the age of three, there's no better, more passionate person to take on the role of associate director of* Riverdance.

Believe it or not, I tried to quit dancing when I was twelve years old. It was taking up a lot of my time and the comments from other kids in school, slagging me for 'wearing a skirt', didn't go down well with junior me. Growing up in the Bronx, those things weighed on me a little bit but not too much. Going to a feis or competition would also take away from football.

I remember my mother saying, 'If you quit dancing, you quit football.' I thought, 'I'm not quitting football, so I have to stick with dancing.' I'm grateful to my mother for that.

I was always a very determined person. I was very, very competitive and always wanted to win. I wanted to try and be the best and that was my mindset from the age of about five or six. I remember my dad telling me stories of when he'd take me out for a run in the morning and I wouldn't let him beat me. I'd ask him to race again. Sure he would let me win, he had to let me win, but I wouldn't let him stop until I did win.

I began dancing at the age of three. When you move away from home, all of a sudden your culture becomes that much more important to you. With my parents, they wanted us to remember our roots and where we came from. We began playing Irish music, continued to do Irish dancing and play Gaelic football and all those kinds of things. It was the Irish-dancing part that baffled kids in New York at first. I never really told my classmates what I did. Some would find out through other Irish dancers in the school. I think I was the only boy in my school that did Irish dancing.

When I went to dance with Donny Golding, there were other boys there and I remember feeling that it was a much more comfortable environment for me because they were my age and also interested in sports. In some ways I felt at home, when I was dancing with Donny. I remember him being a massive influence in helping me grasp that dancing wasn't just about the steps and technique, it was about performance. I realised quite quickly that that was the element of dance I loved most, that performance element. Although I was aware that I had to be technically accomplished, I knew where I really enjoyed dancing and that was on stage performing it rather than competing.

My dad used to give out about my level of dedication to the craft. My extra-curricular activities often took away from my schoolwork. I remember coming in from dancing one morning at 3 AM and I was getting back up at 6.30 AM to go to school and my dad was saying, 'This is ridiculous.' My mom was saying the same thing but it was what I loved to do. I think both my parents realised that this was what I loved to do. I appreciate the fact that they supported me, although they did stop me at other times. They did put their foot down when they need to.

I did Milwaukee Fest when I was sixteen, and that's when I truly realised how much dancing had gripped me. Milwaukee Fest is a huge Irish festival in America. There are about 120,000 people there every year. I remember performing there and there were people as far as I could see. They were all cheering and shouting and I thought, 'This is the life. This is what I was born to do.'

After that performance I overheard somebody compliment me to my dance teacher, Donny. He said, 'Yeah, he's good but he really won't reach his peak until he's twenty-two or twenty-three and then he'll really understand what it's like to perform in dance.' Those words always stuck with me. I remember thinking to myself: there's so much more to grow, there's so much more to go. *Riverdance* came about around that time. I remember watching a taping of the Eurovision on VHS and saying to myself, 'I'm going to do that.'

I decided to cut school one day to audition for *Riverdance*. I didn't think I'd be allowed to go to Boston to audition so I drove all the way there, ditching school and not telling my parents anything about it. Shortly after, I came home one day to find my mom sitting at the kitchen table. I remember walking in the back door to find her with a letter in her hand. On the letterhead it said *Riverdance* and I immediately thought I was in trouble. I got both a scolding and a pat on the back that day. She was very proud that I got in but she was also very unhappy that I didn't tell her that that's what I was doing.

I'm not a rebellious type of person but there was that moment in my life where I said, 'I have to do this.' I was scared that I wouldn't be allowed to do it otherwise. The risk paid off, although that's when my parents sat me down and said, 'You're not leaving school. You can tell *Riverdance* that as soon as September comes, when your school year is finished, you can join then.' And I did: I joined November of that year.

I joined *Riverdance* on a Monday morning, and we started rehearsals that day. I was in the show by Wednesday night, doing a number called 'Heartland'. I messed up. I made a mistake. I remember the two girls beside me talking me back into the dance. There's a section where we do twelve trebles and I only did ten, going into the next piece. Katie Maguire, who was dancing with me, guided me. I remember her saying, 'Two more, two more, here come the toes.' I remember coming off the stage, being so bitterly disappointed with myself, so angry inside that I had let myself and the team down, and also my dance director, Carol Leavy.

She had trusted me to go on after only two days' rehearsals and I'd made a mistake. She told me to not worry, that I'd never make that mistake again and a part of me believed her. I went home and thought how much I enjoyed every minute of that fear; the fear of going on. At the beginning of 'Heartland' you're standing on the steps with a curtain in front of you. The curtain reveals the beginning, the rhythms and the dance and I remember saying to myself, 'I can't wait for that tomorrow night.' That was it, the feeling I had being on the stage in Hammersmith that night in front of 3,500 people, those people beside me and the leads in front of me. That's what inspired me to set new goals, to be better than before.

I also realised that as good as I might have been, I definitely wasn't the best. Once I got into *Riverdance* and saw the level of talent that was in there, I kind of said to myself, 'I'm lucky to be here'. From that moment on I didn't want to take off my shoes. I was pestering people with questions about how they were doing certain steps, that general quest for knowledge. I was on that quest from that moment on.

The best moment of my career was when I played my first lead role. I never told my mother, who is the biggest inspiration and driver in my life in terms or dancing. My father had a massive role to play in keeping that secret from her. I told her I was homesick and that I didn't want to do this any more and that I might come home. I knew what she was like: 'No way, this is your pride and job, you're going to do this, I'll fly out to you.' That's what she did and of course, that was my first lead performance.

My mom was sitting there nudging my dad in disbelief, 'That looks like Padraic, it *is* Padraic.' And then the tears flew down her face. She met me at the stage door and I could see the pride and joy in her eyes. It was all so worth it, just for that one moment. If you never went on again, if you never danced again, it was worth it just for that.

My training has changed over the years and I've had terrific mentors who helped make those changes. One such mentor was, and still is, Enda McNulty, who works closely with the Irish rugby team and has worked with serious athletes over the years. I got to that point in my career when I was twenty-seven or twenty-eight and I was saying to myself, 'How much more is there to go? How much better can I be? have I reached my peak? Do I really love this? is this my absolute passion in life?'

I also realised that there were a lot of younger guys, with a driving force behind them, and I wanted to get a better understanding of my drive and my determination to be at the top. I began to question myself and whether I was physically in the best shape of my life – I knew I was. I was never out of breath; I went and had a full physical. Doctors are always amazed at the heart rate that Riverdancers have. They did not think it was possible. At that point my resting heart rate was about forty or forty-one beats per minute, which they felt was a joke.

I realised, physically, I was there. So the next thing I questioned was my mindset and how I was recovering and all those kinds of things. I studied sports psychology on the road, did a correspondence course and decided I wanted to put it into practice. I knew Enda McNulty was a motivator and sports psychologist so I called him up and asked to do an internship.

We met for coffee one day and it was that meeting that changed my life in many ways. We were completely honest with each other. I promised to give him everything I had if he gave me everything he had.

He was fascinated by the world of dancers. He asked, 'How have you done the same thing every night, to the same music, for ten years and you still want to be better? What is it inside you?' He wanted to learn.

Essentially, from then on, I realised that although it was great that I had rituals, they weren't necessarily the best rituals for me. I would dance the show each night at least three times as part of my warm-up; it was unnecessary. Enda put me in touch with Barry Solan, who is now the head strength and conditioning coach for Arsenal Football C;ub. We watched my water intake, spiritually where was I, mentally and nutritionally where was I, and then we designed more of a functional training session for me so that I could monitor how much better I was getting, or whether I improving at all.

I changed all of my rituals – the only ones I kept were the things I knew were working really well and I knew I was in a very good place motivationally and in terms of drive. I think in hindsight that gave me an additional ten years. I can honestly say my last show was one of the best I ever performed. When I look back at the video, technically, in terms of energy, I felt I was at the top of my game, and it was a good way to go out. A lot of that came down to making sure I was able to evaluate myself in an honest way in terms of saying where I was good and where I needed to improve.

Artists and sports people, in general are the most insecure people in the world. Our spot is never se-cure. Even as a lead dancer in *Riverdance*, there's always somebody coming up; you're always being reviewed.

If you look at the Irish rugby team today, there's always someone on that bench who believes they should be starting in Sunday's game before other people. There has to be a certain belief that when you're given that role, you believe in yourself and you can achieve what is being asked of you.

One of the biggest challenges for me was trying to stay at the top. That was a massive challenge, one that can never really be put into words. You really have to believe in yourself and what you're doing.

Getting to do what you love is the best thing about being a dancer. I've been a part of *Riverdance* for eighteen years and I've never worked for them. It's what I love to do. Even now, with the new role that I'm in, I count myself so lucky to be a part of it and doing what I love. I love *Riverdance*. It's part of my life. I wake up and think: how are we going to improve today, how are we going to make this better; how are we going tell people how good they are at what they do; how are we going give them a clearer idea of what they're a part of; how are we going to give them a clearer idea of where they stand within this company; how are we going to help them improve. That's a great spot to be in.

We have six leads out there: we always have three boys and three girls and rotate them on and off to make sure they have a long career. Within those three, each one is a very different person. What I've been trying to do over the course of the last year is to bring out the personality of each of those persons.

Rather than confine them to the actual role and the character within the role, I want them to understand the character, understand the role and how their personality can improve the role. Each of those guys are very different. What I say to them is, 'Help us see what makes you different, what yourdifferentiator is. Is it your personality? Is it your technique? Is it your physical stamina?' Whatever that is, let's make it stronger. Let's improve the areas you need to improve on and the areas you're strongest at, let's be the best in the world at it. Let's make sure that each one of you make that extra one percent difference.

It's important to continue to learn and always, have that quest for knowledge, that desire for learning and information. I think finding a good mentor will help a lot of those young, Irish dancers.

Sometimes those mentors will be their Irish-dancing teachers, sometimes they will be outside the Irish-dancing world but it's essential to have that somebody who will help you achieve your goals.

Many budding dancers will have desire to join *Riverdance* but they don't know the steps to enable tem to get there, and a mentor will help them understand how to set goals. You may have your big lifetime goal, but you need the little ones in between to help you achieve things along the way.

At *Riverdance*, we hold summer schools for Irish dancers to educate them how they can become a dancer. We educate them on nutrition, mindset, rest and recovery, physical conditioning, setting goals. At the end of the week, each week, we allow them to perform *Riverdance*. It was only a small little showcase we put on in the Lir, but it gave them a better feeling of what it's like to be part of this company. For some of the special ones, we put them on stage in the Gaiety with the actual *Riverdance* cast.

For us, for *Riverdance*, it's a great opportunity to see who's coming up, to know who you're about to hire. You get to know them for a week rather than just a day long audition and you get to see them in an actual performance environment, when they're on the stage in front of an audience can be quite intimidating.

There are a number of people who say that's what I've always wanted to do but when they get there, fears can overcome them. We want them to understand those fears and how they can rise above them. The biggest piece of advice I can give to young artists or people looking to achieve their goals is to share your goals, share your fears, and allow people to help you.

I don't think any of us in life get anywhere in life, *ever*, on our own. Surround yourself with smart people. Surround yourself with a very good team, whether that's your family or people outside your family. Realise that you're never alone and that there are always people who are willing to help.

I didn't get here on my own. I had the most amazing wife in the world who was there to support me when I was insecure and when I doubted myself. I had people there who were able to pick me up, whether they were the directors and producers of the show, my teammates or my wife. There are always people willing to talk but they will never talk to you unless they understand what's going on in your head and whether you're willing to talk to them.

Behind every successful person is a terrific team. The people who can give credit to those who helped them along the way are the ones that are humble and the ones who hopefully able to stay at the top for a lot longer.

Padraic's Tips for Nailing a Dance Audition

Prepare.

Riverdance has been around for a long time; there are a lot of videos out there. You could have a lot of that material before you come in.

Show your personality.

Show that you're a team player.

Stephanie Roche

Professional footballer Stephanie Roche has been kicking balls since she was a little girl. A dedicated Manchester United fan, she followed her team passionately, hoping one day to emulate her heroes success.

Fiercely dedicated to the game, she landed a position on the Irish Women's Football team, representing her country around the world. In 2014, fate waved its magic wand, resulting in a FIFA Goal of the Year, Puskás nomination.

My earliest memory playing soccer was out on the street with my friends who were mostly boys; I must have been about eight. Any time I went outside, it was with a football under my arm.

My two older brothers were big Manchester United fans, so I've pretty much always been a fan too. I'd always watch the games with them. I was always a bit of a tomboy growing up.

My dad used to coach my brother's team and I used to go to their matches quite a lot to show support. Football was all around me.

I started playing for Bellevue in Shankhill at the age of eleven. One of my friends who I kicked a ball around on the street with played for that team, and his mam asked me if I'd like to join. I had never even thought about joining a team until then.

I was the only girl on an all-boy team. That wasn't too unusual in training because they were all used to me playing out on the street; it was when we played other teams that I got a few odd looks from boys who weren't used to seeing a girl play. They could give me a bit of a hard time but never anything too bad. My team was always looking out for me. When I was playing against the other boys, I usually did pretty well, so that kept them quiet. I had proven myself to them and shown them who was boss!

When I was younger my goal was to play for Ireland. I knew all about the Irish women's team and I started playing for Cabinteely when I was about twelve because the mixed rules changed. I had a trial for the Irish schools team. It was only as recently as five years ago that I saw turning professional as an option. A lot of the girls in my team were starting to play for Ireland; all I ever wanted was to play for my country.

At the age of fourteen, I was still playing for Cabinteely Girls. We played against Stella Maris in Oscar Traynor Road, and Noel King was at the match. At the time he was the senior women's team manager. He came over to my dad and me after the match and said, 'Keep up what you're doing and you'll be in the Ireland squad some day.' That made my day. I was delighted to hear the Irish manager say that.

A couple of weeks later I was brought up for trials for the under seventeens. I was still only fourteen and it was a big deal for my family and me. Noel was the first person to recognise me and give me that first little vote of confidence that made me keep going.

Back then I think I put football before everything; my friends will tell you that.

I missed a lot of school days because of the game. Stupidly, in secondary school, I didn't concentrate on my academic work as much as I should have. I've been lucky that it's worked out for me but looking back I wish I had concentrated more on schooling.

My boyfriend used to say to me, 'Something good is going to happen to you,' and I kind of felt that myself. Because I loved football so much and worked hard for it, training all the time, I had it in my head that football was going to be my life. I've had a few very lucky breaks and I'm privileged to say that football is my career; it doesn't always work out that way for people.

Playing for Ireland has allowed me to travel the world. I've been to some of the craziest places you could imagine. I've been to Kazakhstan and other countries you'd never ever even think of going to. It's been an amazing experience to be able to travel to these places that aren't your typical holiday destinations, all the while doing something you love and representing your country. I've seen a lot of the world through football and it's a great thing to be able to say.

I made my international senior debut for the Irish team in Iceland and my home debut in Cork against Kazakhstan. I scored the winner coming off bench, and that sticks out in my mind as a very proud moment. As a striker, I love scoring goals, and scoring goals for your country is one of the most amazing feelings ever.

A lot of my friends don't play any sports. There'd be times growing up when they'd be going away on holidays or weekends away or nights out and as much as I'd like to join them, I just couldn't go because I had a match the next day or I had a tournament to play in. There are definitely times when football gets in the way, but for me, it's all worth it. It's something that I love doing and I never want to miss out on the opportunity of doing it.

I remember I was just finishing up school and I had booked a holiday to Spain with my friends but a tournament came up in Limerick that same week and I cancelled my holiday. I remember being disappointed at the time but then as a result of that tournament, I got picked for the Irish under nineteens team, so it all worked out in the end. There have been times when I've had to sacrifice things, but it's always been worth it.

Peamount was the first team I joined in senior women's football where I really felt at home. I was playing alongside some of my best friends and I really felt comfortable in the team. I was there for three years under Eileen Gleeson ,who was a very good manager.

Every time I played for her and Peamount, I played the way I wanted to play. I had the freedom to do whatever I wanted.

Without that I wouldn't have been able to score that famous goal that I did because I probably wouldn't have tried it. I have so many happy memories and good friends from that team. I'll always be grateful for them. Eileen knew what my strengths and weaknesses were. She has always encouraged me to do what I could do up front. I was always given a free role, even though I was the striker. A few times things mightn't have worked out, but she always encouraged me and she was the same with every player we had.

I was playing in France when the whole FIFA thing happened. I was sitting in my apartment when I got a tweet to say that I'd been nominated. I had been home a few weeks before watching a women's national league game, and somebody said something along the lines of: 'Oh I heard you're going to be in the Puskás nominations.' I thought they were just messing. I don't know or where they heard it from, but a week later it came out and I was chuffed. I was shocked, but I delighted.

All of a sudden there was this massive press interest. I tried to be myself as much as I could. I was new to all of the attention! It was a great goal but I was so lucky that it even got caught on video in the first place. For FIFA to have caught it and put if forward for a Puskás was a lucky break.

I had worked hard at football for a long time and I always said at the time that I knew I was extremely lucky. The run-up to the Ballon D'Or ceremony was crazy. When I got nominated for a top-ten goal, I never thought I was going to get to the top three. I knew the goal was good but I thought, 'These are world-famous footballers and they have millions of people around the world voting for them.'

So many people in Ireland and England and women's football around the world got behind me and got me into the top three, I was just delighted to get the chance to go to the awards. The whole run-up to the awards, all we were doing the whole time was trying drum up support and get votes. I didn't even have too much time to think about it.

I remember the day we were flying out to Zurich, my dad and I did an interview on radio and my dad got quite a bit emotional. I had never seen him like that before. That's when it really hit us that this was reality – that we were going to one of the most prestigious awards ceremonies in football.

The day itself happened so fast. We were treated like royalty and I got to meet some of the best footballers that have ever played the game. It felt like a dream. I had the privilege of chatting to Abby Wambach who is one of the best female footballers around and Martha too who is Brazilian.

The person who I was slightly nervous to meet but over-the-top excited about was Ronaldo. He was a Man United player and I'm a big Man United fan, so he was the one I really wanted to meet and speak to. He was lovely, which made it all the better. It was all a little surreal. It's only now that some time has passed that I think about all the people I've got to meet and share that moment with. It was amazing.

I play for Sunderland now and it's going really well. I'm really happy here and I hope to do well for the team during my time with the club. I'm only twenty-six and want to keep playing, as long as I can. I'm lucky to have achieved a lot of my dreams already but I always want to continue playing for my country. I want to get as many caps for Ireland as I can and continue playing professionally at the highest level that I can.

Going to the Fifa Ballon D'Or was never something I thought I could achieve, and it's happened, so who knows what the future has in store. You never know what lies ahead; it's exciting.

Stephanie's Tip for Soccer Stardom

Have a true passion for the game.

You must love it more than anything. All I ever wanted to do was play the game, and I think that's so important in order to succeed. I never had a football out of my hand when I was growing up. I was always kicking a ball off the wall or playing with my friends.

At a professional level it gets to the stage where it's competitive and its hard and it turns into a job. I always say that coaches who coach girls and boys shouldn't be too hard on them because it's when they get to sixteen or seventeen and it starts to get competitive, that's when it should be hard. Up until then you should be enjoying every second of the sport. Every player should love football for the sake of playing. I think that for as long as you can, you should just enjoy the game.

Rob Kearney

Leinster and Ireland rugby star Rob Kearney is a serious sportsman. With his eye firmly on the prize, this fleet-footed full back has been representing his country since 2007. With over seventy caps for Ireland and three Lions Tours, there's no stopping this fierce athlete.

Growing up my life very much revolved around what sporting event I had next. I was lucky to play many different sports, and my parents were dedicated to driving my siblings and me to a different sports lesson or match every single day. I feel incredibly lucky to have been blessed with folks who were so willing to help out and to put a support system around me and my brothers and sister, to help us do so many different things, and enable us to follow our dreams.

My first real memory of rugby was in my back garden. My mam and dad were having a barbecue and loads of my dad's friends were over. dad was always a huge rugby man. He loved the game and naturally, loads of his friends did too. I remember kicking a ball around the garden. I remember dad's friends were kicking up all these big, high kicks, and somehow, I was catching them, one after another. I couldn't believe it. I suppose my love for the sport dates from that day.

I have another vivid memory of my dad and me in Lansdowne Road. He often took me there to see games when I was a kid. I must have been about five or six years of age this particular time. Ireland were playing and I was up in the stand with him. During the game I nudged him and I said, 'I want to be out there playing some day.'

I played rugby throughout my childhood but it was in the schools' Senior Cup with Clongowes that I first got 'spotted.' I went straight from there to the Leinster Academy. With the academy you train with the senior squad every few weeks and that's what I did back then.

Over time, I managed to get a game. I played well and it all snowballed from there. I was lucky that the whole process happened really quickly for me. It takes some guys three to five years going through the system before they get the opportunity to play for Leinster like I did. A lot of things fell into place for me quite quickly.

I remember my first game for Leinster really clearly. It was a friendly. I had already played two friendlies at the start of the pre-season. It's mad to think it was ten years ago now. I'll never forget the increase in the intensity and just how quick everything was, how strong everyone was and how weak I was. It was a real shock to the system. It was a brilliant day. There are moments in your career that you do sometimes forget but your debut is generally one to remember! It was a day I had beem working towards and looking forward to my whole sporting life.

Back then I looked up to the likes of Jonah Lomu, the New Zealand winger who took rugby to a global level, everybody knew him. I was a fan of Keith Wood and Simon Geoghegan too. When I was thirteen, fourteen and fifteen, Brian O'Driscoll was quickly becoming Ireland's greatest-ever player and I looked up to him massively. I have autographs and photos with him at home. Fast-forward a few years and I'm playing alongside him and we're good mates.

When I first started playing alongside my heroes, it was quite surreal. It was difficult at the beginning to be honest. Here I was, on the one hand idolizing so many of these guys – I had looked up to them for so many years – but then on the other, competing with them for a position. I had to have a chat with myself and say, 'Listen, you can still look up to these guys and really admire them, but you need to have a level of competitiveness too. You're fighting for your place and you want to achieve and you won't achieve if you give them too much respect.'

I'll never forget my debut for Ireland. It was in Argentina and I was twenty-three years old. My dad, my brother and my best friend flew over for it. Dave was at home with my mam doing his Leaving Cert, from what I remember. It was a huge moment in my life. I'd be lying if I said I didn't feel the pressure.

I was just four or five years old when I decided I wanted to play for Ireland, so my first emotion out on the pitch was 'Wow, I'm actually here, I've done it.' There's a sense of relief that you have achieved your lifelong goal up. I was nervous because I was going into uncharted territory. I was massively excited to get the opportunity. There are so many different emotions going through your head on a monumental day like that one. It's probably the same before a lot of games. You're feeling lots of different emotions.

The best thing about being on the field is the fact that you're doing what you love. For that moment, nothing else matters. All those thoughts you have during the week, some of the problems or issues you might have Monday to Friday are gone and it's just you on a field in front of eighty or ninety thousand people. Your country are cheering you on and that's really special feeling. It's all those years of dreaming about doing something and then you're finally living the dream. It's a really cool place to be.

I've always been fiercely loyal and passionate about the game, but as time goes on, I find myself getting more emotional before the start of a game as we sing the national anthem. It's only since Dave got on the team that that side of me has come out. When the two of us are standing beside each other in the line-up and we look to where mum and dad are sitting, with my brother and sister, during the anthem beside our brother – that's such a brilliant moment. It's those little snapshots that are the moments you'll remember for life.

Dave and I are really lucky to be able to share this experience together. We live together and we're really good friends; we help each other out a lot. When games are going well and we're both playing well and we're winning, that sense of euphoria is massively heightened. If we're losing or one of us makes a mistake or one person had a bad game, you share that a little bit with the other person.

There are definitely disadvantages to it too but generally the pros outweigh the cons. If one is going through a tough time, you know what to say, or what not to say – which can often be just as important.

Team sports are brilliant. I've been so lucky in the job that I do and that it's a team sport. Personally, I don't think I'd be able for an individual sport in terms of the mental strength you need to have and the loneliness. When you've got issues with your own game or confidence, it becomes a much darker place. When you're in a team environment, you can look to your teammates. You have a much better level of camaraderie. You share a lot of great moments together; you share the bad moments too. When you're in those moments as a group, it gets you out of them a bit quicker.

Failure can be difficult; nobody likes to lose. Mentally it can take a while to regather yourself. Physically, it's fine. After a week or two, you go back to normal. When you're building up for something for so long, the whole country comes to a standstill, and when you fail so publicly, it's difficult. It's lucky that we're in a team environment: thirty players going through the same emotions; twenty coaches feeling the same thing.

You all rally together; you close ranks and you commit to each other to get yourselves out of that hole. I've lost so many games throughout my career – big games. But when you've got another game to play six or seven days later, you can't hang around in your head too much.

There's nobody in the world who has achieved something who hasn't failed in some way. At the time of failure, it sucks but that's really important on several levels because it drives your hunger even further. You learn from those failures. Anyone who has achieved and become successful learns from those moments of adversity in his or her life.

Everyone goes through it be it poor form, big injuries, missing big games or not getting selected. Injury is the worst part of the game and injuries are becoming more and more common as the game progresses. Collisions are getting bigger. Guys are getting bigger and stronger. For me, it's part and parcel of what I do.

My most testing time was perhaps when I picked up a knee injury, which required surgery pretty much immediately. I was out the game nine months.

During that downtime you go through moments of self-doubt where you wonder if your body will ever be the same again, if will you be capable of doing the things you did before the injury.

What made my injury extra difficult at the time was that my team was doing unbelievably well; they were winning every single game. They were winning trophies in Europe.

Isa Nacewa, who was playing in my position, was playing unbelievably well and that made it extra tough. You're out injured and yet your team is still doing incredibly well and the guy you're competing with is doing amazingly well.

You feel completely forgotten about. That is extremely tough to deal with, and it was a difficult time for me.

When supporters have been watching someone do well, you almost need to prove to them that you're worthy of your position again and that you can offer more or at least that there's room for both of you on the team.

When you've been out for so long it is almost like a clean slate all over again and there's so many people you need to prove to – your coaches especially, that the big injury hasn't affected your game.

Even for the first few months when you're back, there are still a huge number of mental challenges. I was lucky to get back on my feet again.

To succeed in this sport you need to be enjoying what you're doing. You need to train really hard and make a huge amount of sacrifices. There are a lot of commitments too.

Our weekly schedule can be intense. We're usually in training, Monday or Tuesday between 8 AM and 4 PM. We'd do a recovery in the morning, loads of video work, team meetings, weights, a pitch session. You have to get your massage, your physiotherapy, all that sort of stuff. Wednesdays we have off. You'd go into the club in the morning, get a massage, do a bit of pool recovery or rehab work on some sore body parts if you need to. Thursdays we train on the field and there are no weights. Then it's gameday on Friday.

The front end of the week is a pretty heavy work load. The goal of the week is to make sure you're fresh come Friday and you're ready for the game. The training hours when we're in the club, aren't the tough part; it's more everything that we do outside of it that is geared towards that eighty-minute block at the weekend.

Diet is important and you need to sleep right. You need to make sure you're cooking the right food, eating at the right times, taking a certain amount in. If I go shopping I can't walk around for longer than an hour before my back starts to get sore.

All those things, you need to make decisions every day, 'Is this the best thing for me and more importantly, is this the best thing for my teammates?'

If everyone has that sort of outlook, where they put their team first, then the team is going to be in a really good place at the weekend.

To get the rewards, you have to put the work in. That's the bottom line. When you go out onto a field, be it a rugby field or a golf course, if you put the work in, you get the rewards back. There are very few workplaces that have that level of honesty.

Generally, more often than not, you find that the people who work the hardest will achieve, and that's a brilliant state to be in; knowing that if I do the work, I'm going to get something back from it.

I'm really hopeful that I haven't had my proudest career moment yet. As an athlete, you love to win; you want medals; you want trophies. That's what we do it for. Growing up as a kid, you're always taught: 'taking part is the important thing.' That's not the case any longer, now that sport is my life. Winning is the important thing, and it's the only thing. When you don't win, you have that sense of failure, and you need to go back to the drawing board and look at your next task, and you work out how you're going to win. I suppose you want to leave a legacy, don't you? You hope that in forty or fifty years' time, people will still know your name.

You have to accept sport for what it is. Sport is beautiful; everyone loves it. It can be cruel and unpredictable and that's why people love it.

Al Mennie

At six foot five inches, Northern Irish big wave rider Alastair Mennie operates on a different scale to other surfers. Braving ocean swells and giant waves, the Castlerock surfer is a daredevil of the seas. Surfing since the age of five, the ocean is not only his true passion, but also his life.

The very first time I ever went into the sea with anything resembling a surfboard, I was about five or six. I can only briefly recall it but it wasn't a real surfboard, it was a polystyrene thing that I used in the waves. I've seen pictures, and I was wearing just a pair of blue shorts and I was catching little white-water waves lying down. I do, however, remember the time I got a proper surfboard for my eleventh birthday. I couldn't get my arm round it, so dad had to carry it to the beach for me at Castlerock, Northern Ireland.

I remember that the surf was big and stormy and the sea was all brown and menacing-looking – mid-November – as the river nearby was spilling into the sea and staining the water a peat-brown colour. It was really cold but I didn't care, I just remember trying again and again to stand up when I managed to catch the white water but I couldn't. I kept slipping off – we didn't realise we were meant to wax the top of the board for grip! I was totally hooked from the very first time. I was always in the water when I was kid.

If I wasn't surfing, I was in some sort of boat, on a boogie board, water skiing, swimming or whatever. I was born in Belfast and we lived inland for years, so I only had weekends and school holidays to surf for a long time. This time limit on my surfing time actually made me appreciate surfing even more. I would get up before it was bright so I could surf as soon as the sun came up, and I would spend pretty much all day in the water, or not far from it.

Surfing just kind of became the focal point of my life. I was never aware of it happening. It was at the centre of everything. As I grew up, I planned literally everything around the tide, the wind, the weather chart. I wouldn't arrange anything that might get in the way if there was going to be surf.

I started competing when I was fourteen. I didn't know there were competitions or I would have probably started them earlier. That first one was in Rossnowlagh, County Donegal, and I only made it to the quarterfinals. It felt really strange only being given a fifteen-minute timeframe to catch waves and to be judged!

It was especially strange considering that when I surfed in Castlerock, I rarely saw any other surfers except my brother and the odd older guy from time to time.

I've competed at professional, national and international events all over the world but the one that stands out as my best performance in a contest was the British University Championships. The standard of surfers was generally quite low compared to many of the other events I did, but that's not why it stands out for me.

The reason is because it represented my ability to overcome a lot of things I struggled with. The event is one of the biggest in terms of competitor numbers in the world, and there were something like seven rounds to get through before the final. That's a lot of opportunities to get knocked out of the event.

Also I had been training specifically for that event, its locations and its waves. I won it, and it felt like I had done everything right in my preparation and it had paid off.

I'll never forget when I surfed the biggest swell ever recorded off the Irish coast. I surfed it off Mullaghmore head, County Sligo. Believe it or not, the more I ride those big waves, the more nervous I get. I think as time goes on I become more and more aware of the consequences. The more experiences I have, the more the ocean shows me its power and strength. It can make me feel insignificant at times.

That day was one of the most significant for me. The thing is, in order to prepare for a football match, for example, you know it is usually taking place on a certain day, time and venue and against an opponent known well in advance.

It is possible to train in a way that prepares you gradually over time to peak for that precise event. For big-wave surfing, things are very different. I don't know when the next big swell may arrive. It may happen in two weeks or it may not arrive for three months.

All I know is it will probably be winter. There is no way of knowing where exactly I may be able to surf it, or the exact conditions, the exact day or time it may arrive. I need to be in a very 'ready' state of preparedness all through the year, but in particular to be able to hold my peak mental and physical state for the entire winter. If I aim to surf in the Southern Hemisphere too, in their winter, then that requires even more dedication, for even longer.

To be 'ready' for a long period of time takes routine. I have off-season training, which is generally through the spring and summer, and in-season training, loosely around autumn and winter. That's all physical training from gym work to underwater training with my trainer.

In terms of being mentally prepared, I developed a way to increase my physical performance through mental preparation, which I adapted over time for big-wave surfing. It has actually helped in lots of other parts of my life too. I used sports psychology books, subliminal sports recordings, hypnosis and affirmations. I struggled with the level of competition at the time and I needed to work on my confidence and self-belief so I did all of these things and my results rocketed.

I ended up with a list of words linked to various situations, which I used in my head or written on notes around my walls, in my wallet and so on. It might sound like I'm crazy but if you want something badly enough you have to recognise your weaknesses, isolate them and work on them. That's what I did.

Now when I enter the water on a giant day with huge surf, and I'm scared or doubtful, I can perform better knowing I am physically fit and ready but also I am mentally fit and ready. The combination is needed, as having one without the other doesn't work as well. I also plan everything to the nth degree. This is nature, the ocean; it is completely uncontrollable, so my approach when I'm preparing for a big day is put everything into two groups, *controllable* and *uncontrollable*. I deal with everything controllable as early as possible: things like equipment, safety gear and so on.

Then I'm left with the uncontrollable aspects such as weather, people and timings. You can't control them, so you have to accept that and roll with it! Make the best of it as you go. If you spend time fretting about the uncontrollable factors, you will not focus on making sure the controllable factors are dealt with. It's me trying to clear my mind and free up my time as much as possible so I can just get on with surfing.

I'm lucky in that I can go to the beach three or four times a day, be it to walk my dog, surf, train, paddle-board, go out on the boat or jet-skis or even simply sit in the van and make calls while watching the sea. It's part of my subconscious. I thinkit would be weird for me not to be doing something sea-orientated on a daily basis, big wave surfing is simply just part of the entire picture.

Touch wood – I have been very lucky. I haven't had many injuries as a direct result of surfing. Most of the big waves I surf break in relatively deep water, so the biggest issue can be repeated hold-downs under water. The closest I came to a serious injury was falling on a forty-footer and something hitting me under water. Luckily I was wearing a glass-fibre helmet but even that cracked.

When I surfaced I had blurred vision, I was hard of hearing and another two waves hit me before my safety guy got to me on a jet-ski. That one rattled me, but in the next ten minutes I went on two more big waves . . . Back on the horse and all that!

I've surfed in some incredible locations but the highlight for me is a place called Mavericks, California. It's hugely special to me because it was a turning point in my life when I first went there. The last conversation I ever had with my dad was that I wanted to go and surf the spot called Mavericks. I went there aged twenty-two and surfed it, and it sparked an interest which has lasted throughout my life. I came home, borrowed money, bought a boat and some ocean charts and went off searching for similar waves to Mavericks. I knew we had huge swells here; I just needed to find the best places to ride them.

Today, this country is recognised as one of the best big-wave locations in the world and I can safely say we have some of the most terrifying and cold big-wave locations on the planet.

Surfing fits in very easily with my lifestyle and I'm relaxed about it. I have lots of other things going on in life, from business interests to writing. I am a black-belt martial artist, I teach, I travel. I like to continually flex everything I have; surfing is just one part of me. For anyone wanting a piece of the action, remember to be realistic. It's all very well being passionate about something, but you also have to put food on the table.

Education is everything, and the older I get the more I appreciate that. When I was younger all I wanted to do was surf,. But, mum and dad kept me achieving qualifications in other areas too, so that I didn't just know what the wind direction would be and how to get a tube when surfing!

You have to develop everything you have, flex everything you have, use all your skills to enhance everything you are good at.

Being great at surfing does not mean you will be able to make a profitable career from it; unless you are business-minded too. The most important thing is to make use of all your time as best and most efficiently as you can so that every day you are progressing in some way in the things you are passionate about.

If you can do that, keep focused on developing your skills and abilities, then everything else will fall into place. If you would rather think about Friday and Saturday night in the pub all week and pay little attention to training your body and mind and learning and engaging with people then you probably won't allow yourself the chance to achibe your potential.

If I could meet Al junior and give him some words of wisdom, I would tell myself to ask more questions of those older and wiser than himself. There is a world of information and advice that can help make things happen much quicker for you. A perfect example is that you can look at a picture of me surfing a big wave but unless you actually talk to me, then you have no idea what goes into being able to do that. I would definitely advise myself to ask more people more questions when I was younger and that goes for everything in life – not just for surfing.

In Vogue

'People will stare.
Make it worth
their while.'
Harry Winston

For some fashion is just fun; for others it's a way of life.

With a beautiful garment, a stylish pair of shoes, a carefully crafted handbag, fashion can alter your mood, your lifestyle, your habits and your world.

It's a mode of expression; a way of wearing your personality and feelings, a way of exposing to the world who you are. For the consumer it offers a pleasure like no other; for the designer a way of showcasing their view of the world, whether in multicolour or monochrome, snakeskin, silk or the finest wool.

Leaf through the following pages for an intimate look into the lives of some of our biggest fashion names from jewellery crafters to costume designers and haute-couture ateliers.

Don O'Neill

Kerry-born designer Don O'Neill oozes fashion from his fingertips. From humble beginnings to running a New York based fashion house, the style guru has been dressing international superstars like Oprah in his breathtaking Theia Couture gowns since 2009. With stints working for prestigious fashion giants Lacroix and Badgley Mischka, nobody knows haute couture like O'Neill.

My interest in clothes started very young. At the age of seven or eight when I was playing with my sister's Cindy dolls, I would dress the dolls up in mom's silk scarves, draping and wrapping them around to make new dresses. God, those dresses were so simple to make. Cindy never had fit issues!

Mom was quite fashionable and had a wardrobe of beautiful dresses from Bergdorf Goodman in New York and IB Jorgensen in Dublin, and I was aware at nine or ten years old of the excitement around a new designer purchase and what made them so special.

When in I was about fifteen, I saw a fabulous television documentary on Karl Lagerfeld preparing a winter collection at

Chloé. The fashion-show scenes at the end ignited in earnest my fledgling fashion flames – that's when I decided I wanted to be a fashion designer. I didn't seriously pursue if for another few years, however. I had other interests too, many of which were creative. I loved drawing. I loved to cook. I loved science, biology and chemistry but in school, my heart was always in the art room. My art teacher thought I could one day become a graphic artist.

With that in mind, I applied to the Crawford College of Art in Cork and the Limerick College of Art and Design and was luckily offered places at both. My art teacher recommended Cork for its foundation course and suggested I transfer to Limerick for fashion, if fashion was truly my passion.

Two months in to college in Cork, I felt in despair. At the tender age of seventeen, I was homesick and unsure of my career choice. At that time, I would come home every weekend with my cousin Lorraine who worked for AIB in Bishopstown, along with another girl from Ballyheigue who was training to be a chef in the regional technical college with CERT.

Every weekend she told stories of wonderful and exotic things she learned to cook or bake during the week and I was fascinated. I decided I no longer wanted to study art. I wanted to be a chef. I was nervous telling mom and dad about my change of heart but they fully supported me. I dropped out of college and applied to CERT, and fortunately was accepted to begin classes in Cork the following September. I was thrilled. I studied there for two years and loved every minute.

I really excelled in culinary college and came third in the national apprentice competition and represented Ireland in the junior culinary-olympic team at Hotelympia. I never forgot about my love of art and fashion. All through college, I was doodling fashion models in the margins of my books and even designed my sister Deirdre's debs dress.

I graduated with distinction and went on to begin my career at a restaurant in Galway. The reality of being a chef the long hours, working weekends and holidays began to take its toll .

Ironically as I write this, it is the Labor Day bank holiday weekend in America and I am on my way in to work to prepare for fashion week which kicks off in three days.

Fashion was always on my mind. I was in a bit of a dilemma and once again told mom and dad, that I wanted to switch careers and go back to college to study fashion. Like always, they were fully supportive and promised to help in any way they could. I resigned and began applying for courses. A few weeks later, I received a phone call at home, congratulating me on winning a fully paid tuition scholarship to the Barbra Bourke College of Fashion Design in Dublin. Fate had decided I was definitely going back to fashion and was helping to pay the costs too!

College, I now know, is essential in learning the basics of the craft; how to draw and sketch fashion illustrations, how to make a paper pattern or drape a dress on a mannequin, understanding how clothes are cut and sewn together, what all the different types of fabric are, how they are made, how they drape, how to push and nurture creativity and design a collection, merchandise it, price and sell it, and learning about the various business models and fashion career choices within this enormous industry. Internships while in college at established fashion houses are wonderful for seeing what is being learned and put in to practice, and to really learn from witnessing how it all happens.

My time with Christian Lacroix in Paris was my most extraordinary and magical fashion experience ever. To be an intern in the number one couture house in Paris was such a privilege. I had worked unpaid and very hard for a costume designer in Paris – the pay-off being that if I helped her, she would introduce me to her friends at Christian Lacroix where she herself had worked for many years. As promised, she set up the meeting and they liked my portfolio, much , they offered me an intern position to work on the Autumn/Winter haute couture collection.

I worked side-by-side with Monsieur Lacroix every day for three months and witnessed this incredible man make magic happen. Nothing was impossible and his ateliers could breathe life into even the simplest scribble on a tiny post-it note that he doodled while on the phone one afternoon. I was nervous on my first day. My French was terrible and I continually addressed Monsieur Lacroix in the familiar 'tu'. It was a terrible 'faux pas' to the horror of the entire studio, for which I severely reprimanded several times! However one evening, Mr Lacroix confided in me that he found *it* and my clumsy French and Irish accent adorable and that he didn't mind at all, but that was just to be between us.

My trip to America was almost fated. Before working at Lacroix, I was barely surviving in Paris and had entered the Morrin Visa lottery in the hope that New York would provide better work opportunities. I won a green card just before starting at the fashion house and unsure of what to do, I confided in Christian. He proposed I go see his astrologist who told me my future was indeed, in America. I headed off to New York with an armful of introductory letters to America's top designers, each handwritten by Monsieur Lacroix. I was a very lucky man.

My first job in America, as design director in an evening-wear company, lasted ten years. I was then head hunted by one of the evening wear industry's top sales executives who had just joined JS International. They had just secured the license to revive the bankrupt, defunct Badgley Mischka brand, which was once America's leading red carpet glamour label.

My job was to create a high volume, affordable luxury evening wear collection for them. It was the most challenging and transformative period of my life. I walked through fire and the burden on my shoulders felt crushing I thought I would collapse. I regretted many times leaving the comfort of my previous job, however, *miraculously*, I made it through the testing times and we went from zero to eleven million dollars in sales in our first year, exceeding the company's two million dollars projection for year-one.

We had grown Badgley Mischka to an eighteen-million-dollar company but working as a licensee to the giant Iconix Corporation, that owned the trademark, was proving to be a nightmare for the

CEO of JS Group. At least the collection was hugely successful and everyone knew that Don O'Neill designed it. The license contract was due for renewal and the company decided not to renew. The contract was being terminated and I was handed the exciting opportunity to create a new evening wear brand.

At the time I had just completed a white chiffon strapless gown with a very ornate jeweled waistband, from which a huge ft skirt flowed in the breeze! When our model tried it during the fittings, she looked like a Goddess. I researched the names of Goddesses, Celtic, then Roman and Greek, and fate drew me to 'THEIA', the Greek word for Goddess. She was a Titan, the Goddess of light, from whom all urces of light radiate. A woman feeling like a Goddess radiating light – it was the perfect name for a new evening wear brand. That was the birth of my business.

My job as creative director is varied. I set the tone for the brand. I tell the story of who 'THEIA' is and incorporate that story in to each collection, creating the brand 'truth' – that a woman feels like a Goddess radiating light in my dresses.

The collections start with a light bulb going off, an emotional reaction to mething. It can be a piece of furniture, a picture in a book, a walk in the botanical gardens – a seed is then planted and it grows to form a collection. The fabrics come first, and again it's emotional. I buy fabrics that I love. Then, I drape the fabrics and allow them to tell me what shapes they are best suited to. Next, I sketch, letting my mind wander freely as I fill pages of scribbles and doodles and dresses. It's from these pages the most interesting and most successful designs come from.

The sleepless nights occur when I feel as though the muses of creativity have abandoned me, deadlines approach and my mind is a blank slate. But thankfully those moments, weeks at times, pass and the flow begins again.

It is always surreal and thrilling to see my gowns on the red carpet; pinch me moments like – 'How on earth did I do that?' – I remember watching the red carpet of a big award show one night with mom, dad and Pascal, my life partner for twenty-two years, here in New York and Carrie Underwood arrived on the carpet looking stunning in THEIA. Seeing all the hundreds of photographers going crazy as thousands of flashes lit her up, you could feel the excitement on the red carpet. I was excited; mom and dad were excited and proud, proud. It was lovely.

Oprah is the most famous celebrity I have ever met. I was nervous at first but she put us as easy immediately and we thoroughly enjoyed her company, that meeting was a huge highlight of my career.

For any budding designer, there are a few things to know. This industry is very, very hard work, with very, very long hours. It involves a lot of thankless, unpaid hours of interning, but remember you are learning your craft.

There is al the fact that you are only as good as your last dress – you don't get to make very many bad dresses, or dresses that don't sell because when sales plummet you either go out of business or get fired – this business is ruthless.

Finding a job can be tough – the competition is fierce. Going to a good school is very important and getting great industry experience is even more important.

This industry is full of very insecure yet powerful influential people hiding behind crazy, big glasses and über expensive designer clothes, terrified of sharing their contacts, giving a helping hand or allowing anyone in to their tiny privileged fashion circle. They will only open doors to you if you are prodigiously talented, or have managed to work at prestigious design houses.

Be prepared and know if you do not qualify for that club that you can still succeed and be very happy in the world of fashion without being featured in Vogue magazine or having dinner with Kendal Jenner or being best friends with Karl Lagerfeld.

Having your own company is expensive – hugely expensive and when you launch your first collection; know that you will not receive any payment until almost a year after you start. Signing away your name for a big injection of cash to keep the company going is generally a bad idea, as that deal has gone ur for most designers who end up being fired by the company that owns their name. Jil Sander being a prime example, Prada fired her after they invested and bought a majority stake in her company, only to turn around and fire her because her design development expenses were too high and she wasn't making enough 'commercial clothes'.

Of course, it is an exceptionally rewarding industry too. My advice? Work hard, be nice, work harder, treat people with respect, help people when you can, travel. Intern in London, Paris or New York – learn how to make clothes, how to sew them, how to drape patterns. Learn, learn, learn – never stop learning. Don't let fear stand in the way. Follow your drape, know that no matter what you do, there is always, *always* meone who will do it better, just do what you do, what you believe in and do it to the very best of your ability.

Al, be open to opportunities and don't let an opportunity to learn during an internship go to waste. I missed many opportunities at Lacroix that I wish I could go back and have a do-over, many more things I could have learned there – you can never learn enough.

Joan Bergin

Few costume designers have an Emmy to their name; Joan Bergin has three. The Irish designer fell into the business as a budding actress and has never looked back since. From the Vikings *and HBO's the* Tudors, *to silver screen favourite's* My Left Foot *and* Veronica Guerin, *Joan has enjoyed working on me of the biggest film and TV productions ever made.*

I rt of fell into costume design by accident and to this day I look around and think how good it's been to me as a profession. I often look at everything from lighting to directing and wonder, why not *that* end of it? I'm interested in the whole concept of theatre and filming and the arts.

My main passion, alongside costume, has always been acting. Becoming an actor was all I ever dreamed as a child and I certainly chased that dream in my early days. I remember my parents saying, 'Acting isn't a real job. What else do you want to be?'

Despite that, I kept it at the back of my mind the whole time and then finally began to pursue it properly when I started acting in the Focus Theatre in Dublin, which used the Stanislavsky system, with Luke Kelly's wife Deirdre O'Connell treading the boards too. It trained everyone from Gabriel Byrne to Tom Hickey – lots of people who went out to do very big things.

My passion for acting had begun as a child. I used to act in the school plays and my mother said she could never come to watch me because that's where the wedding china was, up on the stage – I had literally snuck it out the door! Anything to show my passion and enthusiasm for the craft and the roles I played.

For a small theatre, the Focus was very successful. I remember I was playing the lead opposite Gabriel Byrne in *A Month in the Country*, a role I did for six months. I remember one night watching Olwen Fouéré, who's gone on to great things in Ireland and abroad.

For me rean I stepped quite outside my character and I was assessing how she looked and thought how great her performance was. It was at that moment that I thought – I actually would rather be backstage.

I think I made up my mind up that very night that while I would never be a great actor, maybe I could be a great designer. What I did there and then was very practical. In a very small theatre like the Focus, everyone was dying for mebody to take over the design; everybody wanted to be an actor and nobody wanted to design. Most young designers who come in to me these days have all been thoroughly trained and it's a totally legitimate course like anything else you study. But back in those days and certainly in my case, I just went for it. I made it up as I went along, learning on the job. I was always good with people and I often say my job is being fifty percent a psychiatrist!

One thing I've learned is that you shouldn't be afraid of a change. Back then I had a very light speaking voice. I was very aware of it. I just felt I would never that successful an actress. I realised that while it was mething I was definitely interested in, maybe it was best to leave it as a hobby and look to another aspect of the industry. I would say to anyone that it's quite hurtful and a little demoralizing when you have to let go of a dream but you never know where it will take you. It's worked out well for me.

As a kid I could be shy and I was al quite self-conscious. I grew very tall, young. I was a bit of a ringleader. I was captain of the class, obviously I wasn't that shy but I was always quite watchful which I think is part of being a designer.

I must admit that I didn't make the break immediately. I was still acting while working costumes. The Focus was a fantastic theatre in that it did a lot of the international classics, which most small theatres in town at the time couldn't afford to do. They were much more inclined to do Irish plays. I remember the producer Noel Pearn of *My Left Foot* and *Dancing at Lughnasa* came to see the shows one night.

He must have been impressed because he asked me to do the Dory Previn's show on Broadway and that's exactly what I did. It's amazing how a career can take off. By now I've done five Broadway shows.

People always ask me, which would I rather do, theatre or film? I think it's very good for you to go back to theatre now and then because no matter how romantic film unds, it is a huge machine and every day, you have to have decisions on the spot. It makes you ready for a war cabinet. You have to be very secure in what you want because as the camera goes to roll, you can't change your mind. Whereas in theatre, you've got six to eight weeks rehearsal. You sit in on the rehearsals and it's quite hand-crafted. I like doing both; it clears the head, I think.

Epidic television is relentless and it can be completely exhausting. I much prefer movies because no matter how intense it is, you do a piece of work and then it's over. I just did Anna Friel in Jim Sheridan *The Secret Scriptures*, which was very sensible of me.

Even at this stage in my life, I see a need to keep testing myself. I think once that is gone, then you are phoning it in and that applies to any actor out there and any production designer out there – you have to keep a step ahead of the posse the whole time.

In mething like *The Tudors*, there were one hundred and ten secondary principles in the cast. *Vikings* is big, but it's not the same kind of scale. mething like *The Tudors*, which is based on historical fact, you better do your research or meone else would have done it for you. That's a huge part of my job, even now.

There's nothing like a laptop on your desk to double-check historical facts. I al read a lot and I'm a great believer in cial history, I always say this to anybody training to design. To this day, how we are and what we wear within a ciety is governed by how a society is at that time.

During *the Tudors*, I'd always try to read some chapter of a book that someone had written about people of that time. It would often unlock the doors to where the mystery was about something you wouldn't understand.

With something like *Vikings*, you're clutching at straws sometimes; it's quite ambiguous. Bloggers always comment on the vikings' clothes, 'That's not what the vikings wore'. We're on our fifth series of the show; you can't leave the women in aprons and pleated dresses for the whole time.

One of my great stories is that I never understood or liked Picasso until I went to the museum in Barcelona, which has some of his young work between the ages of fourteen and eighteen. When I understood the photographic detail he captured then, it more than allowed him to move into anywhere he wanted to.

What I do now is give a very accurate, one might even say a little dull, recreation, and then I fly and I say, if I lived back then, my team would be the bad ass kids on the block and this is what we would have interpreted what we wore then.

It varies from production to production, but you can be given as little as six-to-fourteen weeks for design depending on the project. Some actors will walk in and go with what you give them, others, like Daniel Day Lewis for example, would be in on most of what was being done and would bring a lot to the table.

I think people think the elves wave their hands and make the costumes appear.

They are astounded when they hear how much time it takes. It takes two-to-three people, at least, a fortnight to make one costume. The details, the embroidery, all of that, it takes time.

You do need, as a designer, a kind of humility about other people's talent. I often think at this stage in my career, I'm more of an editor. I am the person who says, 'No, take that sleeve back a bit,' or whatever but regularly my team will come to me with the concept and I'll develop it further with them. I know several very famous designers who just hand in the sketches to the workshop and then check back to make sure it's made that way. Maybe it's because I haven't formally trained and that kind of frees me up to be more hands-on for the entire process.

Nowadays, because of the structure of education and the structure of how you train, people are inclined to be a bit rarified. I always say to a trainee, nothing is ever lost. It's astonishing what you sieve through to bring things up to the front again. You can use an awful lot of experience – one of my team, who is very gifted, the leather-maker, who does all the armour, he showed me a photograph of a shutter on a window in Madrid which he's now thinking of incorporating into an outfit. Keep your eyes open the whole time, if you want to go into design. There's inspiration all around.

Any time I have a second free, I work on a new project. I have a good relationship with *Riverdance*, having worked closely with them over the years. In 2015 I revamped the show's costume. People often ask me if I find it hard to say 'no' and I think it's rather, that since childhood, I get bored very easily. Naturally my energy isn't what is used to be. I have an amazing supervising assistant in Susan

O'Connor-Cave. She takes over a lot of the logistical work and I do most of the creative work.

Posh Spice's wedding dress influenced one of my earlier *Riverdance* designs. John McColgan – one of the owners of *Riverdance* – was up in the gods in the theatre one evening, looking at the show. Whatever way the dancers bodice was constructed, he thought he could see down to her navel. Around the time there was picture of Posh Spice that became quite famous. I still remember it. She had a sequenced bra and then another piece built up on top of it and that design has stayed to this day. It's a great way to give somebody curves.

The only time my knees shook working on a production was when I went to New York to meet David Bowie. I walked into the room and had a complete fan-girl moment. I lost the ability to speak for a few minutes. It's the only time I've ever been extremely nervous on the job. When I started to speak, he asked me where I was from and of course, I said, 'Dublin.' He had assumed I was American.

Some women in the industry can be a bit intimidating but the better they are, the nicer they are. I always think the ones clawing themselves up; they always become pussycats when they get there. I've enjoyed dressing Meryl Streep, Julianne Moore, Cate Blanchett, and Kate Winslet. I've been very lucky to go from this tiny island to working with most of the biggest Hollywood names. More recently, I've started working with the younger crowd, Rooney Mara and the younger ladies yet again. Sometimes I smile when I think of the people I've worked with.

Your biggest fear is when you or the actor you have dressed goes on set and the director doesn't like what they're wearing or feels it's wrong – their decision is final. Amazing things happen, but that's why you've got a big team behind you.

In the American film industry, they call your name over a tannoy if and when they need you. It must be one of the few moments that really gives me butterflies is when I hear 'Would Joan Bergin go to . . .' In one particular case it was to Brad Pitt's Winnebago.

As I arrived in, the director, now dead, was with Brad. Brad had a balaclava and as I walked in, the director said – 'How do you wear this?'

It came out as, 'Well, where I come from, you'd wear it down.' I looked in the mirror and Brad Pitt winked at me and it was a very funny moment. Actors on the whole can be quite kind to costumes, particularly if they've been in for several fittings because they'll know it's pretty hard work.

In the Name of the Father is the production I'm most proud of. I'm very politically interested and it was amazing to re-enact that whole story and to work with Jim Sheridan. For all the madness and the talent, I can remember sitting in on the rehearsal where they bring them into court for the first time and that feeling of 'creating history,' swooping over me.

The whole Emmy thing is quite astounding. We were on the dining bus on a rainy day when I heard about my nomination. It was very romantic. I think Gabriel Brien my assistant came in and told me I was up for an award. The win didn't really hit me until awards night. The scale of it – *my God*. It's exactly the same as the Oscars; the same theatre, the same format, the same thing. They all tell me when my name was called; I knocked them out of the way like a football and ran up on stage. The second time I won I felt great justification and the third time I won, I was gobsmacked. I never expected to win for the third time. That was the icing on the cake. I keep those awards on my kitchen mantelpiece.

It's false modesty to claim that the awards don't matter. One can argue why one show wins over another, I definitely agree with that. Such a big award is fantastic for the people you're working with. It's a brilliant morale booster and sometimes when we're doing promos and thing, I bring the awards in as a sort of motivational thing. I have fourteen awards at this stage. It's a lot of gongs.

It's gotten tougher and tougher to get into this industry today. You would think it would be the opposite but there's so many training courses and courses in college now and there's such growing talent. I always make a point of going to Dun Laoghaire and several of the people I've trained are teaching there as designers. It's quite a tough profession and because Ireland is such a small country, there's only really room at the top for half a dozen people. That's a worry. What will all the others do? Where will they go?

I remember asking one of the best young designers I met what she wanted to do and she said, 'I want your job.' I always say to them, if you have to start polishing boots in the wardrobe department, at least you're there.

There's nothing like getting your foot in the door. If you're there and you work hard and show some initiative, you'll get further. I think Irish people are shy to push themselves. Often I have to go to people and coax them to do something if I can see it in them that they can do it; sometimes they won't even realise it for themselves until I tell them.

If I was still acting now, I would have loved to have been in *Mama Mia,* I'm a huge admirer of Meryl Streep. I think I might

have made it but I don't like living with regrets and it's more than too late to have regrets. If I could give advice to my teenage self, I'd say trust your instincts more. Above all, do not be afraid to make mistakes. Also, don't forget your friends. I've seen such sadness from people who have made it and have forgotten everyone around them.

Nothing on the shelf compensates to be left on your own without family and friends at the end. It sounds a little *Little House on the Prairie* but it's very, very true.

Chupi

Chupi Sweetman is the name on everyone's lips. But who is this delicate jewellery designer taking the world by storm, one sparkly accessory at a time? Did you know she's also a cookbook author and a former Topshop designer too? Meet the ambitious entrepreneur who has never been afraid to dream big.

I find it quite peculiar how when we're kids we're told to dream big, that we can be anything we want to be, but how when we get older, we're sort of told to pick something sensible. That's always such a shame.

I suppose you could say I had an unconventional childhood, but I would never change it for the world. When I was young, I was really sick and as a result I couldn't go to school. My amazing mum took it upon herself to home school my little brother Luke and I.

I don't ever remember mum saying, 'You can be anything you want to be,' but I also don't remember ever being told that I couldn't *not* do anything. If I had told her that I wanted to be an astronaut, she would have said, 'Ok darling, let's go get you a physics book.' There were never any limits put on what I could achieve.

My mum is Rosita Sweetman and she is one of the founding members of the Irish women's movement. She was audacious and bold and bossy enough to think that they could change the world. mum had a different way of looking at things and it really rubbed off on me as a child.

Being homeschooled was such a privilege. I was exposed to so many more grown-ups and I was treated like an equal. I never felt like a kid. We had a pretty boho lifestyle. My mum brought us up on almost nothing, we had no money. We lived in a beautiful house in the middle of nowhere that had lots of space and land and wilderness but we weren't privileged, we were just creatives. Every child's experience of homeschooling is different. Ours was very non-vigorous. We learned to read and write and do maths but we didn't have a formal structure.

We'd go for five-hour hikes to learn about nature or spend days with our grandmother who thought us real living history. It wasn't very regimented but it meant there was room for exploring our hobbies and interests. It was an incredible gift for mum to give us. She have us a lot of her time and a huge part of her career and to this day, we have an incredible relationship.

I was always a creative child. I remember I had this tiny kitchen when I was a little girl. On the back, it had a picture of a writer, a ballerina and a cook. I remember thinking, 'That's what I want to do when I grow up. I'm going to be a writer, a cook and a ballerina.' And that's kind of what has happened. I've gone on to write a cook book and with fashion and jewellery design, I get to tell stories. I know it sounds mad, but I got my first sewing machine when I was five. It was a real electric machine with a real needle. How anyone gave it to a five year old is bonkers but I guess it was meant to be!

While not quite yet a cook, the first of my dreams began to take shape when I was sixteen. It was around then I began writing a cookbook with encouragement from my mum. I was a little fed up as a teen when my nutritionist took me off pretty much every-thing – dairy, wheat, sugar and yeast. We were always big eaters in our family so once my more restricted diet came into play, we'd write down recipes for new ways of making things. Mum suggested my brother and I wrote a cookbook and we thought that sounded like great fun! Through a family friend we met with an editor from Gill and McMillan with about thirty organic recipes. My brother Luke and I had it all beautifully laid out and they really liked it.

I was eighteen when *What to Eat When You Can't Eat Anything* was published. We had an amazing reception and we sold out on our first print run. We're on our tenth print run today but I think back then people didn't really know what to make of our book because there weren't many kids writing cookbooks! It was such a pleasure to be a part of and people still come up to me to this day and tell me they own a copy in their kitchen! We sold the American and German rights too, so it didn't do too badly for a first foray into publishing. It helped that mum was a writer; we had some guidance along the way. I plan on writing another one in the future but very, very, slowly.

When I was about seventeen, I started a womenswear label. I've always made things and I've always loved the idea that someone would actually care about what I'm making and that it could actually make another person happy. The label was tiny and we sold our stuff in Temple Bar in a tiny little shop that sold all sorts of things by different designers. It was an interesting space and lots of really interesting people came through it. I was making little party dresses and bags. Business wasn't huge but it was really great fun.

I eventually decided to go to Sallynoggin in Dun Laoghaire where I did a little PLC course. I think it's really important not to commit yourself to a four or five year degree if you're not one hundred percent sure. My PLC was two years and I feel like it was the perfect time for me. I had been enjoying selling my small line in Temple Bar fashion market and decided I wanted to make something bigger of it.

Just at the end of my first year, Topshop were scouting for designers and probably one of the most exciting times in my life was getting a card from a Topshop scout. That was amazing, it took me completely by surprise and caught me off guard in the best way possible.

We had this little company called Chupi and the whole collective, my two friends and I, owned what was called Taylor, Bright and Young. One of my friends was a Taylor, the other loved really, really bright colours, and I was the baby of the group because I was only twenty years of age at the time.

For whatever reason, I was absent from the stall the day Topshop came knocking but my friend almost immediately called me rather excited and said, 'You're not going to believe it, Topshop has just scouted us!' We had to wait about two weeks before they called us back. That was followed by interviews to show off our collection. I spent an entire three weeks designing a full collection for them, putting my heart and soul into it. The wait in between was a month and that felt like the longest time ever. I had no idea what I was doing and I had no one to ask. I had just finished my first year of college and there was nobody to turn to for advice.

We eventually launched in Topshop on Grafton Street. I remember it really, really well. I was the youngest designer; everyone else was in their mid and late twenties. At that stage I was still too broke to shop in Topshop and yet there was my collection on the shelves. Launch night was wonderful. I invited some of my friends to the store and I remember watching people I didn't know buying my dresses and feeling so incredibly excited and terrified and overwhelmed. I was the same age as the staff working the floor, I wasn't a 'proper' designer. I remember at the end of the night everything had sold out, with only five or six things left on the hanger. In the run up to the launch I had my friends come in to sow labels onto dresses and skirts – they were unbelievably brilliant and I remember them all selling out and thinking, 'Oh my god, what am I going to do?'

The entire collection was my baby and I was involved in every stage of it. I worked with Topshop in the UK and Ireland for six years and loved it completely. What I learned from that experience was that I didn't know how to ask for advice. It wasn't that I couldn't take it, I just didn't know who to ask or even that it was OK to ask, 'Is this right?' and admit that I wasn't always sure if I was making the right move.

Topshop is a wonderful business to work for but it's very serious and there's not much hand-holding. As a young designer, I did find it overwhelming at times but I learned so much. I loved fast fashion. The idea of wearing dresses you'd love and then maybe not care too much about them afterwards. It's only when I was twenty-six or seven that I began to explore the idea of working on something that might last a little longer and soon fell in love with all the sparkly things. I've always liked taking risks and I've never been afraid of hard work, putting my heart and soul into everything. I felt I had done that with Topshop but that perhaps it was time to try out something new.

People are often too afraid of failure and to try out something new but what's the worst thing that can happen? It might not work out and you'll have to re-gather and rethink and try again in a new way. It's normal to fail. I fail every single day.

I realised I wanted to design and sell beautiful things that were going to last forever; a ring you give to your daughter, something that lasts thirty years, and with every piece I wanted there to be a story. I loved the idea of being part of people's milestone moments in life. It's an incredibly magical thing. In seventy years we'll be gone but my pieces of jewellery will carry on. They hold a story and that's what appeals so much to me.

I have my hands for friends and I've always loved making things. That part of bringing, Chupi the jewellery brand, to life was not too difficult for me. The skills I lacked were that of a goldsmith and I decided that if I was going to do this, I was going to do it *really* well. I wanted to do something epic. I went and met an amazing silversmith called Cormac Cuffe. He's a gentleman and a master goldsmith and he taught me everything I know. I can be quite impatient. I want to know everything right now but Cormac was brilliant and I had a lot of fun learning. I spent eighteen months learning the craft necessary to become a goldsmith.

There are a couple of moments that really matter in my business. The first thing I made was a tiny little wren bird. There were these tiny wren birds resting in the wall of the house where my studio was and they would fly out every day. So I modelled this little flying wren out of clay. It was the first thing I created in gold and silver and it was just so unbelievable to see something go from my head into a physical thing. One of the frustrating things with fashion is that you're very dependent on fabrics and cut and colour but I loved that with gold I could literally create anything I wanted. Anything I thought of, I could make appear into the world.

What shaped what I make and how I design was trying to make this one feather out of silver. I knew I wanted a swan feather ring. I had this ring in my hand and I knew what I wanted and I made version, upon version, upon version, and they were awful. But then I realised that what I loved was the flawed beauty of them. Cormac worked with me and we worked on casting from feathers – taking a mould of an actual feather. It's how I work now and influences what I do. Taking wild things and casting from them. I remember getting that feather back front the mould and being blown away. I think good design has a kind of magic.

And it was the same with the ring. It has this luminosity. It's not world-changing design, it's not the best thing I've ever designed because I'm really critical of my own work but I remember with the swan feather ring thinking, 'I've made something beautiful.'

For every one good thing I make, though, there are so many that don't see the light of day. I'm a big fan of a creative crisis. I have a wonderful team of ten people at Chupi and they've heard me mutter, 'Nope, it's horrific, nobody can ever see it', on far too many occasions.

A big part of why I started designing is because I couldn't find the jewellery that I wanted to wear. It's incredible to think how much that's grown.

Today we ship to over sixty countries worldwide. People say, 'You can't sell good jewellery online,' but it seemed only logical when I started making jewellery that we'd go online. You can reach as many people in the world as possible that way and get this whole extra audience who otherwise you might be missing out on. I mean, we're shipping to Korea. Who is buying my jewellery in Korea, why are they wearing it, and how did they find it? I love the idea of it being out in the world for enjoyment.

I wish I could condense all the wonderful things I've been taughtt by all the brilliant people who have influenced me. Running a jewellery line is a lot about hard work but so worth it. I'll always tell anyone who is curious enough to give it a bash to do whatever he or she wants to do. You've got to really, really, really love it – your heart should be in it fully. It should be the thing that wakes you up in the middle of the night because you're so passionate and excited. It should be part of your heart and soul.

People ask me if I ever switch off and I say, no – *when* would I and *why* would I? In life you have to find something you love and do it. But also remember not to beat yourself up if you haven't found anything you love yet. I think sometimes people have found what they love but are maybe too scared to take the risk and do it.

It is terrifying. It's absolutely terrifying to go and tell your parents you want to be a clown in the circus as opposed to something more conventional like a barrister. The happiest people I know are the ones who are kind of obsessed with what they do.

Some people are excited by the idea of making one beautiful thing that costs €5,000 and makes one person really excited; others are excited by making 5,000 pieces that make 5,000 people happy. As a jewellery designer, you have to figure out where you sit. Do you want your pieces all over the world worn by loads of different people or do you want one incredible person wearing what you make? The same for furniture or other products – what excites you?

I know that I've always been excited by the idea that someone, somewhere who has never met me, who doesn't know who I am, who doesn't know that I'm in love with sparkly things and inspired by feathers, but they just see something beautiful and gold and it makes their life happier. So figure that really important question out – where do you want to be? Then go and find your people. Get yourself out into the world. There's no point having beautiful pieces that never see the light of day. Find a local market – that's what I did when I was thirteen and designed my first piece.

The excitement of people buying that you've made and love is so unreal. Find who you are as a designer. Ask yourself what your thing is.

For me, statement necklaces are completely lost on me. I don't know what to do with them. I feel like the necklace is wearing me. I feel like this huge thing around my neck is like a huge sign pointing at me. I love really tiny, delicate things.

Also make mistakes, maybe your designs will be horrible and they won't sell – it doesn't matter; maybe what you've made is disgusting – it doesn't matter. Everyone makes disgusting things. I make disgusting things all the time that I hate. The glorious thing is, you can take it apart and start again.

Life is filled with ups and downs and mishaps. It's how you overcome them that matters. I regularly fail in the studio where I design and create things that are spectacularly boring and I step back and think, 'What happened there?'

The worst thing in your life would be to have a life of regrets. To look back and go, I could have, or would have or should have done that. There's always ways to find out how to do what we love. I've never had a moment where I felt like I've achieved it, whatever 'it' is. I'm constantly chasing bigger things. I'm always embarrassed and pleased if anyone says well done but I've never felt like I've reached my full potential. I always think if only you knew what I'm trying to do, all the plans I have, all the stuff I want to achieve.

Paul Costelloe

Dublin born designer Paul Costelloe is one of the most established names in British and Irish Fashion. With a strong sense of style and the desire to create wearable designs with a fresh feel, the real *Paul Costelloe has been the head of his successful label for over 30 years. From Paris to New York, Milan and London, the fashion mogul has dressed some of the world's most elegant and influential women, including the late Princess Diana.*

It might sound like a funny thing to say but I've never had a career. It's been more of a nomadic adventure, swimming in a pool on the edge of fashion. Sort of like a spider in a room on the wall. He's there but he's not that visible and he builds his own web in the corner, catching the odd good moment.

From the get-go my career has had its interesting turns. I went from dreaming to be a real life cowboy in Texas to studying fashion and running my own label. My father was in the textiles business so I guess it was always in my blood.

As a teen, I wasn't very good in school. I excelled at art but that's a gift from God, nothing to do with studying or going to college. Between various interesting job – like working on a pig farm, grading pigs – I went to the Grafton Academy for a year; it was *the* school of fashion in Dublin when I was about seventeen or eighteen. Funnily enough, I didn't excel at that either. I was simply no good. I found making patterns a bit boring- even to this day I get other people to do that for me! As a student, I didn't mind saying, 'Sorry can you help me?' and I still don't mind. It's a great way of being humble. You can use it to your advantage.

I have my older brother to thank for my trip to Paris where it all sort of kicked off for me. He encouraged my parents to send me to Paris where we had some family friends. My mission was to find an internship and I was very luckily taken under the wing of Jack Esterel. My Irish charm worked a treat and we got on very well. He gave me a chance to start and I'll be forever grateful.

At Jack Esterel, I worked on a launch at a big long table with designers from all over the world. For a full week, we had to design suits – it was certainly an interesting induction. At the end of the week they piled up all the drawings and brought them to a client who came in, went through all the designs and made a selection on his favourites. We were paid on whether our specific drawing was going to be made into a garment or not.

I was so skinny during that time. I was like a rake – starvation. I lived in a little flat rented by the week in the Odeon on the left bank of the Seine. It was damp and green and I had a little camping stove which I bought. I'd have a tin of ravioli in the evenings. It was modest times. But I did have a bedroom view of the Eiffel Tower. My poor late father would come to visit me. He hadn't travelled as much as I had. He walked up six flights to my little room, looked out the window and said, 'Oh you've got a wonderful view.' In those days the franc was quite strong and the Irish pound was rubbish. My father tried to help me out in any way he could. He was very dear to me.

Because I was associated with an international name and living in Paris, somehow Marks and Spencers heard of me. In those days there were very few people from Europe working in Paris, and they contacted me and asked me to come to Baker Street where the headquarters were. They wanted to develop their market in Italy. They thought they could be as important in Italy as they were in the UK and that's how the ball started rolling for me. I still couldn't cut a pattern. I still couldn't sow but I could sketch somewhat reasonably. Somehow I managed to pull it off.

After being trained by M&S, I was sent off to Milan one Friday night. I ended up in the highest building in Milan, which was so heavy in fog. I remember stepping out on the street the first morning and it was amazing. That Monday I started work in a zone called Quattro Jarro, in a studio, without a word of Italian and hardly a word of English. I was *so* Irish. My French was poor too. Working there set me up and once again it was by being associated with a well-known brand that I ended up there.

In Paris I learned that it's a very competitive world and that your fellow designers are as ruthless as you are. Don't pretend otherwise. There's a lot of jealousy. I was quite naïve because I was out of the sticks.

There was one particular girl who was Japanese and she used to say to me, 'Paul, you're not a designer, you don't look like a designer.' I can see what she meant. I was a mad, wild Irishman, not very chic.

Moving to America happened by chance. My late brother was a successful painter and sculptor. He got married in North Carolina and I went over to his wedding which was awesome. Post-wedding I went to New York by Seventh Avenue and knocked on a couple of doors. I went into 557 Avenue, which is the building where all the relevant designers are.

I ended up talking to a man called Leonard Sunshine. I discovered not long afterwards that he was no sunshine but he had company called Anne Fogarty. I was a bit extreme for the American market which was quite formal but he liked me. We worked together on the wedding dress for Tricia Nixon who was the daughter of the president of America. Before long though, Leonard decided that the company no longer needed me and that I wasn't right for their brand.

I had a few other interviews after that with Oscar de la Renta and a bunch of other companies. I also went to see the guys at Ann Lowe who designed the wedding dress for Jackie Kennedy. I was a little bit stuck at the time. I couldn't get any work. I had a little flat on Midtown Manhattan and I needed to make money to support myself. I didn't want to go back to Dublin a failure so I ended up taking a job as a messenger boy for an adult magazine. It was part of a chain of adult magazines and newspapers. Over time they put me as editor and I used to be in charge of adult novel manuscripts coming into the office. It brought in some money and I also did some translating from Italian into English. I'd fall asleep on the underground, I was working 24/7.

New York brought me on many adventures, you could say. Before long I found myself working for a very tough lady in the Empire State Building on the eighty-fourth floor. I designed hosiery and body wear. It was very different to anything I had worked on before but I quite enjoyed it. It's when I first started getting mentioned in magazines too, with *Womenswear Daily* throwing my name down on their pages on a couple of occasions.

All of that was great but what I really wanted to do more than anything was develop my own Paul Costelloe brand. I eventually decided to leave New York and I go back to Ireland. I found a factory in Northern Ireland that would finance me to develop my ground. That was really the beginning of the Paul Costelloe brand. It's gone through lots of valleys since then but it's had its good moments too.

My brand is like one of those old Mercedes cars. It's got a good engine and it keeps going. I always describe myself as a jockey competing in the Grand National. I don't fall off the horse and I don't win the race but I finish. I'm consistently there and in some cases, annoyingly to other people – 'What's he doing showing up at fashion week? Why is he taking up the space when someone else can?'

I enjoy women and dressing women. I enjoy dressing men if they've got the right attitude and home ware is something I seem to have an eye for. Having an American mother helped to bring out my creativity. That mix of Irish and American. There was a certain standard at home – how you sit at a table, posture and so on.

I wanted to live in New York and take advantage of that. It's a lot easier to fail away from home. You don't have the same restrictions in a city that big where you are a complete unknown. I'm very critical of myself.

My first major break was designing for Princess Diana. That really helped to establish me as a brand. I should have taken more advantage of that at the time. I got a lot of press in Ireland in those days but not in the UK. Back then it was frowned upon to exploit a Royal connection. Of course that's all changed now and whenever the Duchess of Cambridge pops out, there are endless articles about what she's wearing with stores selling out left, right and centre.

The Diana story is a special one. There's a little shop in Windsor where my clothes are sold. A lady in waiting saw my garments at the time and contacted me to bring some garments into Kensington Palace. The first time meeting Diana was amazing. I went in a mini cab, pulled up to the gates and to my amazement I was allowed in. I remember touching the couch where we were doing the changes, looking out onto Hyde Park. I was pinching the couch thinking, 'Am I really here?'

Diana came down the stairs as I was hauling up the garments and it felt very surreal for a few moments. She was very easy to get on with and we enjoyed a cup of tea with biscuits.

I remember my son went with me to one of my fittings. Gavin was playing behind the couch in the drawing room with William and Harry. As I was leaving, I kissed Diana on the cheek. When we got back to the office Gavin blurted it out to everyone, 'Dad kissed Princess Diana!' It was a big scandal at home. Seeing Diana in Hyde Park on a pouring wet day was very special. Pavarotti was singing on stage and she came up to him with wearing a Paul Costelloe double breasted suit looking absolutely gorgeous. It's a sight I'll never forget; she was happy at that point in her life.

Like everyone else taking a chance to follow their passion, I've had tough times. The toughest time of all was recent. I had a ladies wear license in a company called Signature Brands. It was an exclusive license for middle to better-end market, which had about thirty outlets in the UK and concessions in all the John Lewis department stores and a lot of the House of Fraser department stores. The bank came in and closed Signature Brands. My name was part of their stable. That unfortunate event affected me and my family and our security. Other than my wife I have one other very significant person in my life and that's the financial director I have, who is incredibly good and very careful and wise. It's essential to have that in the fashion business when you set up on your own.

We went out into the city and spoke to investors. Yes they want your name, but that is it. They'd exploit it and expose it and you'd lose control of your name. I decided I couldn't do that because of my family, my culture, my Irish pride and my stubbornness. I've gradually got back on my feet and worked in different ways to keep myself not tied down in any specific way. I've retained all of my brands.

If you start with quality, people will always remember you for quality. Quality gives people confidence to invest in you, in your brand.

That goes back to my association with the factory in Northern Ireland who make beautiful, high quality clothes. For anyone setting up a fashion business bear that in mind in the early stages and be careful. Once you go down the other route of looking to make a lot of money – and you will, it can be short lived. Longevity is what you want and that's why I'm still here today.

I've had many highlights on my adventure. Designing the British Airways uniform was a wonderful experience. I did that for twelve years. I went to China and Hong Kong and Brazil – I got such a thrill out of seeing the crew step off the plane in my designs.

My proudest achievement has been getting married to a woman who gave me seven amazing children. She was from the north side of Dublin. I was from the south. She's fifteen years younger than me and has been my best critic and my best support. She also wears my clothes incredibly well.

Being married to a designer is not fun; she's got the patience of an angel.

I work alongside two other people at Paul Costelloe. Coming up to showcases I also team up with a studio and I have freelancers on board too – patternmakers from Greece and Poland. I pull in these people during show time. It keeps my overheads very tight. It's very expensive to showcase. I don't use thirty models like other designers. I use twelve to fifteen – max. For me to put on a show it costs about £50,000 per season, minimum.

Like most designers I work seasons ahead. When it comes to designing, I do about forty or fifty sketches, editing down to twenty-five styles. The sketching happens in a burst and I really need to focus and concentrate. Sometimes I might go to Italy and work from there during that time. Isolation is quite relevant; I need to find that space. It's like giving birth each season, it's quite hard.

Once I make up my mind on something, that's it. When I draw, the garment usually looks like how I would see it. All the details are there and it's quite visible. You see everyone else's shows, you do your research; you see what's in stores and get a feeling of what others are doing. I saw Charlize Theron in *Mad Max: Fury Road* recently and that inspired me – there are so many beautiful women in that film. It's long and lean and fluid lines. The collection can't just look sexy, it has to look upmarket and rich and expensive.

There was a show I did on *The Assassination of Jess James by the Coward Robert Ford* with Brad Pitt. Remember those coats he wore? I always thought that collection had interesting shapes and it didn't get much recognition so I'm considering pulling that back in a little bit because I did think it was a unique looking collection. Magazines and critics never love me. But I don't mind. All I want is it to make money. If you don't show the catwalk, you devalue your brand. There are only two people from Ireland showing on catwalks now, myself and Simone Rocha.

I love the creative element of my job, bringing things and ideas to life. Travelling to source fabrics is such an important element and I get such pleasure out of it. You can't study textiles. It's a gift. Nobody can teach you the magic and the feeling of a beautiful fabric in the hand. That's what I go for.

To any budding young designer, remember – don't kill yourself because all success leads to the grave anyway. I used to keep to that much more than I do now. Having done it myself, I think it's important to leave home to work on your own once you've come out of college. To make your mistakes away from home so you don't feel constricted. Enjoy that freedom. Don't allow yourself to get too complacent in your work because months can amount to years and then you're stuck in a job and you can't move forward.

It's very important to sketch. Sketch while watching TV or in a coffee shop. Always have a camera with you and observe the world around you. Keep doing that little extra and keep building on your portfolio. Keep renewing it. If you're caught and are unhappy at any age – twenty, thirty, forty or fifty. Don't be embarrassed about changing. It's never too late. Do what you love. Follow your heart.

Blanaid Hennessy

Blanaid Hennessy knows a thing or two about fashion. Single-handedly reforming the Irish red carpet with her expert stylist's eye, the Kilkenny born entrepreneur and owner of hip celeb boutique, Folkster, is living the dream, sourcing beautiful threads around the world while running a string of successful businesses.

I was a late-bloomer – as a sporty teen I was more likely to be found in my kit than any attempt at a decent rig-out. I was around twenty-one before I even got half a clue as to what suited my shape, and I think I was around twenty-seven before I finally figured out my own style! I'm lucky to be surrounded by creative people like my parents who definitely gave me the confidence to have a bit of fun with the fashion when I was eh . . . 'experimenting'.

I was definitely the not-living-in-the-moment-at-all-type child – I wanted the sixth class homework when I was eight. By Leaving Cert I became more and more impatient to get out and try *all* of the things. I knew I wanted to learn as I worked, rather than going the college route. So I started working in every field that interested me – radio, retail, newspapers, photographic editing and so on. I worked seven days, and nights, a week trying to learn as much as I could and I'm still learning every single day.

My brother Eoin is a fantastic photographer, and at the ages of twenty-four and twenty-five we started Shutterbug as a media company. We had €500 to start the business. I worked on photo editing, radio production and fashion journalism, and he did all the photography.

We learned as we worked – we always asked questions and sought advice when we needed it – it's all about that constant education.

We were definitely nervous, and I don't know if you ever stop being nervous either but you just have to challenge it into positive energy. You have to face the issues making you nervous, find the solution, solve it and get to the next issue.

I love the saying, 'It takes a lot of hard work to get lucky,' – and that really is the secret to success. You just have to work hard, and when you think you're working hard, you have to work even harder. If you're not getting results, you need to work smarter. If you're still not getting where you want to go, you need to figure out how to work harder and smarter. It goes on and on like that!

Luck is the people you meet along the way – the incredible, generous, selfless people who will advise you in a storm, who'll remind you why you're there, who'll connect you to your next stepping stone or who'll work hard for and become part of your dream.

When you combine your hard work with the luck of meeting those people, then you have the perfect combination for success.

The first few years of any growing business revolve around 'fire-fighting' – you're running around, putting out fires that flare up unexpectedly. That's how you learn, and that's how you refine how you can prevent that particular fire too. It's been an incredible adventure, and even through tough times, I wouldn't change a thing.

We have a running joke that I'm Folkster's 'courier and general labourer' with the amount of driving between stores I do, and how often we spend nights redesigning the new or old spaces, shifting furniture and dragging boxes and so on.

I am involved in every single aspect of the company, supported by a small but fantastic team. My current focus is on buying and design, developing folkster.com, researching markets and territories, setting up internal systems and the most important thing – ensuring we can afford to open our doors every day. That's the main role of any business owner I think, when you get down to it!

When going into business, you have to surround yourself with people you trust. Almost all of my close family are involved but the team feels like a family too. We have a team of close to thirty people now, and I can honestly say that every one of them contributes massively to fulfilling our motto - 'Work hard and be nice to people' – every day.

If I had to choose one, then I think the one thing that fundamentally changed Folkster was opening our second store in Dublin. We have such support in Kilkenny that it was always going to challenge us to see if we could take what works there and make it work in a different city.

Dublin really focused my vision on what could be achieved. Also, making the decision to expand, and learning how to grow with that expansion – has defined how we run as a company. Now we joke that in a way all the work with Dublin was like getting some kind of Masters.

It's wonderful to be supported by so many incredible women – I'm equally excited if I our clothes on the red carpet or someone just out and about. I have a terrible habit of smiling madly at anyone I see wearing Folkster. They must think I'm really odd!

In the world of well-known women, we have particular love for Angela Scanlon, Sinead Kennedy and Amy Huberman – they have been incredible to Folkster from the start. I am hugely grateful to anyone who spreads the word about Folkster, and they do it on such a national and international scale. I'll always be thankful for the support.

The best things in business are a happy customer, and a happy team. I feel so much pride when I hear a customer genuinely delighted with their find or the customer service they have received. There is no real downside to my job. I love being my own boss – but being the leader of a team and company brings many responsibilities, which can at times of course, be difficult.

You just have to take time and learn to become comfortable having the responsibility though.

Blanaid's Tips For Setting Up Your Own Mini-Fashion Empire

You have to be ready to work hard, that's a fact.

Be respectful and courteous, and smile. Learn when to ask for advice. Listen to your instincts as whether to take the advice or not.

Choose your battles.

Remember that you are always learning. Every mistake is a part of your education, and it will take time. Educate yourself as much as possible, increase your skill sets. Aim to have a general understanding of every aspect of your business, but know what you uniquely offer to add to its success. Do that a lot.

Learn to be decisive.

Keep an eye on the cents, have savings for a tough time and remember – this is business, don't take it personally. You will have peaks, and you will have troughs. How you respond to the troughs will determine the height of your peak.

Also – have fun!

If it doesn't make you happy, make a change if you can at all.

Darren Kennedy

TV presenter, producer, columnist, stylist and designer Darren Kennedy has a jam-packed daily schedule, living his ultimate dream. As if hosting for the BBC, ITV, RTÉ, FOX and E! isn't enough, the stylist and Telegraph columnist is also the proud designer of menswear range DK x LC in association with Louis Copeland.

It's important to have passion, drive and direction in life. Sometimes people get so bogged down in the impossibility of what they're trying to achieve, they miss the obvious steps in front of them. You just have to start something, no matter what sphere it's in and a door is going to open. It also boils down to working hard, not being afraid to make mistakes or taking measured risks.

I'm living my dream but I don't mean I'm living on a bed of rose petals. I just feel very privileged and incredibly lucky to be able to do it what I love. I think everyone can live his or her dream; you just have to be ballsy enough to reach out for it. Growing up I took a lot of risks and chances in order to follow my dream. School was never a place I enjoyed and I wanted to get out of there as soon as possible. My academics were fine but the environment didn't suit me. I never felt at ease. I didn't hit my stride until later on in life. Some people peak very early in school and I just wasn't one of them.

When the time came to choose my subjects that would earn me a place in college came up, I asked myself what I really loved. I thought, 'Speaking French and Spanish and going off and living in France would be amazing.' So that's what I did. I got accepted into a course in Trinity but got offered a course in DIT too, a new degree that came on stream that year, which was international business with French and Spanish. I remember my dad going, 'If you can do one without business and one with, you're probably better off doing the one with business.' It was the best decision I ever made.

All throughout college, I was trying to figure out how to worm my way into the media. Working in broadcasting was always my dream but I didn't want to study it. I wanted to learn by doing.

It all kicked off with Alan Hughes putting in a good word for me in TV3. He lived around the corner from me and my mam encouraged me to go knock on his door and ask him for advice. I eventually met him walking my dog one afternoon and stopped for a chat. Not long after, I began working as a runner on *Ireland AM* TV3's breakfast show which had just began airing at the time. I went in two or three times a week, do the meet and greet with all the guests and then I'd hop in a taxi at half nine to make it to lectures on time.

What followed was a love affair with Paris and France. I lived in France for a year and then I came back and did my finals and started working in *Ireland AM* again. I went back to Paris and lived another year on a graduate programme with IBEC and it was amazing. When I returned, I still had this desire to work in broadcasting and began working for a little company called Google. I was employee number forty in Google, European Headquarters. I started out in a little office on Earlsfort Terrace and I stayed there for a year and a half.

For the first three months, I absolutely hated it and I would have rather stuck pins in my eyes because it was computer based. But then they offered me a job in training that involved working with people and travelling to San Francisco on assignments. It was a great year and a half. I set up Google TV while I was there, again following my own passions.

I was only twenty one or two and I remember getting a budget of a £1,000 to go off and buy a camera for Google TV. I loved my time there and I interviewed the founders of Google, Larry and Sergei, it was cool.

I eventually left Google because it wasn't my passion. I took a leap of faith and took a job as PR manager with the French tourism board in Ireland. Again, it wasn't exactly what I wanted to do, but I was getting closer. I went from working in this amazing Google campus where the food is free, and people are young and fun, and we had drinks on a Friday, to this two room office opposite the government buildings in an old Georgian house where our kitchen was the cubby hole under the stairs. I remember the first morning making a coffee and I put my heads in my hands and I thought, 'What have I done? This is such a big mistake.'

From the word go I hated it. I said, 'OK, what am I going to do?' I decided to give it a year. I wanted to make contacts. I wanted to learn and do everything I could to further what I wanted to do. I wanted to do my job to the best of my abilities and leave with something tangible.

Around this time I had started a radio a programme on Dublin City FM called *Kennedy's Couch*. It was a half hour chat show where I'd interview luminaries of Dublin and Ireland, politicians, authors, TV stars etc.

While I was doing that, a TV production came in to us to talk about a show in France involving wine – they were looking for money and sponsorship. Randomly, I met the producer a couple of weeks later when I was going to interview an author in the Merrion Hotel. I told him about what I was doing and my interests and a couple of weeks later he phoned to say, 'I have a new travel show coming up, would you like a job as a researcher?' I said, 'Hell's bells, yes!' I handed in my notice a year to the day that I had stated a year previously. I was never so relived. I used to nearly cry at lunch breaks, it was that bad.

I started worked in production on a show called *The Holiday Quiz* with Seán Moncrieff. I got to travel all over and it was fab. As my career in TV grew legs, I continued with my radio programme and they kind of went in tandem. I had really made strides and when it came to an end I thought, I can't go back to not pursuing this further. I got my stuff together and send my tapes to the UK and long story short, I got to present a thirteen-part series on the BBC, which was incredible.

At the same time, I went back to the soul searching. I have always loves aesthetics, be it interior design, be it gardens, be it fish tanks or of course, clothes. It's something that came naturally to me. I wanted to nurture that. I went off to London and did some courses, set up my own business as a personal stylist and that grew and grew and grew.

Eventually those two worlds collided. On the last season of *Operation Transformation*, not only was I the reporter on the *Gerry Ryan show*, producer and doing a daily web show, I was also the stylist for the final of the show. That's how I got into it.

There's an element of faith in there but there's also an element of taking a chance and going for it. The risk of failure was huge, especially leaving Google. That was mad. Who leaves Google? They employ only one in twenty-five people they interview, it's a massive company to get into. It was the beginning of the tech bubble and it was very exciting. They made it very difficult for you to leave.

It's about having belief in your own self and following your dreams. That's my approach in life. I can fall flat on my face and fail, but if I fail, I will do it gloriously and at least I'll know I tried. I'm not afraid of failure.

When you're being honest, true to yourself and authentic, that really comes across. The one thing you can't be on TV is fake. I grew up watching *This Morning* on ITV so to work alongside Philip and Holly and the crew is really special to me. On *This Morning* you're going live to an audience of three million people, it's quite mad. Normally the show is studio based and it's all very rehearsed, you block it off and you know what space you're going to be in.

My very first show, we were doing a surprise makeover, live on the Southbank. It was outside in an uncontrolled environment, crowds, weather, wind and so on. And also the person we were doing the makeover on had no idea. Would she turn up, how would she react? Would she cry, run away, be happy or overwhelmed?

Emma Bunton threw to me from studio, 'And now we go live to Darren on the Southbank who is about to surprise an unsuspecting passer-by,' and this lady literally had no clue, which was a little bit nerve-racking as a presenter! The lady, Tina, was almost backing away but I grabbed her and got her on air. It was pretty intense for a first time on national live TV on such a big morning show in the UK. In a way the fact that it hadn't been done before, meaning there was no structure producers could guide me through in advance sort of made it easier. I did my best to just own it. My years of training in Ireland really came into use then. If I'd never done any TV, I'm sure I would have completely sunk.

I love the variety of my job. What I absolutely adore is making excellent TV, TV that has meaning. On the *Unemployables* we do actually help make some changes in people's lives.

I love when I can stand back and know I've made somewhat of a difference to someone, even if it's one person, even if it's with something like his or her clothes.

You can really change someone's outlook and affect their confidence and bring them to the next change in their life very simply. I love the really meaningful element of TV making.

A few years ago, I've worked on a couple of very personal documentary called *Gay Daddy* and it wasn't something I did lightly. It was something that came organically from me. I pitched it. I was working with a team of producers who I know and trusted for years. The executive producer is a friend of mine and we've worked on so many different things in the past that I trusted her. I had to sit with my family to make sure they were OK with it too. And then I had to sit down myself and go, hold on, do I want to do this?

Especially at the time, I thought it was a very important story to be told and be looked at. I was shining a light on an area of life that wasn't protected or recognised by Irish law, that was kind of being brushed under the carpet and that nobody was talking about.

A lot of people have misconceptions about gay people, that we're all flamboyant little queens running around dancing and not caring and actually, I just thought well this is me – so like me or loathe me, this is who I am.

I just kind of thought, I'm doing this. I was very nervous because I thought I was going to get so much hate mail. For about two months after the documentary aired, I was inundated with emails and messages on Facebook that had me in tears. People were literally opening their hearts to me. The most powerful thing about *Gay Daddy* was that it wasn't just about being gay, it wasn't about sexuality; it was about anyone who couldn't biologically have a family. As a result, it touched so many people.

I had guys coming up to me in bars and they could all relate, telling me their own personal stories. I think when people see you're not out to get them or make a mockery of them or do anything, people respond. It was described at the time as a watershed moment on Irish TV and that's something I'm really proud of. I pushed RTÉ more than I realised. At the time there were a lot of things going on politically which I didn't hear about and I know that there were certain factions that weren't in favour but that's fine, we all have free speech. Two years later, Ireland passed marriage equality.

In life it's human nature to dwell on the negative and the things that might not have gone to plan or gone so well but actually it's really important to take stock of the things that have gone well, to live in the moment and enjoy the moment.

We live in a world where everything is about planning ahead; we're stuck in our heads. It's important to take time out and acknowledge success and appreciate it and look at it and think, that was a good achievement. If you're an ambitious person, always focusing on a goal, it's important to remember to be flexible because otherwise you can miss opportunities.

Be courteous and treat people with respect. Working behind the scenes is invaluable and it makes you a much stronger presenter when you do finally make that progression on screen. It also means you can bond with your team and crew more if you understand their job as much as they understand yours. No TV programme is about one person; it's a team effort. Often there's tight budgets, tight turnarounds, high-pressure environments, things go wrong and you have to roll with the punches.

It's funny how things come round. When I was doing my radio show *Kennedy's Couch*, one of the people I approached to interview was Louis Copeland. We got on well and I build up a relationship with him and got to know him well over the years. I'd won the award for Ireland's most stylish man around the time and I decided to design my own suits – it seemed to make sense timing wise. I approached Louis and said, 'I want to design a collection of suits and you're the best man in the country to make them, what do you think?'

In fairness to him, he took a punt. I subsequently found out that he had been approached many, many times over the years and he had never ever done anything about it. It says a lot about him. I had a vision for it and I was honest with him. I told him how difficult it was for the modern man to find stylish suits and I told him being a modern man, I knew what other men wanted to find in stores. I knew about aesthetic and I wanted to make something original that would sell. Louis' brand is incredible and he's known for his immaculate tailoring but for people my age, Louis was not the obvious choice for a guy wanting to wear a sharp suit. I said this to him.

The whole experience has been very good. It has absolutely captured a new market for Louis Copeland and it's been a very powerful branding reposition. I design the suits from scratch. I'm very involved and I get free reign, which is great. I also work very closely on the artistic direction of our shoots, on the PR, on the marketing and all that. My background is in business and branding so I love to do those things. It's not just a vanity project by any means. It's a business, its part of my brand and I love it.

It was an extremely steep learning curve but I chose my battles well and I worked with pros. I learned so much from them, from the language of tailoring to everything else.

The fundamentals I knew, in the sense that I was very much in tune with style and I had a very definite point of view of what I wanted and how I wanted it cut, how it should fit, how it should fall etc. That might have jarred with what our team was used to so I had to bring people with me and I learned a lot from them too. They totally took a punt. It could have been a glorious failure but something told me it wouldn't be. I was prepared for it not to be.

Luckily I have nothing to worry about, we've done over five collections! I get a great buzz from it. I've had guys in their sixties stop me in the street to tell me they love my suits and that they've bought three or four or however many. I remember one particular time a lady stopping me and asking if her son could take a photo with me. It was his eighteenth birthday and all he had wanted was a Darren-Kennedy suit. That for me was amazing. People often tweet me pictures of themselves wearing my suits and I love that!

Our tag line is 'life is the occasion' and I love that my suits are part of people's stories and their special memories. Success for me is people enjoying my designs.

You have to enjoy life because who knows what's around the corner for any of us and therein lies some of the difficulty but all of the adventure.

It's funny but there's no clear path in life. You have to do your own thing, your own way and remain true to yourself.

It took me a long time to figure out who I actually am, to be really comfortable in my own skin and know what I am and what I bring to the table; what my strengths and weaknesses are. I think it's once you really discover that, that you hit your stride.

Darren's Top 3 Tips For Impressing When it Matters.

Bring ideas.

Do your research and know who you're meeting.

Try and find a connection.

Let them see who you are; it doesn't have to be all sell, sell, sell. Some of the best meetings are the ones where you actually connect with someone. Oftentimes you may not know what's around the corner. There may not be any work for you but they're just giving you some of their time. If you can leave them with an impression of who you are, that will stand to you. Again, it's about being genuine and authentic. That's the most powerful thing.

Work hard.

Even if you're somewhere making a coffee, make sure it's the best coffee you could possibly make.

On Air

'It's not true that
I had nothing on,
I had the radio on.'
-Marilyn Monroe

Nothing brightens your mood like the booming sound of the radio; whether in the car, in the office, in the comfort of your own home or keeping you company on your daily chores, whether on a cold winter's morning, a dull autumn afternoon, a clear and crisp spring evening or the sunniest of summer days; Radio is the perfect companion.

We've all got that favourite DJ, the best friend we've never met but feel like we've known for a lifetime. Whether it's music, news or general chit chat, radio has been around since 1895 and is the longest running form of entertainment. An intimate medium, its power to connect with people is like no other and over the following chapter a host of radio presenters and DJs give an insight into their 'on air' world.

Ryan Tubridy

As the host of the world's longest running chat show, Ryan Tubridy is a familiar face to Irish households, bringing TV screens to life and brightening up living rooms every Friday on the Late Late Show. *A successful radio host, a published author and the next best thing to Santa, this broadcaster has many strings to his bow.*

I often think that there's been a terrible mistake, that I shouldn't be in this era at all and that some day I'll be tapped on the shoulder and told, 'The 1920s have been on, they said you could go back.' Ever since I was a child, I've liked old-fashioned things in life. I love the old world. As a kid, I was a fun-sized nerd who loved books and history and cartoons. I grew up on a diet of *Bagpuss, the Flumps, Mr. Ben* and *Mr. Men*. They all informed my world. Roald Dahl and *Charlie and the Chocolate Factory, The Twits, George's Marvelous Medicine* were all really important to where I am now because I realised from a young age I liked the quirkier side of things.

I loved watching TV, particularly cartoons. I went to the movies a lot too; *Superman* and *Star Wars* and *Indiana Jones and the Raiders of the Lost Ark* and *ET*, all those wonderful movies. They were big movies with big themes, big music and big acting on the big screen. When you're little, the big screen isn't just big – it's enormous. The cinema back then was something special. You went there for a special occasion and it was a very big deal. You worked hard to be able to afford the trip there and you'd queue on the street to get your ticket. It was almost a ceremony.

My dad, brother and I went to the movies so much, back in the day, we soon ran out of films to see. Encouraged by my dad, I wrote a tiny little letter to the *Irish Times*. The headline over it was 'Too Few Films for Twelve Year Olds' and it said 'Dear Sir, what about us twelve year olds? We need more movies.' To my surprise they published it. Something magic happened after that.

It began with a letter headed with 'Anything Goes' that came through the door in the post. *Anything Goes* was a program for children on RTÉ, and that letter might as well have been a letter from Mickey Mouse sent from Disneyland – that's how much is meant to me. I couldn't believe it. A researcher had seen my letter in the paper and decided to get in touch, asking me to review some films for the programme. I couldn't believe they had written to little twelve-year-old me. It was as if Mr. Wonka himself had sent me the golden ticket and I was Charlie Bucket. My heart was pounding. RTÉ was the equivalent of the chocolate factory.

They sent me to see two films, *The Adventures of Young Sherlock Holmes* and the other was *The Journey of Natty Gann*; two films that died without trace but I remember them because they were so important to me. I went with my dad and brother to see them in the Savoy in Dublin and the three of us then went into RTÉ to do the review. The cameras, the lights, the presenters – everything, made me feel I had found my natural home. It felt absolutely right.

It wasn't long after that, that I was listening to kids reviewing books on a radio show called *Poparama* on RTÉ Radio. With my newfound confidence, I thought, 'I could do that! I've done film reviews; I'm a veteran now.' I wrote to them and they sent me a big envelope full of books. They asked me to review them on tape and that's exactly what I did. I sent a cassette tape of me reviewing them at home. I had a little old tape recorder and nice little microphone. They sent a letter back saying we'll see you on Sunday. And that was that. I went in once a month for two years. I got an unnatural kick out of it. I really loved it. It combined two of my great loves, reading books and showing off and it was a magic collision of two things that I'm good at. I got paid twenty-five pounds – a king's ransom and I thought, 'This is something I could do.' I spent that money mostly on books. I was also a sweet fiend and I was able to buy a bigger packet of fizzy cola bottles with my new funds.

When my voice broke, I was no use to anyone. Too old for children's radio, neither boy nor man, neither coming nor going. That was bit tricky for a while. I remember there was a thing called Aertel on TV that had all the information about the weather, cinema and flight times. It's very old fashioned now but it was a thing back in the day. The BBC had a version called Ceefax. I used to read that aloud to myself, off the TV screen, imagining that I was on TV. It was almost like an autocue. That's a sad but honest admission because I just wanted to see what it would be like. I could almost see my reflection on the screen as I was pretending to be on TV. That was my pre-leaving cert idea of the media.

When college called, I decided to study Arts in UCD. I did History and Greek and Roman civilization. It sounds very grand but it actually was for the less bright academics. I did an alright Leaving Cert but I definitely wasn't the brightest kid in the class. I was nerdy but I wasn't geeky. I had interests in things but I wasn't brilliant. I was also easily distracted – I still am to this day. I couldn't concentrate for long enough. I was good at the things I liked and I was rubbish at everything else. In my Leaving Cert, History and English I did well in, everything else I was only OK at. I loved college. I had great fun for three years.

Once I graduated, I toyed with doing law, because it required a lot of spoof, and media which requires even more spoof. I settled on law and studied it for a week in the King's Inns before deciding I just didn't like the smell of it. I thought it was really pretentious, it felt like a slog and I wasn't sure that my head was ready for it.

It's about that time that I came into RTÉ. Someone who I had worked with when I was a teenager doing research pointed me in the direction of somebody else and I started making coffee for Gerry Ryan, who was a famous broadcaster before he sadly passed away. Gerry was a larger-than-life figure in Ireland. When I was making his tea and coffee, we hit it off. We just got on well, like an older brother or uncle and nephew. He decided that I was a good guy and we had fun. We liked American politics and we had similar things in common, including a very dark, bold sense of humour. If ever there was something wrong or I had trouble, Gerry always had my back and he always had my corner and sadly, when he died, it put an awfully large hole in my career and my life because he was always somebody I wanted to talk about things. I miss him to this day. He was very, very important person in my life.

In the early days, when I was making tea and coffee and bringing down the Danish pastries for Gerry in the mornings, I would look around at other programmes to try and find an opportunity, an 'in'. Where could I do something to get on air? I always felt I was an on-air person, not a behind the scenes. It's amazing the confidence I have but my parents loved me and that would explain that. Radio was a great medium for me because I didn't have any confidence in my looks but I had good confidence in my personality. I never thought of TV. I thought you had to be an ex-boy-band member to be on the box and unfortunately, that wasn't on the cards.

In radio, I learned how to work tape recorders, machines and put radio packages together and they really liked what I was doing. Slowly I began to get more attention and in time I started to work as a reporter on Pat Kenny's radio show. Eventually I got my own show called *Morning Glory* which went down quite well because it was a mixum-gatherum of things; the sort of things that Emily would have seen through the window when she went to see *Bagpuss*. It was just a bit different and they liked that.

And that's something that one has to be – a little bit different. You have to have your own thing. My thing was the nerd-thing, the young fogy, the love for history and the old world – but it's not fake. I love all that stuff.

TV-wise I did a small quiz show called *All Kinds of Everything*. Somebody saw me talking to the audience in that and said, 'You'd be great at presenting the Rose of Tralee,' which I then did for two years. It's off the back of that, that I got a Saturday night chat show – my own one, called *Tubridy Tonight*. Then *The Late Late Show* came along and there I was hosting the longest running chat show in the world. Initially I didn't know if I could do it but six years on, I'm doing OK. It's a dream job! In the beginning, I definitely felt the pressure. To this day, I still get nervous every Friday. The show starts at about 9.30PM and around 9.15PM I go into my special zone. It's like a bungee-jump-thing. Then you're in and it's show time and that's addictive and gorgeous and every interview is like playing a match. Did you score, did you win, did you lose, did you draw? It's gladiatorial and it's hugely satisfying. I love it, it's challenging.

Choosing a favourite interview is difficult because there are so many. I was very surprised by Professor Green. I wasn't sure what he had to say because I didn't know him that well other than a few tunes. He turned out to be amazing. He gave this extraordinary interview about his life that was really dark and difficult but he told it in a very articulate and intelligent way. He was a lovely surprise and I love when that happens. Joanne O'Riordan is another favourite guest. She had a condition called total amelia – no arms, no legs and a personality that would fill Croke Park countless times over. She's extraordinary.

Editorially, I have two teams of people who do what I call, the heavy-lifting. They make the calls to the agents, they make sure the guest is OK, they will do a briefing document on the guest that I will read with them. If you choose a sporting analogy, they set up the goal, I knock it in with my head. I'm very, very keen about the make-up of the show, the feel of the show, the direction of an interview. I'm very, very engaged in that sense. I help choose the questions, the clip we might play – I feel the talk show or chat show has been taken over by stand up comedians and I'm definitely not that. All the chat shows around the world are pre-recorded and they're presented by guys who are funny and sometimes who are too big for their guest and the guest gets lost. I'm trying to preserve the art of conversation. Parky would be one of my idols. It was a dream come true to interview someone like him – and Terry Wogan. They were journalists and hacks and they asked questions, their interviews were investigative and that's what it has to be, otherwise it's just 'wakka, wakka, fozzy bear'. I think the world has to have chat shows with conversation as well. *The Late Late Show* is a real honour and I love being there every Friday.

If I really, really had to choose between radio and TV, I'd choose radio. It's warmer and more intimate and less judge-y. If you go on the radio in the morning and you're talking to somebody, they're not looking at your shirt or commenting on how wrecked you look and equally the guest isn't being judged. They're just being judged on what's inside the head, the heart and the soul whereas on television it's just jazz hands, you could talk to somebody but people at home will just spend a lot of time commenting on that persons shoes or hair or whatever as opposed to saying, 'What a great story, what a great interviewee that person is.' TV is maybe more fun to watch but presenting-wise, it's all about the radio.

For anyone wanting to work in radio, my advice is to go local. Don't be afraid of approaching Radio Kerry or WLRFM or whatever it might be. If you're in college, go to the college radio station, if you're living in a town where there's a radio station, get involved, regardless of the size. Learn how to use the equipment. Learn how to interview people. Be curious. Don't read everything from a book; just be curious about the world.

You have to be relentless in this business. You have to be almost disturbed in your ambition. You should also never be afraid of your ambition.

This is a word in Ireland that is considered dirty. It's sort of been made into a curse word. I celebrate the American approach to ambition which is a 'Yes, we can' vibe. I say, 'Go for it'. Knock on the door and if that closes or doesn't open, knock on the next one. If you want it and believe it that you're good enough, you just have to keep knocking. It'll never happen instantly. If it's taking a while, do something else; don't just sit at home wondering, 'Why aren't they answering?' Find something to do. If I lost my job tomorrow, I'd go and write books or I'd research or try to make documentaries. You've got to be proactive. You've got to go out there and tell them how amazing you are.

When I started out, I definitely kept on top of critique and criticism. Sometimes I would read reviews that weren't so nice and my morale and ego would be bruised. As my career got bigger and I got more attention, it became water-off-a-duck's-back stuff. Then online came along and honestly, if you want to depress yourself as a broadcaster, read online. I made the decision to go offline a couple of years ago and it's the best thing that's ever happened. Of course, I use the computer but I don't read stuff. I don't interact with trolls. If I could switch off the Internet sometimes, I would. Especially for kids and bullying and all these things that are so easy to do for cowards. You used to go to school from nine until three and then you could switch off. Now it follows you and bullies can follow you now wherever you are if they want to. I'd rather read a good book than what some guy in a bedsit watching *Star Trek* thinks about me.

I've been very lucky in my career. Between radio and TV, I've got to do so many wonderful things. I have to say, I was very proud of my book, *JFK in Ireland*. When I first saw it, I nearly cried. It was like my third child. That was a really big deal for me. I still go into my local library and I see the spine there and it tells me two things: I've a book in the library and nobody's taking it out. I get a kick out of that. I'm also exceptionally proud of my children who see me as dad only. They don't watch *The Late Late Show*. They are gorgeous and warm and kind and funny and great company. I'm their dad, I'm not the guy from the television and that's wonderful. They're my equilibrium. When they're beside me, the world disappears and that's all I want.

Louise McSharry

Writer and 2FM radio presenter Louise McSharry loves everything about her job but it wasn't until college that she found her true calling for going 'on air'. Inspired by her uncle and college radio, she made it her mission to follow her dream, letting noting stand in her way, not even a battle with cancer.

I often think sixteen-year-old me would be blown away by where I am now. It's funny, as you achieve your dreams, you begin to have more dreams, bigger, bolder, and wilder.

From a young age I was reaching for the stars. I was one of those kids who liked attention – that was my primary goal. I wanted a grown up job where people would be looking or listening to me.

I remember there was an exercise my teacher had us doing when we were about thirteen. We had to write our obituary. It sounds really morbid, but the idea was we had to write down all the things we hoped to have achieved by the end of our lives.

At the time I was living in America and I was like – 'Louise was an Oscar winner and the first non-American female president of the United States.' I think I'd won a Grammy too. I wanted to be everything – a lawyer, an actress, a singer; I just wanted to do it all really.

I began to really explore my media dreams as a teenager, certainly that's when a seed was planet with radio. My uncle used to work in FM104 at the time and I would often help him come up with ideas for the show.

As appealing as it was, I didn't really think radio was a job that I would *actually* get to do – like a football player, rock star, whatever- it seemed a little unattainable. One of those jobs that nobody *actually* gets to do in real life . . . bar my uncle, but he was special!

By the time CAO came by in my final year of school, I chose all the media courses. I didn't know what I wanted to do specifically but I knew it something in media. I also put down Arts in UCD. I think I only put that down because I thought I could definitely get it and because I wanted to go to a 'proper' university. I was a bit snobby about that. I blame it partly on the school I went to and the people I hung around with and also the fact that my parents had gone to UCD and they seemed to have the best time ever – they met each other there and they had this brilliant great social life.

As a teen that was a little bit socially insecure, I thought that if I went to UCD, I would have this amazing social life and everything would fall into place for me. I would have my first proper boyfriend . . . you know, everything would happen for me – magically!

In the end I missed three of the courses that I wanted to do by five points. I was gutted. I had a choice between Arts in UCD or Audiovisual Communications in IT, Tallaght and because of my aforementioned snobbery, I decided to go to UCD. It was a big mistake. Down the line I had met people who had gone to Tallaght and they had such a great time. All of the stuff they'd done and all of the stuff that they'd studied sounded amazing and right up my street. Instead I ended up in UCD in lectures of like two hundred people. I was doing English and Psychology and Sociology and while they're all things I'm interested in, I simply didn't care enough about them to put in the necessary work.

If I was talking to myself now, I'd say pick what you're interested in because you probably won't be successful in things you're not.

It was not all doom and gloom though because UCD is where I got involved in the college radio station and that's really where it all started for me.

I realised radio was something I was actually quite good at and I felt like I had a natural aptitude for it, which wasn't something I'd felt before. For the first time I though, 'I'm good at this, *this* is my thing.'

The first time I did a show, I think the only person listening was the station manager's mother – it was a test broadcast for Belfield FM in UCD and it was the first time I'd ever sat down in front of a microphone, played CDs and talked about them. I had my own CDs, I got to talk about the music and why I liked it and what I knew about the people and I just really enjoyed sharing that passion and introducing people to music they might not have heard before.

Radio also made me realise that I am articulate and that was something that I wasn't necessarily aware of previously. I would say that's probably my greatest skill. There are loads of things I'm really bad at but that is, I think, my biggest gift.

I realised in UCD that it wasn't really happening for me, primarily because I wasn't going to any lectures or sitting exams. By the end of first year, I hadn't done any actual college work.

Sure, I was in college, all day, every day but I wasn't focusing on course work. Instead I was involved in the drama society and the radio station, putting all my time and effort into my passions.

It seemed like a natural decision to leave college but even though things worked out for me, I still regret it to this day.

A college drop-out, I went off and I tried my best to get work experience in any radio station that would take me. I was working in Extravision at the time. I was applying everywhere but not with much success – I wasn't really getting any responses. It's funny but sometimes it really is about being in the right place at the right time.

It's only when I volunteered for the Special Olympics that I managed to find a tiny connection and a potential way into radio. One of the girls who was volunteering with me had done some work in Newstalk and she gave me the name and email address of the editor at the time.

I emailed him and told him my story and that I'd really love some experience. He got back to me and said, 'Listen, you've got a little bit of experience so I'll put you in the maybe pile. We do get a lot of these emails and unfortunately we don't have much space at this moment in time.'

I don't know what came over me because it's very unlike me but I replied and said, 'I promise you, if you take me on, you won't regret it.' I wouldn't be very ballsy normally. Usually I find confrontation hard and I sometimes even find it hard to push myself forward in work situations – it's a thing I'm working on. My cheekiness paid off in this instance. I got a call the next week and got three-weeks work experience in Newstalk and I didn't leave for four-and-a-half years. It was amazing.

I think it's a combination of being in the right place at the right time and also making sure that you're talking to people about the opportunities that you're looking for.

If you're walking around never letting people know that you want some work in radio or whatever, nobody knows and therefore if somebody hears of an opportunity that might suit you, they're not going to think of you. You have to have your eyes and ears open and you have to be looking for the opportunities. When I got into Newstalk, I didn't have a clue what I was doing. I knew nothing about current affairs. I fell in there just because it was the only radio station that would take me.

But I loved it. I loved being around that kind of radio. I didn't even know how the Oireachtas worked because I grew up and was educated in America. I used to go home and study.

For the first six months I was working there for free. I used to go in at 5AM and finish at 12PM and then go across town and work in an office to keep myself going but I loved every minute of it. I was so excited to be doing it that I was just seizing the opportunity.

After the six months I had made myself indispensable, I had taken on responsibilities within the breakfast programme that I worked on. When I went on holidays, they had to get another work-experience person in to fill in for me. I made myself invaluable. Anything they needed done, I said yes; nothing was beneath me, I did absolutely anything. Because Newstalk was a startup, I got to do loads of different things – I wasn't just getting coffee.

Getting my job on 2FM didn't come easy and the opportunity definitely wasn't handed to me on a plate. I worked hard for many years behind the scenes, as a reporter, as a writer, building up my credentials, gaining experience and topping up my skills and knowledge. I feel so privileged to present my very own show now and the fact that I get to play new music and I'm in control of the playlists. It's a dream.

My job doesn't stop once I set foot outside the studio, I'm always working around the clock, reading blogs, listening out for new bands, checking out gigs. I adore what I do.

There are of course other types of radio I'd like to do one day. On a few occasions I covered for Ryan Tudridy and I revelled in those opportunities. I adore talk radio. I love people. I love hearing people's stories, I'm genuinely fascinated and I hope one day to be able to combine that into the type of show I present. Radio is such a strong medium, I think it's very personal.

Some of the most powerful experiences I've had with media are things that have been on the radio – you know these experiences where you have to do something but you don't want to walk away from the radio or you're in the car and you don't want to get out because someone's telling a story that's just so powerful, you're captivated and it awe. I have always found people talking about their own experiences to be completely gripping and way more interesting than any fiction.

For me, in many ways, I'm more at ease in a studio in front of a microphone that I am anywhere else. And that's the way it's always been for me since my very first show.

I'm really picky about what I play on the *Louise McSharry Show* because I think that if you're doing a music show, your credibility is very important so people need to trust you and trust that you're only going to play good stuff. That means even if you play something somebody doesn't necessarily like at first, if they trust you, they'll give it a chance.

Sometimes I really agonise over whether or not to play a song. I keep a database of everything I play on the show so if anyone's ever filling in for me they can look at what I've been playing because I'm bit of a control freak over what gets played.

When I decided that I wanted to go into radio and my radio presenting opportunity came up, my uncle who worked in radio for years told me not to take it. At first I thought he was nuts but now, I completely understand what he means.

When you're a presenter, there's no security. You're contracted for very short periods of time and sometimes you can even be out the door before your contract even runs out. I remember I was doing a breakfast show and I was doing well. My figures were good too but there were redundancies and I was one of the people who was made redundant and that was it.

Also, your job is public and people are always critical of you. People send you abuse. I've learned not to take it personally. It's only a certain kind of person who decides they're going to send a mean text to tell you you're a terrible person or that you're bad at your job.

The same goes for tweets. I don't particularly value the opinion of someone who is that kind of person, so that means that whatever they say is not of value to me. I try to rationalise it that way.

At times it can be hard. I had someone text in something really horrible and personal about my family one time which I hadn't been too public about. It was obviously someone who knew some-one in my family and decided to text into my radio show about that while I was on air. That was really vicious and hard to take.

You just have to accept that everyone has an opinion, in life, on radio, in your day-to-day dealings and not everybody is going to like you, and that's OK. There are going to be people who find you annoying, but at the end of the day, you're the one who's doing your job and you have to do it to the best of your ability - that can be a challenge.

It's essential to have other skills. That's something I learned when I was made redundant. That was my first on-air job and I had always worked in production prior to that. If you're good at production, you'll always find more work one way or another. When that presenting gig ended, I had nothing else going on and I had a really, really long difficult time. It was during the throes of the recession, I was applying for jobs and not even getting responses, it was really awful.

What I love about the fact that I worked behind the scenes for years before I was a presenter is that I understand the jobs that the people around me are doing and I would hope that that means that I'm never going to be unreasonable about them. I can remember when I was a researcher or a producer. I might have worked all day in getting the right people for a story and the presenter might have come in and be like, 'No, I don't want to do that.' You had to learn to fight your corner and say, 'We're going to do it and here's why.' You had to convince them. It's been really valuable for me to work my way up rather than just become a presenter straight away.

I've been quite open about my cancer experience. I've spoken about it in the media and I feel like I shared the experience with the public. I made a documentary called *F*ck Cancer* too which was really special to me. It was a difficult journey to capture but I wanted to help others through my own experience. It might sound or look a little unusual to say, but I am grateful that it happened to me and there are loads of different reasons.

Being so ill, showed me that work isn't everything. We should not let fear get in the way. My illness also made me feel a lot differently about my body. It thought me to really appreciate it and realise what it's for. My whole life I had thought of my body as something that was for show, to put clothes on and decorate, forgetting that it's actually there to keep me alive. Your health and happiness are the most precious things in life.

I certainly don't feel like wasting time any more. I'm much more tenacious now about the things that I want because I think you have to be.

And especially as a woman, I think you have to be. Women have a tendency not to ask for what they want and sit back quietly and hope that it will happen. In order for us to compete we have to be more confident about ourselves and more tenacious about asking for what we want. I'm no longer shy about reaching for my dreams or making my wishes vocal. And neither should you be. Go out there and make it happen.

Louise's Top Radio Tips

You have to persevere.

When I lost my job, I emailed every programme in Dublin, every single one. None of them came back to me. I emailed them again and the head of 2FM got back to me. That's the only one that replied. Not any of the more local stations but one of the big ones! He said that there weren't any opportunities but that he'd meet me. I persevered and eventually I got a 'in'. I didn't go away. You can't give up at the first hurdle. You have to keep going.

Treat everything as a learning experience, even if you get a job that isn't exactly the one you want.

Take it and do it because you'll get something out of it that will stand to you down the line. Experience is the most valuable thing in radio, across the board.

Be yourself.

Nobody likes to listen to someone who is pretending to be something that they're not. People see right through that. You are good enough. If you don't know something, don't pretend to. Just ask. That's how you'll learn. Sometimes people say to me, 'Have you heard such and such a song?' and I feel like I should say yes, because I *should* know everything but I don't do that because, why should I pretend like I've heard every song ever? That's not possible.

Be honest and be true to yourself.

Rick O'Shea

Radio DJ Rick O'Shea has been on Irish airwaves for over twenty years but did you know that Rick isn't his real name?

A self-confessed bookworm and cinema fanatic, the broadcaster's insight into the industry is filled with golden nuggets of advice for any budding radio disc jockey.

I was one of those kids who didn't spend a lot of time outdoors. I spent a lot of time with computers, I was nerdy, I was geeky, I spent a lot of time watching TV and I read an awful lot of books. I did see the sunlight sometimes, but not overly often. I went to school in a place that was relatively far away from where I lived. I grew up in Crumlin and I went to school in Drimnagh Castle – so it's not as if I just walked home three minutes and everyone who was in my class was near where I lived. The school had children from everywhere. There was nobody in my class from Crumlin and it kind of created a little barrier. I spent a lot of time at home, doing stuff by myself.

Back then I wanted to be an astronaut. It was never going to happen but I loved reading stuff about space travel, about NASA, about astronomy – that was my thing. Ideally I would have liked to have been an astronaut but of course it was complete nonsense and it was never going to happen because I was a pudgy kid, growing up in Crumlin. When I was fourteen or fifteen, I decided I wanted to be an accountant purely because it was one of the few things in school I was really good at. Maths and English were my subjects but I didn't realise how I was going to make some money out of being good at English. Accountancy seemed like a good idea. It was probably when I was sixteen or seventeen that I realised what a terrible idea actually was and that dream died off – sharpish.

By the time I finished school, I didn't know what I wanted to do. By that stage I'd done a little bit of radio – I had been on a radio competition. It was a competition run by one of the pirates in Dublin. I was lured in by the prizes more than anything else. They had £50,000 worth of prizes, which back then, was a lot. I did an on-air demo and ended up in the final but of course I lost. You're not going to give a fifteen-year-old kid £50,000 worth of stuff. It was one of those moments when I thought, 'Oh, radio might be interesting,' but it kind of fell by the wayside. I didn't do anything about it after that.

I decided to go to UCD to study Arts, mainly because my career guidance teacher said, 'You don't really know what you want to do and a good general arts degree will go a long way.' In the summer between school and college I got in touch with the hospital radio station which had just been relatively recently set up in St. James' hospital. They said come on in because there weren't a lot of people interested in doing it at the time. I ended up doing little weekend shows for them here and there and when I did go to college, I fell into the student radio station. It was the first year they'd done student radio in UCD, so it was a bunch of guys who knew nothing about anything – including me. By the time I reached the end of first year, I was running the station. At that point, I thought maybe there's something in this and I should be looking into it.

I was terrible in college. I didn't even go to my exams in my first year. I dropped out and decided I was going to do a broadcasting course somewhere else. I went to Ballyfermot and did a broadcasting and journalism course there for a year and by that point I had been doing a little bit of local radio and got offered a real, full-time job and I've been working ever since.

I should point out that I didn't choose my radio name, it was given to me. When I first started my first radio job, I was in East Coast in Wicklow. I was there for about a year and a half. I then went to work in Wexford in South East Radio for seven weeks – seven weeks because I was then offered a job with Atlantic 252. Atlantic isn't around any more but at the time, it was run partially by RTÉ and Radio Luxemburg. They ran it out of a tiny little town called Trim in Meath. They were a very big deal at the time. It all seemed very sexy and very exciting. I took the job.

It was only when I walked in on the first day that I was told, 'Welcome, there's your desk with everything you need and your name is on top of your desk and we'll see you later.' I was twenty at the time and you don't think of questioning things like that at that age. I come from a long line of Sandy Beaches, Dusty Roads. I just took the name on board. A part of me thought it would just be temporary. That's twenty-two years ago and I'm still lumbered by it.

Radio had been just a hobby up until the first time I was given a paying job with East Coast radio in Wicklow. I'd been doing weekends there for about ten months and I was getting on OK as far as I could tell but they didn't even pay your bus fare, that was the nature of the gig. It was entirely voluntary. I had a conversation with a guy who was the programme director there at the time and he said, 'Look, at the moment, we have this late night radio slot, from ten-till-one in the morning.' They had six different presenters six nights of the week and they wanted to amalgamate it with one person. I straight-up said, 'Me, me, me, me, me.' I wanted a proper paying job where I could move out of home and make some money.

I got it fairly quickly and I moved out to Bray and it was brilliant. I had an open playlist, which for a lot of presenters, they never get in their career, ever. I was twenty, I knew nothing about love and yet there I was playing late night love songs. I played a lot of mellow, laid back stuff and it seemed to work. It felt like something was starting.

The best thing about having your own show is the freedom to do whatever you want. And again, not a lot of people get that. It's something that's afforded to 2FM presenters most of the time but I haven't always had it. There were times when I was doing shows here and I was very strictly, rigidly told, 'This is what the show is, this is the box you need to tick.' For the last six or seven years I was very lucky to do a show with Cormac and Michael. We'd been told 'We trust you guys. Go off and make your thing.' Our music was playlisted but it was about the bits in between, not the songs. I loved the freedom of coming in every day and working alongside two people that I liked – that freedom to say 'what sort of utter nonsense will we chat about today.'

I've been doing radio pretty much every day for twenty-two years so nerves no longer affect me. It's like breathing in and out, it's second nature to me. Luckily I love people and they seem to enjoy talking to me too!

I love interviewing people but you never really know how someone's going to be when they come in. A few years ago, I interviewed Russell Brand when he did *Get Him to the Greek*. I didn't quite know what to expect from him. I'd done a phoner with him about two years before that – before he started becoming super-political and he seemed really intelligent. I decided that I'd try to build a rapport with him and do something different. He turned out to be one of the most intelligent people I'd ever interviewed. I had him for twenty-six minutes on the show. We were supposed to do ten minutes but he just kept talking and talking and talking. He was absolutely fascinating. I've seen him do terrible interviews too but it could be just something about the atmosphere.

Music-wise, I was interviewing the Manic Street Preachers a couple of years ago. I was hideously intimidated because they're incredibly political and intelligent guys and I felt totally out of my depth. A few minutes before we did the interview, I had a quick chat with them. The smoking ban had just come in to Wales where they were recording their album. We got into a chat about the ban and they were like, 'It was terrible going outside and having to smoke,' and we had this lovely chat and warming up which had nothing to do with them or the interview or their new album and by the time we got to do the interview, they were pussycats. They were one of the best interviews I've ever done.

Usually most people are great because they're aware that you're there to interview them, you're there to have the chat with them. Most people fantastic. It's very rare you come across someone who is having a really off day.

I love my job but it's a risky industry. Back up plans are crucial when you're doing this job. If you're interested in other things and this job allows you to participate in those other things, then grab those opportunities if and when possible. I've known so many people over the years who were just 'radio presenters' and that's how they define themselves. Maybe they were interested in other things too but they never chose to try to interact with that world or embrace any work outside of broadcasting and it ends poorly for them quite frequently and they find out that some day, you're not wanted any more but you've got nothing else in your life to do and no other strings to your bow. That's quite a cliff to fall off in that situation.

Doing what you love is hugely important. If you ask a number of people if they enjoy what they do, very few will say 'yes'. Whether you're working in McDonalds, sweeping the streets, or maybe a civil servant, if you enjoy your job, that goes a long, long way. Of course there are enormous perks from getting asked to do stuff like interviewing famous people, which can be quite cool. Sometimes it's part of the job but sometimes they're people you've always wanted to meet.

Another perk can be being asked to go to press junkets and meet famous movie stars. Or even down to the simple stuff like getting sent books by the truckloads. It's fantastic. I get new books, sometimes three or four months before they come out on the shelves. For me being a book anorak, you may as well send me gold bars. Being asked to become part of that world over the last while has been fantastic. I've always wanted to do that kind of stuff. There are perks and they are great but they wouldn't make up for it if you didn't enjoy the job you're doing.

Perhaps the biggest fear for a radio presenter is JNLR ratings. Every three months you get a set of figures that tells you what happened in the last few months. It's an impending terror, particularly when you're young and you're thrown into this and you're not quite used to it and it happens every three months. It's the focus of your life. The older you get and the more you do this, the more you realise it's like getting the Leaving Cert results every three months and if you allow yourself to obsess about that, you will go mental. You have to think, 'Feck this', my job is to come in and make a radio show every day, the best one I can and to do it within these parameters. The ratings come out and then it's the job of sales people to sell ads off the back of that. I can only affect what I do when I walk in here in terms of making a radio show; I can't affect all the other stuff outside of that. I can't control it. You shouldn't obsess over things you have no control over. You focus on the things you have control over and you get on with it.

I was only fired from a job once in my life and it had nothing to do with JNLR or ratings, it was completely different. Changes were happening in FM104 and I got moved along. I was unemployed for nine months and it had nothing to do with listenership figures. I felt desperate at that time. My son was quite young and I spent nine months scrambling around, talking to people, looking to find a job, almost taking a job down the country and eventually a slot became available here in RTÉ.

I always felt confident as a young man that I could land my dream job. One thing that might have deterred me was when I developed epilepsy at sixteen but I stayed strong and powered on. Having epilepsy never got in the way of me chasing what I wanted.

I think there's only one way of getting what you want in life and that's by throwing yourself into what it is you want to do and making it happen.

For some people, that's not going to happen but that's true for everyone, not just people who have medical problems. If you don't throw yourself at what you want and what you want to do, then you're never going to have an answer whether it will work out or not. That's the same for pretty much anybody.

For anyone considering radio as a job, I would say be sure that this is what you want to do for a living and not just something you want to do for a laugh or a hobby. Talk to people in the business, who have done this forever. Grill them about the workload and about stress, about how hard a job this is to do long term. If you want to be a presenter, nothing is a substitute for actually doing the bloody thing.

Find a local radio station, a community radio station, a hospital radio station, anyone who will let you behind the mic and will give you the chance to do stuff regularly. It's like wanting to be a professional cyclist but having never actually gotten on bike. The way you do that is by continually cycling. You've got to practise, practise, practise and it doesn't matter if there are only five people listening to begin with. Sometimes that's the best thing because then there's only five people who hear you mess up. Start small and don't worry about whether or not it's a big radio station or whether anyone is listening. The first hospital radio station I worked in, we weren't even on FM, we were on speakers in the hospital and I'm sure that ninety-five percent of them were turned off most of the time. Nobody was listening but it was a great way to learn and make mistakes without people coming down on you like a ton of bricks.

Budding radio presenters should remember not to obsess about radio all the time, that's a very insular, naval-gazing, way to treat yourself. I think the best radio presenters are those who are interested in everything, those who are interested about the world around them. If you're the type of person who obsesses over radio and only ever listens to radio – that's going to make you a dull presenter.

You have to be able to relate to your listeners and the world you live in.

Rick's Top Interviewing Tips:

Research your interviewee or topic properly.

Don't go in there without the right information. Researching doesn't mean looking up someone's Wikipedia page. That's a terrible idea. What you need to do is dig around a little bit, look at interviews they've done in the past, look at stuff that's appeared on their website or just things out of your own head from movies you've seen or the songs and albums you've heard.

Don't ask stupid questions.

I see people ask these questions all the time these days when they're doing press junkets or interviews, 'If you could be a colour, what colour would you be?' No movie star cares about that. Ask intelligent and interesting questions, or just ones you want to know the answer to yourself.

Make the interview not about you, but about them.

So many times I see people interviewing famous people and they're attempting to prove how brilliant they are by asking long involved questions or by interrupting or making the interview about themselves. Your job is to make *them* and interesting interview, not the other way round. That your job. Your job isn't to be the star of the interview.

Adrian Kennedy

*Adrian Kennedy is Irish radio chat show royalty. A favourite amongst
listeners, the broadcaster had been the voice of late night talk shows for
over seventeen years at FM104 before moving to 98FM to shake up
daytime radio and inject some fun with his sparky attitude and love for a
good debate. Bullied as teenager, Adrian initially turned to radio for
company and escape. Today, he's one of Ireland's most successful
broadcasters.*

My earliest memory of radio is when RTÉ Radio 2 opened. I was
in sixth class at the time, just about to finish primary school.
Because I was so mad about radio, I made it my business to bring
a small pocket radio in with me and I listened to the opening of
broadcast with Larry Gogan. I was obsessed with the thing, music
radio in particular.

Larry Gogan was one of my inspirations as a young fella. I also
loved Tony Blackburn on BBC Radio One and Two. In the 80s when
the pirate channel Nova went to air, I thought, 'Oh my god, this is
how radio is meant to be done.' They blew radio wide open here in
Dublin and created a good radio station. Up until then,

RTÉ Radio 2 was OK but when Nova came along and Sunshine and all of the big super pirates of the 80s, they really blew the lid on radio. It was good, American style radio in Dublin and I listened in religiously.

I often used to play pretend, hosting my own radio show in my bedroom. I actually have some tapes, which I've since transferred onto my computer of some of my recordings from my bedroom from 1979 and 1980. They're kind of cringe worthy but I was only fourteen or fifteen recording them.

For me radio was escapism. I hated secondary school and I was very badly bullied and picked on by a gang of young fellas, all the way throughout. Radio for me became company.

I was at home making these shows in my room and I realised that actually, I was quite good at it. I thought, 'I can do this.' It was from a very young age that radio was everything I wanted to do. I was in school and hated it but as soon as I'd get back home to making my little radio shows, I was happy.

When I was sixteen, the 80s version of Radio Nova ran a school of broadcasting course. It was aimed at young people interested in going to radio. I begged my mam and dad to do the course. I loved it. I got to make my first halfway decent demo tape and sent it to all sorts of radio stations around the country – it was eventually picked up by a radio station in Bray called Bray Local Broadcasting, BLB for short. That's where I got my very first radio show. I was sixteen years old. From that moment, I was hooked.

When I finished school I considered college. I would have got enough points to study journalism, which I was sort of interested in, but at the time, because I hated school, college was the last place I wanted to go and the last thing I wanted to do. I did odd jobs here and there but all the while I was working voluntarily in BLB radio. I didn't mind that I wasn't getting paid because I was still getting my airtime. I did a show on a Wednesday, I did a show on a Saturday, and I became involved in the management committee of the station. All the while I was working in the Apollo record store in Dublin. It earned me a few bob and I started getting into DJ'ing around that time too. I worked in a nightclub in Bray called O'Shea's, so I was keeping the wolf at the door in terms of earning a few bob but I still wasn't making money out of radio. I took a couple of years before I actually got a job that paid me money.

My very first show was a Saturday programme between seven and ten in the morning. Thinking back, there were only about ten people listening and most of them were probably my family members. It still gave me the experience of being in a studio and using a mixing desk and perfecting the craft. At the time it wasn't computerised like it is now. You were playing vinyl records. There was a lot more work involved then than nowadays. Everything is playlisted now and I just have to press the next button. I guess there was more creativity back then too.

From that I went to do the stations top-thirty countdown every week, which I absolutely loved. I did that for several years. Even though I wasn't getting paid and it was voluntary, BLB radio was the best experience I've had in my life. It set me up for my life in radio and that's all I've really done. I had one instant it the 80s when I was doing a radio show and I was wet behind the ears and getting used to it all. One of the jobs that we had to do back in the day in this pirate station – I was on a Saturday morning at 7AM – The first thing we had to do when we came into the station was switch on the transmitter, seems very logical.

Nowadays radio stations are on air 24/7 so their transmitters are on 24/7, but back in the day we started at seven in the morning and my first job was to switch on the transmitter. Little-old-me forgot and I did an entire show for three hours without the transmitter switched on, talking to myself in the studio until somebody came in at ten to ten and said, 'Eh, I don't think we're on the air.'

I literally sat there talking to myself for three hours with nobody else in the building. You learn from your experience. I've made loads of funny on-air gaffes over the years. I've made loads of silly mistakes. Everybody makes mistakes but that's part of the fun of working on radio. The radio I love is live radio. I've never been one for prerecorded radio.

Obviously it has its place. Live radio keeps you on your toes – you can't edit it. What happens on live radio stays on live radio, bar a ten second delay where you might be able to edit something out. Live radio literally keeps you awake because you can't afford to make mistakes. Pre-recorded radio, any time I've ever done an interview or something that's prerecorded, it just doesn't have that same edge. I don't know what it is that it's missing.

The thing I loved about radio when I started in radio is that for me, as a young fella, at that time in my life as a teenager who was getting bullied in school, it was a complete and utter escape from the crap that I was putting up with in school. The people in the radio station treated me well, there was no bullying of any sort and it was quite an enjoyable place to work.

Today I love the intimacy of radio. I love that as I talk, people are listening to me in their own home, in their own cars. Ninety percent of people listening to radio, probably more, are listening on their own. It's a solitary medium. We don't all gather around a radio and sit down and have a chat and listen to the radio in the background. When I'm on the radio, I'm talking directly to that one person and that's one thing that I've tried to teach people who want to get involved in radio. It's not like TV. You're not talking to a group of people. You're speaking to one person and you need to remember that. It's what makes radio so personal and it's what I love about it most.

I doubted myself in the early days. One of my problems I couldn't crack any of the big radio stations in Dublin. I couldn't get in. I applied with demo tapes morning, noon and night and none of the bigger radio stations in Dublin ever picked me up. I stayed with the station in Bray. What I did during that period in the 80s was get into management. I got into commercial production, I tried loads of stuff. Bar radio sales, I've done pretty much everything in radio during that time in the late 80s. I enjoyed management initially but it wasn't for me. When the business became licensed and commercialised, I probably didn't have a good enough business head on my shoulders to run a successful station. I kind of moved sideways and moved into news and a talk show. I didn't have a fall back plan then and I still don't now! Radio is something I've always done since I was sixteen. I've done all sorts of different things in radio and I'm kind of pigeon-holed now as a talk show host.

My lucky break was only days after my son was born. At this stage I was working as a journalist and a morning talk show host on East Coast radio in Bray. Out of the blue I got a phone call from Scott Williams who at the time was programme director at FM104. He asked me was I interested in filling in for the nighttime talk show and I said, 'What night time talk show? He said, 'There's a fella called Chris Barry who does a talk show here at FM104. Have a listen, ring me tomorrow and let me know what you think.' I listened to it; it was called *The Phone Show* and still is to this day. I thought, yeah I could do that. The next day I rang him and he gave me a gig filling in for Chris for two weeks.

It was nerve-racking at the start. The reason it was my lucky break is that I was doing a morning talk show on East Coast Radio in Bray County Wicklow. Scott Williams happened to live out that way and happened to hear me one night and happened to give me a call. That was a lucky break, I have to be honest. For the next year, any time Chris was off, I was used as the fill in presenter while still working out in East Coast FM. Then a job came up in the news department. I was still working in Bray in news and a job came up in the news department. I applied for it and all of a sudden, I had a full time job in the news department. I left East Coast after many years and moved to FM104. After a couple of months I was promoted to head of news which I did for a couple of years and then the opportunity to take over the phone show came up. I jumped at it. I packed in news and I went hell for leather doing the phone show. I did that for seventeen years.

The main reason I took the opportunity to move to 98FM was not because of better money or anything like that. The reason was seventeen years of working on nights, seventeen years of going to work at 8.30 in the evening and coming home at 2AM, trying to wind down until 3 or 4AM. Seventeen years of that kind of gets to you. When we got the opportunity to do a daytime show, I said, 'Yep, I have to do that.' I have to take a risk. We had a very successful show on FM104, there was no sign that it was going to end anytime soon. Maybe I was bored and just needed a new challenge. That's what we have at 98FM.

On *Dublin Talks* we have a small team of three people. There's myself, there's Jeremy Dixon and there's Katie McNally. We are the team; we are the show. We do everything ourselves. Jeremy is the producer and his job is to come up with ideas and topics for the show. We have production meetings twice a day so I'm totally involved in the editorial decisions on the show deciding what we're going to talk about. It comes with a degree of responsibility. I'm enjoying the show and the challenge that it's offering. I'm enjoying bringing a different type of radio here in Dublin. The sort of radio we do is controversial at times but it's completely listener driven. They are the ones that dictate to us what we talk about and they are the ones who talk to us about it. My main motivation is to involve listeners in everything that we do on the show.

The reason our show was successful for all the years that we did it was mainly because it had a history. The show had been on for twenty years and that really helps. That's what we find with our new show. It doesn't have a history and it's going to take a couple of years before it does. We weren't afraid to be cheeky; we weren't afraid to offend; we weren't afraid to push the boundaries. One of my favourite memories from all those years was the week that we lived in the window of Cleary's on O'Connell Street. At one stage we had five thousand people outside the window of Cleary's on O'Connell Street to see Westlife in the window with us.

I get a kick out of riling up listeners or having tricky listeners call on. Only the other day I had a guy ring in. We were having a conversation about people's fears of going to Paris in 2016 for the Euros, in the wake of the bombings and this guy rang in to say it was the most pointless topic we had ever had. I absolutely ripped him apart. Sometimes a call just gets to me and says something that triggers something in me. Some might say it's not very professional but if someone annoys me I just lose the plot with them sometimes. That wouldn't be my personality normally but when you get people ringing in with the most ridiculous things, it just winds me up to breaking point sometimes.

I think radio jobs suits all sorts of people. I started off as a complete introvert; someone who was afraid of his own shadow because of the way I had been bullied in school but radio actually brought me out of my shell. Radio gave me a new lease of life. Now it doesn't bother me to stand in front of ten thousand people and speak publicly – as I do sometimes. I'm very comfortable doing it now.

Radio suited me as an introvert and gave me a new lease of life but it's very suitable for extroverts as well. Is there an ideal quality? I don't think so. I think interest in what you're doing is essential. We get people into the station on placement and you know within ten seconds of talking to them whether they're there for the sake of it or if it's something they're truly passionate about.

You can spot the people who are enthusiastic, who want to get involved, ringing in and asking if they can do free work – they are the people that I admire.

College degrees are important but it's most important to get experience. First hand, fingers-on-the-button, experience in radio. I've met student who have done four-year degrees in communications and broadcast and when you meet them they haven't a clue. If you need to work for nothing in a radio station while you're in college, then do it. That's the sort of experience that you need. It's all well and good to have it on paper but if you don't have any practical experience, you're wasting your time. No radio station is going to look at you, no matter what sort of degree you have. If you want to get into radio and onto radio and if you haven't already got experience on the radio, a station isn't going to be interested in you.

I know one guy who is doing a course in DCU, he voluntarily worked in Newstalk for a couple of years. He didn't get paid, he didn't ask to get paid, and he just offered to work. He was a runner and he was lining up guests and stuff like that, but he was getting experience. I know another guy who for the last three years has been working in a small community station in Dundrum. He does a show every week and he has experience. He's already much more appealing to a potential employer who has never set foot in a radio studio.

Ok, they may have done programmes in college during the course in college but you need practical experience on radio. College is important alongside that. The toughest part of the job is coming up with ideas that people are going to want to talk about, topics that are going to create interest, that are going to create debate, get people and annoyed and most importantly, get them talking. Some days it's going to be easy because there's plenty to chat about in the news, other days we have to be a little more creative.

If I could give me teenage self advice, I'd say don't do it. I hate to say it because I've worked in radio all my life but that's what I'd say. I'd tell myself to go to college. My son has got a marketing commerce degree from DCU, he speaks French fluently as a second language. I don't. I don't have a degree; I don't speak a second language. I kind of look back on that and go, 'Oooh maybe I should have.' I'd say, 'Pursue the whole radio thing if you want but get a degree and go to college. College isn't like school, you're not going to be bullied there like you were in school.'

I'd advise myself to get a college degree as a fall-back if the whole radio thing doesn't work. I've been lucky that it did but I do think what would have happened if it didn't. I didn't have much to fall back on. Go to college and get some sort of a qualification.

Tracy Clifford

Warm, bubbly and super 2FM DJ Tracy Clifford has loved radio ever since she can remember. From pirate stations, to East Coast FM and SPIN 1038, the on-air bug bit her hard at a young age and she did everything in her power to chase her dream and nail down what is in her heart, the perfect job.

I can honestly say that I am working in my dream job. When I was a little girl my dad used to drive me to school and it was then, listening to breakfast radio in the car that my love of radio began. It was radio was where I heard all my favourite songs and what was going on in the world. From my communion money, I remember buying a cassette tape recorder complete with a microphone. I used to interview my brother and sister and then pretended I was a newsreader, reading the teletext news into the microphone. I had my sights on being Anne Doyle.

As much as I loved radio in my teens but I didn't really know how to get into it. I used to listen to a lot of pirate stations, but I didn't have the confidence to actually become a presenter. So I chose to study radio journalism in college. I loved current affairs, music, and talking – of course – so it seemed like a way in to get a feel for being on air. It was in college that I met a guy who worked in setting up pirate radio stations. We shared a love of dance music at the time, so we talked about doing a radio show from his house. We turned our words into actions and that was it; the 'on-air' bug bit me.

I started doing my own weekly pirate show – while studying broadcast journalism and it gave me a great start. I must say I was absolutely awful. On my first show I stole all the radios out of mum's house so she couldn't hear me! I specifically recall the one time I went to put up the fader to go live only to completely lose my nerve and pulling it back down again. I think this happened about six times before I eventually plucked up the courage to talk!

The only way I can describe why I chose radio is because I loved listening to it. I loved music, loved knowing what was going on in the world, and I loved being made laugh. Some people who work in radio may be enticed into the industry by the 'production' and sound side of things, but for me, it was about getting to know personalities and hearing great music.

To this day, there is nothing like the buzz of having a great time while you are 'working' and making someone smile by either telling them something funny, talking to a listener on air, or playing awesome music. It really is a fantastic job to have and I'm really lucky.

I suppose I took the traditional road to working in national radio. I studied radio journalism and then went on to get a degree in media production and management. During this time I worked on a pirate station for on-air experience. Anyone wanting to work on-air nowadays has the option of working on online stations – for me the only option before legal radio, was pirate. When I completed my degree, I sent my CVs out to a lot of different stations and East Coast FM got back to me. There, I worked in the newsroom and I progressed to reading news on air and producing a current affairs show called *The Morning Show with Declan Meehan*. It was the best learning experience and training I ever had.

I then went on to Spin 1038 and worked as the news editor for four years until I started working on *Fully Charged*. I actually think I got the job on breakfast radio because I was a bit of a messer in the office.

From years of working experience, I can honestly say on-air gaffes are the beauty of the business. Working on a breakfast show was the funniest time in my life, because it was a fly-by the-seat-of-your-pants sort of show! On live radio, you sort of forget that you are actually on air talking to thousands of people and not only talking to that one person in studio with you. It surprises all my friends and family that I haven't ever sworn on air – that may still happen!

When I do mess up – I always find that you have to laugh at it and move on. There are too many gaffes to mention, but doing awkward interviews with pop stars is always something which you can make fun of it later, if the interview doesn't go too well. Some interviewees may be tired or bored with doing press all day but then again, some are absolutely brilliant to chat to. I always find that people with the ability to laugh at themselves and not take things too seriously are the best to chat to. I have also found that some of my not-so-great interviews are not actually because the celeb is rude, it's probably because they are exhausted or maybe having an 'off day'. We all have them. But then of course there are interviews when you are a bit star struck- Kanye West and Tom Cruise being prime examples. It always feels like the interview isn't going great – but then when you watch or listen back to it, it's totally fine. That's the nervous energy taking over, so you need to ignore that.

I have to say, having worked on *Fully Charged* with Ryan Phillips for seven brilliant years and leaving on such a high, I am so proud of that show. Working on a national station is every radio presenters dream, and I feel darn lucky to be honest! I also feel that there is a responsibility to represent women on air. I am proud that I am a national broadcaster and hopefully more girls will follow suit in the future. Some of my peers told me that RTÉ hiring me sent out a great message to girls so I am chuffed about that. Now my responsibility is to deliver. I want people that listen to my show to feel part of an afternoon gang, and get excited about the music I play.

I have two people to thank for my gig on 2FM. I met Dan Healy after a chance encounter at *The X Factor* show in London where we chatted about radio, and Colm Hayes mentioned my name to the powers that be in 2FM. I think my name came up a few times over two years and then when I left SPIN 1038 the timing seemed right. When I got the call that 2FM were interested, I remember being in complete shock and disbelief, but also excited to get cracking.

Like most people, there have been times when I've doubted myself; especially in those very early days of my career. I think it's natural to question yourself, and the radio industry is quite insecure. But I found that if you relax, have fun and be open to learning, it will all work out.

It takes a couple of years for a show or personality to establish so putting focus on the work you do, rather than the big listenership figures that you want is a great approach. Radio is game of chess. Someone has to move slot before another slot is opened up with a new opportunity. So it is wise to have a back-up plan. My back-up plan was journalism and news reading

Variety is the spice of life – there are all walks of life working in radio. To work in radio, first and foremost you must have a love of radio. I think you have to be genuine. People spot a faker and insincerity a mile off! I think it's important to be warm and personable, with a good knowledge of what excites you. Creativity is always key too, as well as an irreverent view on things.

Remember that college is always a good thing. But passion and love is paramount. I also can't express enough how important work experience is. Get it anywhere you can.

For me, my job doesn't feel like work. My dad told me when I was a teenager, 'Find yourself a job you love, and you'll never have to work a day in your life,' and that's very true.

If I could go back in time and give myself advice, I would say, 'If you want to do it – then just do it.' Have confidence in what you do. It's ok to not want to get a 'normal job.' Don't let knock-backs throw you and keep on keeping on. Take the first step. Don't be afraid, and knock on those doors! Oh, and always be open to learning from others – that's exceptionally important.

On silver screen

'For me, cinema is not
a slice of life,
but a piece of cake'
Alfred Hitchcock

There's so much more to the movies than lights, camera, and action! It takes a mini army of incredibly talented people behind the scenes to bring our favourite stories from Star Wars, the Hunger Games, Despicable Me, James Bond and Harry Potter to life

Immerse yourself into the world of film in this chapter, as award-winning actors, producers, stuntmen and special effects directors share their tales of glory, from little kids with big dreams to life both on and behind the glittering silver screen.

Neil Corbould

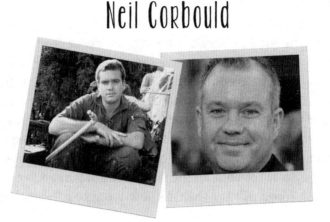

Special effects director Neil Corbould has been working in the movie and TV industry for over thirty years. His wealth of experience has earned him multiple BAFTAs and Academy Awards for blockbuster movies like Saving Private Ryan, Gladiator *and* Gravity *not bad for a kid who left school prematurely with nothing more than barrels of enthusiasm a massive dream.*

Movies were always a big part of my life. I have fond memories of watching films with my mother every Sunday, all the cowboys and Indians flicks. By the time the credits rolled, my siblings and I would be jumping around on the chairs pretending we were shooting each other. Subconsciously, seeing how these movies could take you into another world was a sort of inspiration to me and my career path later on in life.

I have my uncle to thank for sparking my curiosity in film. I found out at a young age that my uncle, Colin Chilvers, was in the film business. I didn't really know what he did but as time went on, when I went to my grandma's house where he was staying, props used to appear. I remember rummaging through the attic once and seeing a spitfire. At that time it was as big as me, this huge model in this house in Kentish Town. I know now it came from the movie *The Battle of the Britain* and that there was also a German plane up there.

Not long after, I began bugging my uncle to take me into Pinewood studios where he worked. It took many months of convincing until he eventually did. By that time he was working on *Superman: The Movie.* I was fifteen-years-old at this point and I remember walking into the Bond stage where the set for fortress of solitude was – that's the big ice set and my first film set experience was watching Christopher Reeves flying down the length of the Bond stage on wires with all the smoke and steam and sparks and everything going off. It's then I knew I wanted to work in film forever.

I was still in education at the time so I applied to my school for work experience. Back then they called it a 'day release.' They'd release you from school to go to work for a day but I sort of turned it round because I loved it so much and only went to school for one day and went to work for the other four days. It grabbed me and took me in from those first few trips to Pinewood. It was like going into another world. What was unusual was that you'd walk into all these sets and you were pretty much in America – American streets and American signposts, seeing that in the UK as a teen was quite surreal.

Work experience consisted of making the tea and sweeping the floor and basically just being nosy. I'd hang around the set as long as I could before somebody told me to do something. At that time I lived in Wimbledon and I used to have to get three trains to get into Pinewood. It would cost me ten pounds go get to work but the production would only give me a fiver a week – my mum subsidised my early career by giving me the money to get to work.

I'd stay there as long as I could before they'd shut the doors at the workshop. I'd be going home late in the dark but it was worth it and to be honest, I still have that feeling now. Instead of a train, I've got a car and I drive from here to Wales, from Wales to Cornwall, from Cornwall to Liverpool. I did that in one day on a couple of movies.

I went back to school just to do my exams and came away with basic grades. The rest I learned on the job. I was very fortunate to be around some very talented people that were happy to show me how to do stuff. I had basic knowledge of engineering, of art and design but it was working with talented people that thought me everything. I'd get in early to work and do some welding stuff on my own, at lunchtimes I used to sit there working on stuff and often after we'd finish for the day, I'd stay on and carry on working. There was always the odd guy that would stay with me and show me different things.

The first time I worked on the smoke machine, being treated as one of the crew, rather than just running around getting them tea and sandwiches, was a special moment for me. I was actually a part of the film making process itself. I was just in the background putting the smoke in but they would tell you where they wanted it and it was my job to get that bit of smoke in there and make it look right.

It was quite an important moment, even when I see the movie now, I know that's what I did right at the back of that scene thirty seven years ago. That was *Superman: The Movie.*

I had to wait five years to get my first credit. It would be unusual for a work experience kid to get a credit, even back then. When I did eventually get my first credit for *Amadeus*, it was a huge, very proud moment for me and it's there forever. It's always going to be there.

I love the challenge of figuring out how to execute big feats on set. The beach landing on *Saving Private Ryan* was quite a feat to achieve, especially with a director like Steven Spielberg. We had a very tight schedule to shoot that sequence, just two weeks. Steven wanted realism. He didn't turn up until one day before we started filming so everything had to be right. It was a very tough shoot. I went and saw dailies each night and was amazed at the look of the movie and what we had achieved. Steven was very happy with everything as well so that was definitely a defining moment.

Working with Steven Spielberg was such a big step for me. He took a chance on me being a very young supervisor at the time and trusted in me to produce all sorts of effects. I must have been in my early thirties.

Ridley Scott is probably one of the best directors I've ever worked with. He's got such a vision and knowledge of the business and life in general; his knowledge of old films is second to none. He can explain it to you but then he can also draw it. He would draw an exact replica or a room or a location and he'll put the explosions in there and bullets. He'll give you a picture at the end and say, 'That's what I want.'

In *Gladiator*, Ridley had a picture by a famous painter and said, 'That is what I want.' It was a gladiator standing on top of another gladiator that he's just killed; the crowds in the background are cheering. The colours, the look, the feel – that spoke loads to us about the look of the movie and what he wanted it to be like. The scene in *Gladiator* in the arena was another special one to execute; the big, long fight sequences with the girls and the chariots.

We had a crowd of two and half thousand people there, cheering and clapping and reacting to the events that we were doing – it was just like a football stadium. Ridley was like the master of ceremonies, rallying the entire crowd and team up to produce mind-blowing chariot effects.

Gravity was again, another movie where I got to work with an incredibly talented director, Alfonso Cuarón. That was a long, long job. I did about two and a half years on and off. It was all about sitting down with him and the team and devising how we were going to shoot these shots. There were no camera rigs in existence that could actually produce the camera angles that we needed or liked for the movie. It was a long slog with all the key people on the movie, going through it scene by scene, shot by shot, figuring out how we were going to achieve the shots we needed for the movie. It was building this specific twelve-wire rig that was the highlight for me. It was something that hadn't been done before.

I was specific about it being a twelve-wire rig so that it would give Sandra Bullock as much support as we could to sell that she was in zero gravity, so that all she really had to concentrate on was her acting; so that she didn't have to tense her muscles up to keep her body straight. It's always a giveaway in films where you can see that the actors clipped from their waist and they're bent over, it never quite looks right. I was part of the Oscar-winning team that produced those effects and that twelve-wire rig we designed, developed and got to the screen, has been talked about a lot since.

When I saw Gravity for the first time, I was so over-whelmed with how good it looked. It was beyond my expectations. All those talented people pulling together, putting their everything into those scenes and for it to end up like that – the sound, the lighting, the visual effects, everything coming together in perfect harmony.

Before the Academy Awards we had all these world renowned visual effects supervisors coming up to us asking how we pulled it off and what technique we used. It even blew away the special effects world. *Gravity* was definitely the toughest production I've ever worked on but also the most rewarding. Because none of the rigs were around, we had to design from the floor upwards.

Often times in my job, we get only one take and everything has to be planned meticulously. On *Saving Private Ryan* we blew up a lot of buildings that we could only do one take on. It was a similar story with landing crafts.

On *Fifth Element*, we had that big spaceship hotel that we blew up and again, we only had one take at that. Those shots are quite thrilling to do. You know you've got one take at it, you know it's got to be right, you've got to put everything in place to make sure it's going to be right. Even on that *Fifth Element* set we put sprinklers up in the roof because we knew there would be a big fire, I mean we could have burned the set down! You just make sure everything's in place and the adrenaline gets pumping and you go and do it and get it in one take.

I love playing with explosives and creating different looks. You've got the Hollywood explosion, which is loads of fire, and I don't like those. I like to play around.

In *Saving Private Ryan*, Steven wanted realism so we studied a lot of WWII footage, how shells blew up and the look of them. On each different movie, we bring a different look to the movie. It's like being an artist. When we shoot tests, we shoot frame by frame and analyse it and if it doesn't look quite right, we'll put a bit more red or yellow.

A few years back, visual effects people were saying our job was going to be a thing of the past but we're stronger now than we've ever been. Directors and productions and audiences like real, practical effects and the movies are now designed and produced around special effects rigs.

I think this job would suit anyone who is into technology; somebody who is very dedicated to working. It's a very antisocial business and you really sell yourself to the devil.

You have to be being willing to put the hours and learn from the people around you. You never stop learning, I'm learning ever day that I come to work.

It's not all about the money. When you're younger, the money's not there and it's definitely not as good as some other jobs. If you stick at it and you love the job and you've got the dedication, the money comes later on. Even now for me it's about working on the right projects, with the right directors and producers and the subject matter. The subject must be right.

It's funny but I don't remember much about my first Oscar win. It's like a flashing dream. We didn't think we were going to win on *Gladiator* because it was a tough year. Thinking back on my career to date, the first shot on *Saving Private Ryan* on the beach brings back the fondest memories for me. Once everything went off, everyone, including Steven, was clapping and cheering– the actors, the extras, everyone. It just went so well and it sort of set the tone for the rest of the movie. *Saving Private Ryan* is the movie I talk about the most. *Gravity* too, because it's still so fresh.

My advice to any budding special effects enthusiast is don't give up, don't take no for an answer. Be very determined in what you want to do, be knowledgeable about the film industry because that's always an important part. It's having the knowledge of what people do, what actors do, what directors do and just enjoy the movie business. It's not about the money it's about creative input.

Work hard, play hard. If you don't know something, never be afraid to ask somebody for advice or help. I still ask people now and I'm sure Ridley Scott and Steven Spielberg still ask people about stuff. Nobody knows everything and you're learning every day. Anyone who says they've never made a mistake hasn't done every much.

Barry Navidi

As a young Iranian boy, Barry Navidi dreamed of making movies. After a move to the UK, years of hard graft, and a chance encounter later, he had that lucky break he'd always dreamed of . . . or so he thought. Life had a few lessons for the budding producer before a firm relationship with Al Pacino and Hollywood could be forged.

As a kid growing up in Iran, I remember going to the drive-in cinema. I was seven-or-eight-years old and I was a complete film buff and watched a lot of movies. When we moved to England I wanted to go to film school. As a kid, from the age of fourteen I had a little camera glued to my hand. I made a lot of little movies, some that I even used in my application to the London Film School. There, I studied directing, writing, camera work, editing – the whole lot. I learned the whole visual grammar of filmmaking.

My mentor was John Huston, the greatest film director of all time. He was a maverick director and through him I met everybody- talent, actors and even Paul Newman. It was a dream come true, meeting all those wonderful people. Producing came into my world by sheer accident. I had my heart set on being a director until one day John Huston said to me, 'Why don't you become a creative producer? You would have complete control of your destiny.' I loved the fact that I could sort of control my destiny a little bit and so from the age of twenty-four or twenty-five, I started producing.

My first gig was *Mr. Corbett's Ghost*. I decided to give it to my buddy, the legendary Danny Huston, to direct. We went to school together and he's an actor now. It was John Huston's last movie before he passed away. Paul Schoefield is in it, one of the greatest English actors. I couldn't get the money from anybody so John Huston made a phone call and there you have it, the money was there and the movie could be made! John really was so good to me.

I'm a big chancer. From day one, I was never afraid to ask for anything and that's an important quality. In life you have to have to be able to ask for help. If you have a passion and a desire and the perseverance to do something, you simply have got to ask.

My passion was film and I got the opportunity to ask, so I asked. All they could say was 'No'. You're going to get rejection throughout your life no matter who you are - you could be a major movie star or nobody, that's part of the game and you have to deal with it. A lot of people are often too scared to ask. You just have to say to yourself, 'Let's go for it.'

When I look at producing a potential screenplay, I have to have a complete passion and love for it. I never rush into it. I nurture it, I massage it, and I keep reading it, working it, giving it around - testing it. Anyone in this industry should always be open to criticism because it's the cheapest bit of the business. It doesn't cost you anything to read a script. Once you become too insecure about your own material, that's no good.

My biggest success and perhaps failure was and is the *Divine Rapture*. I loved it from my first read. Originally it was set in Italy. It was all about questioning your faith, Catholicism and all that stuff. It was a no-brainer for me to set the script in Ireland. I wanted to be in a place where I could do the English language version. It took about a year to adapt the script and work it. Everyone I spoke to wanted to do the picture but I just couldn't get the money. Twenty years ago, it was sort of blasphemous to question the church. I kind of gave up for a little while.

The whole project became possible again one night when I went to a party that I didn't want to go to. It was my agent's, Dennis Selinger, birthday party and I'd been going for years – that year, I simply wasn't feeling it. It sounds spoiled but I didn't want to go to a party and be surrounded by Michael Cane and Ben Kingsley. I'd been before. I'd seen them. I'd met them. I was fed up and wanted to get on with making my movie. I have my sister to thank for changing my mind and I'm glad I did.

At the end of the night I was tired and contemplating leaving when the lady next to me asked me what I did. I went into my story about being a producer and how the agent throwing the party was a dear friend of mine. And then, coincidentally, at the same time, my agent came down and sat next to me. He hugged me and I could tell this lady was impressed. Dennis represented everybody. I told her about my Irish project. I told her how much I wanted to make *Divine Rapture* and that I was still casting. She listened politely and then said, 'What do you think of Marlon Brando?'

That caught my attention immediately – she was his lawyer. She liked my story so much, she promised to pitch it to Marlon. Sure enough, Marlon called me some time later to say that he loved the project and would love to be in involved. Marlon loved the underdog and I was exactly that. I wasn't a Hollywood producer. He was great to me and nobody will ever come close to him. He was one hundred percent behind the project. Still, I should have known the project was in danger. Having Marlon on board was like being on a small boat with a big, elephant. The boat was no doubt going to tilt. Sometimes people call and ask me if they can have Al Pacino in their project and I say, 'No, he won't do it because he'll tilt the boat.' He's simply too big for a small picture. It just doesn't work.

My movie was a small movie but Marlon said 'Yes' and Johnny Depp and Deborah Winger were on board too. Sadly the investors were not forthcoming. Even though I knew there was a risk, I decided to keep going with production and that I wasn't going to stop. Nobody was getting paid, we were all in it for the love. I was working, showing the film to distributors hoping they would pick it up.

We didn't know about the financial situation until a week before filming. I had no idea what was missing, but I knew the cash flow wasn't coming. And then two weeks into filming the investors found out there was money was missing from Deborah Winger's account. Everyone smelled fraud and the whole thing collapsed. Everybody bailed out. I went bankrupt. I had lost everything but Marlon and I became closer. Deborah Winger stood by me too.

Funnily enough, I don't look at it as bad luck, I look at it as a luck that didn't work out.

I took a chance with a passion and my heart without knowing what was really going on. I don't look at it as unlucky because of where it got me to –it would have been unlucky if I had jumped or it had finished my career. I'm a positive guy. When I had cancer, I was lucky to have testicular cancer, which was treatable.

If I had finished the movie, it would never have had so much press as the collapse did. It would have been just another film, perhaps. I was on the front cover of major papers. I didn't pay any attention but it was a huge scandal and to have Marlon Brando involved added extra attention.

The moment the project collapsed, I went straight to L.A.. I wanted to face the music. In Hollywood, they all loved me. Those guys love a comeback. I suddenly became famous. I was being handed movies but I didn't take any. I needed to recover. To lose a picture with this kind of cast was devastating but fate knew what it was doing. It's because of Brando that I ended up meeting Al Pacino and doing a *Pacino* film. From one Godfather to another, it was like winning the lottery.

It if wasn't for the collapse of *Divine Rapture*, I can assure you I wouldn't have made the *Merchant of Venice*.

I hated Hollywood at the time because of what happened to me, the greed in particular. So what did I do? I went and made a movie about greed. I made the *Merchant of Venice*. I asked Marlon if he wanted to be in it. He said, 'No, but give it to that Italian dude, Al Pacino, I'll put you in touch.' One thing led to another and six years later . . .

In this game, honesty is important. Megastar actors are megalomaniacs, all of them. They're crazy. They don't have any friends because of their status. Can you imagine? You're the most famous, iconic figure. Who do you trust? For me to be a part of Pacino and Brando's lives, it's really about trust and likability. You can be passionate, talented and work hard but unless they like you or trust you, you're not going anywhere. They have a lot of choice in producers and directors. They know I have no other motives, no agenda.

I met Al for the first time at the airport in London, when he arrived for the rehearsal of the *Merchant of Venice*. I'll never forget this character walking in, he's kind of tilting to the right and limping, he's bearded. Little did I know he was in character. We really hit it off well and we liked each other immediately. Al is warm, humble and he's got that sweetness about him that you see on screen as well as that same vulnerability –that's why people love him. When we started production, money wasn't exactly in position but I knew that there was a plan and it looked quite good. We had Al. We had Jeremy Irons and Joseph Fiennes. We went for it and everybody showed up, even though the money was tight until the end because the cash flow wasn't there completely.

After the first day of filming, we had dinner afterwards with the entire cast. I decided to have dinner every evening for the cast and crew out of my own pocket. I wanted everyone to get to know each other. Because I wasn't paying them a lot of money, I thought

I might as well look after them in Italy and Luxembourg where we shot the film. Al came every night and sat with the cast and crew. We talked about the day's work, what worked and didn't work. Those dinners encouraged communication and if something wasn't working we were able to resolve it so that the next day, it did work. It was great. If you're going to spend six weeks with anyone, you might as well make the effort to get to know each other. You can see passion and chemistry on screen and I was encouraging that.

A lot of my friends won't read about me for a year or two and suddenly they'll hear I'm doing a movie. I like that element of surprise. People say to me, 'Seven years of doing *Salomé* with Al Pacino, are you nuts, why would you want to do that?' The answer is simple, I love the journey and I love Al.

Salomé was born based on Al's passion. It was his baby. He had done it on Broadway many times. He had personal reasons for wanting to be in L.A. and was quite attached to the idea. He didn't have a script, we didn't have investors but we decided to try it as a pay-as-you-go project. It was a challenge. I asked how long it might take and he suggested three years.

I thought, 'Ok, I've never done a docu-drama but that's fine. I'll spend three years with you and we'll figure out everything together.' It ended up taking six years.

It's funny, because of social media and too much publicity, not too many stars faze me. When they're accessible, when they're on television every day, when you see them all over social media, it's not that exciting meeting them in person. They're almost too accessible, too available. That's almost why movies don't work anymore. Movies that are working now are Marvel movies that have nothing to do with who is in the movie and everything to do with the action. Instead I get more excited by meeting someone completely new with raw talent.

At the moment I have *King Lear* on my radar. There's been a few versions of *King Lear* made but none of them have been all that amazing. It's a challenge because Al wants to do it. Al being a friend now, I'd love to do it for him. If it weren't for him, I'd think about it twice. I'm also making a documentary about acting called *Don't Talk About the Method* with Amanda Palmer.

Honestly speaking, I don't like the film industry because I don't like the film business, the politics and drama but I do love the dream of creating. Creation drives me. The industry itself is not something that excites me as much as creating does. Give me something creative. I love my fellow artists but the business side of it? That really doesn't excite me. That's why Deborah Winger called me a semi-hustler and not a full hustler.

Producing is a vague title. Some producers are only about finance. I'm a filmmaker. In order to be a filmmaker, go to film school and learn a little bit. Read as much as you can. Film school was very helpful to me because I met the right people. I also learned my craft there, or at least a little bit of it. I'm not going to hire you because you have a degree. The degree helps but I would look to other more practical attributes first. If you have the opportunity to work on a production, you'll learn a whole lot more. Make your own short movies. That's what I used to do but it was much more complicated when I was doing it.

Today you can get your cellphone and make a movie because the quality is amazing. I always advise everyone to just go out there and shoot a movie. If you don't like it, delete it. The only way you can get noticed is by your work. No matter how pretty you are, no matter how ugly you are, it doesn't matter, it's about you work. You can put it on Youtube and get noticed. Whether you're an actor, whether you want to be a director, that's what you've got to do. The beauty of it is, it doesn't have to cost anything There's no pressure on you. You just have to keep trying.

The problem is that everyone is impatient today. They want to make it really quickly and be famous. I'm not in it for the fame. Al Pacino isn't in it for the fame. He hates it. He's rebellious about it. He's a stage actor who happens to be movie star and with movies comes fame. Nowadays ninety percent of the kids out there just want to be famous and that's a big mistake. Remember your work *becomes* famous. Go out there and create.

Chris Newman

Former child actor Chris Newman's star is continuously rising. From the small screen to the silver screen, the Irish thespian has been chasing his dream since a very young age. Cast as the young Delaney in Irish feature Song for a Raggy Boy *at the age of thirteen, his passion for acting has grown with him, landing him roles in* Love/Hate, the Clinic, *TV3's* Red Rock *and numerous features.*

My favourite TV shows growing up were *Kenan & Kel, Sabrina The Teenage Witch, California Dreams* –I can still sing the whole theme tune! Basically anything that was on Nickelodeon. It was probably the only TV station my sister and I didn't fight over. I was also all about the blockbuster films. I remember watching *Jurassic Park* in the cinema with my mouth open. Then buying every dinosaur toy I could. I had that Arnie-movie *Last Action Hero* on video and I must have watched it every day for a whole summer.

I decided I wanted to be an actor when I did *Song For A Raggy Boy*. I had been on a few auditions before that and didn't really think much about it. It was something I enjoyed doing but everything changed during *Raggy Boy*. I had the most incredible time on that set. When we wrapped, I was devastated but I thought, 'I can do this for a living!'

My first audition was about two years before I was eventually cast. I met Aisling Walsh in my stage school. It was just something I did for fun on the weekend and once a week after school. We chatted about some pantomimes I'd done the previous year – that was it. She came out to my mam and introduced herself. She didn't seem to do that with anyone else so we thought maybe she saw something in me. But after that, as I've experienced many times in my career, nothing. I quickly forgot about it.

Two years later, I had an audition and my mam immediately recognised Aisling's name. We didn't know I was auditioning for the same film until I was there in front of camera. Due to financial reasons the film had been delayed but Aisling, as she later told me, never forgot me.

I auditioned for the part of Mercier about three times before being asked to read for Delaney instead. We were sent the full script and I saw what was required.

I knew it was a serious film with a serious story but it didn't bother me in the slightest. People forget that I was thirteen. I understand that it's quite young but I'd started secondary school and I was aware of what happens in the world. And at the end of the day, it was just acting.

My brother who was twenty-three at the time was a little more reluctant and told my parents it was too much. Thankfully, they listened to me and said, 'If you're comfortable, we support you.' I went in for the final audition and had to perform the confession box scene where my character describes in great detail what had happened to him. The next day, the part was mine.

Every day on set was great. We played football at lunch and when we weren't needed for a scene. Obviously some days were a little darker due to the subject matter but it really was like a holiday. We all lived together in a local house; a non-stop sleepover with my mates. One day stands out though. We were filming Christmas scenes so there was loads of fake snow. There were a lot of snowball fights to the point where we had to be reminded that we were here to make a movie!

The cubicle scene was the toughest for me. My character is

sexually abused by one of the Christian brothers. It was a closed set so only the people that absolutely had to be there were present; a handful of people. My parents were also there outside the room. It was a weird one because I do so much work nowadays on my characters but I don't remember doing any work at all back then. I would literally just turn up and try to react as naturally as possible to the circumstance. I didn't think through that scene at all. I arrived on set, walked through what would happen then shot it.

When Aisling called action on that first take, I just let go – screams, tears, the works. You have an idea in your head of how scenes will play out, but when you hear action, anything can happen. We only did two takes.

We had a big premiere in Cork where we filmed. It was a little daunting being on a red carpet but my whole family was there with me. It went on to appear at so many amazing film festivals around the world from Sundance to Tribeca. I remember John Travers and I got flown over to Norway for the Bergin Film Festival.

It was an amazing experience. We were treated like kings. Greeted at the airport by a group of people who drove us to our hotel where we discovered we had each had our own king suite! I was fourteen; the day before I was in school in Swords!

I was working on TV shows on my summer holidays throughout school so thankfully I had school to keep me occupied in between jobs. I did a few things after school but there was definitely a period between nineteen and twenty-three where I struggled. I was still doing odd things but nothing like what I'd done as a kid. It was difficult but I always believed I was good enough. I knew I had the talent. The odd time I'd think, 'But is that good enough?' There's so much luck involved in this industry.

Because I'd been working throughout school, I never went to college to train. I decided to go to L.A. where my friend lived. I had a couch to sleep on. I joined an acting school and spent the next year or so going back and forth. The longest time I was there was three months. It taught me so much and made me grow a lot as well. Not just as an actor. The day I landed back in Dublin, my agent rang me and said 'You have an audition tomorrow for a new show. It's called *Love/Hate.*'

Every actor faces rejection. Ninety-nine percent of auditions you go on, you won't get. It will have nothing to do with you. Most directors already have an idea in their head of how the character will be. Chances are, you won't physically be right. It has nothing to do with your ability as an actor. You have to learn to accept that. Obviously that's not always easy. I've been so close to some big parts, only for call back after call back, to be told, 'It didn't work out.' I've cried a few times. It hurts because you want it so bad and you know you can do it. But you just have to take a deep breath and accept that it wasn't to be. You'll get the next one.

I've been privileged to work on many great projects. Filming *Saving The Titanic* was the most rewardingof them all for me. I played an electrician who stayed at his post keeping the lights working until the very end. Every day I'd go on set, my character was facing death. They were long days and I'd leave the set emotionally drained.

When you finish something that you've put your heart into, it's always a proud moment.

Shooting For Socrates was perhaps the most fun I've ever had on set. I'm a huge football fan so to be given to chance to play a living legend such as Norman Whiteside was just incredible. We shot in Windsor Park in Belfast recreating all the goals scored in the qualifiers and then went to Spain and did the same for the goal in Mexico '86. It was a dream-come-true.

I'm currently working on *Red Rock* for TV3 and you couldn't ask for a better group of people; from cast to crew. Another reason I'm enjoying it so much is that I feel I've finally completed that transition from child to adult actor. I've played a lot of characters that seem younger or have an edge of vulnerability to them. In *Red Rock*, I'm playing a detective. It's a great challenge to play someone with authority, who has a swagger about him – he's got a gun for god's sake! I feel like a big kid playing cops and robbers.

Every day in this industry is different. It's tough when you're not working but when you are, you remember why you do it. You get to experience things you never thought possible. The perks of what I do is seeing my work and having people respond to it. Being able to move people feels great. Sitting in a packed cinema about to see your work, with your heart beating out of your chest, there's no other feeling like it. I honestly can't think of a single con.

I have no interest in being a 'celebrity' or anything like that. I'd consider myself 'Z list' so if someone recognises me from something, it's always a lovely feeling because it doesn't happen very often and they're always very complimentary. Come back to me if I'm ever Tom Cruise level!

My dream role is anything emotionally challenging. As humans, we naturally hide our emotions. We don't 'show' how we feel. Sometimes it's nice to just be able to let go.

Chris' Tips for Nailing an Audition:

Preparation is key;

You have to walk into that room comfortable. If you're not prepared, you won't be.

Bring your own traits and quirks to the role.

We are all unique. Don't be afraid to shine through your character. But remember to elevate yourself to who the character is. Don't drag the character down to who you are.

Try to make interesting choices.

Everyone is going into the audition and acting well. But everyone is interpreting the character differently. Try not to play it safe.

Remember, every audition is an opportunity to impress a director or casting director.

Even if you think you're not right for the part, go in there and blow them away. They'll remember you.

Evanna Lynch

Like a lot of teenagers growing up, Evanna Lynch adored Harry Potter.
Unlike a lot of teens, at the age of fourteen, she found herself with a star-
ring role in one of the world's most successful movie franchises of all time.
Quicker than you can say 'wingardium leviosa,' this Termonfeckin girl's
life spiralled, going from small town girl to Hollywood starlet as part of
the J. K. 's 'big seven', alongside Harry, Ron, Hermoine, Ginny, Neville
and Draco

From an early age, my parents really instilled me with the belief that
I could be anything I wanted. I've been through the whole gamut
of potential career paths from 'magical cat' to playschool teacher to
acrobat, to artist. I feel like I settled on acting because I couldn't
make up my mind and acting allows me to do a bit of everything.

I know this will sound daft but my very first urges to take the
stage and become a part of the story was at Sunday mass. Our
church had one mass a week called a 'children's mass' where
basically a bunch of children would sit up on the altar and sing
glory to God and stutteringly answer the priests' questions. I didn't
care about the content of their words or the quality of this little

pious production. I just felt terribly frustrated that I was part of the boring, blank-eyed mass of people who were sat mutely observing the storytellers. I had a lot of questions for my mum. Who were these very privileged children? How did they get up there? What gave them the sacred right to ascend the two plush golden-carpeted steps up the altar and hold our eyes and attention for an hour each week? And it wasn't that I wanted to be the centre of attention and have my friend's grannies tell me how movingly I'd read that prayer of the faithful. It was simply that I wanted to be part of the story, inside the action, making things happen, rather than on the outside, silently looking in. Being a mere audience member made me feel like I was missing out on life.

So I started starring, as I saw it, in the children's mass and entered the holiest period of my young life. As soon as I realised that the people on TV were playing princesses as a job and that there were pure acting classes available in the Little Duke Theatre in Drogheda, my fascination with the world and art of acting began and my short-lived but pivotal role as a holy servant of God swiftly came to an end.

I attended the Little Duke Theatre for several years, taking drama exams before making the decision to audition for *Harry Potter*. I was aware that the Potter films were ongoing and casting people from my age bracket. I had fallen in love with Luna Lovegood when I read the fifth book and from that moment on I had my heart set on playing her. But the main reason I wanted to play her was because I felt I understood her and that she meant more to me than she would to a professional actress or any young girl for that matter. I felt a fierce protectiveness over her and the determination that the movies should not 'mess her up'. I've never really felt so right for anything in my life, I usually get nervous and start to doubt myself. But her story and the desire to honour her was a greater concern than my own and I think that's what gave me confidence. I was able to transcend my petty insecurities and self-consciousness because I had so much love for her that I forgot myself. I was just a portal for her soul.

That's kind of what has become my process, I have to fall in love and have the utmost respect for the character I play. Otherwise I'm too in my head.

The opportunity to audition came through an open audition. Jo didn't have anything to do with my casting process. I don't say that proudly, it is just a fact. We were in touch already for a different reason and that was because I'd wrote to her as a fan and told her about an eating disorder I was struggling with. She helped me so much through those few years and her encouragement definitely gave me confidence when going to that audition and stepping in front of the casting directors. I wasn't nervous at first. I had a purpose and my mind was set on that. I felt utterly ready to play Luna. I wasn't thinking about the possibility of a career or fame or any of that stuff that comes with it – those were things I certainly wasn't prepared for. It wasn't like a maths exam I hadn't studied for or a cute boy I couldn't look in the eye. I felt like I was exactly where I needed to be.

You only feel nervous when you feel like you're not enough for the given task. If you shift the focus and make it about something outside of yourself, a higher purpose, a service, then you can go beyond yourself. That said, there was a heart-poundingly tense moment during the initial stages of the open audition, when we were brought into a room and told to line up in rows of approximately thirty. All we had to do was step forward and say our name and where we came from. And I knew that this was a moment of total surrender to luck. This process of elimination was simply based on superficial things like your look, height, voice quality, demeanour. You could be the perfect Luna but if you were six-foot-two and towering over Daniel Radcliffe you wouldn't make it through the next door!

I really felt for the girls who didn't get past that part as there was nothing they could have done. But I breathed a sigh of relief that I got through.

When I finally got seen individually by the casting directors I felt calm and centered and read the scenes they had provided naturally. The Luna they had written for the movie was my Luna. It was only when they started inviting more and more casting people in the room and I, as a Potter fanatic who had scoured the film credits and written to the casting directors numerous times, began to recognise people's names, that I got nervous. It was all getting a bit real. But I got through it and a week later I had a screentest with Daniel Radcliffe and David Yates.

The scene took place in Dumbledore's office. It was all completely, absurd and overwhelming for me. They were leading me around the study casually introducing me to my teenage crushes and striding hurriedly past giant chess pieces. There were moments where I just couldn't speak because I was trying to process every-thing and I often giggled to myself – that state of awe must have contributed greatly to my dreamy, spaced-out Luna air that the producers loved. I remember Daniel Radcliffe talking to me, trying so hard to put the superfan at ease but I was so used to watching him on screen that I kept forgetting to talk back and I would let him awkwardly keep rambling. He was really kind to me.

At the end of the day David Yates gave me a copy of *The Order of the Phoenix,* which I thought was a bit daft because of course I already had three, and he signed it, 'It was great working with you!' and I took that as a sign-off. I went back to the fancy hotel room Warner Bros had provided and I sobbed my heart out while my dad tried to console me because I thought I had messed it up and the dream was over. Thankfully, it turned out to be paranoia.

The casting agent had said she'd call and I had this irrational fear that if we missed the phonecall, they would give up and give the part to the next best Luna. I was absolutely driven mad.

Suddenly I got a call on my mobile and it was the casting agent and I distinctly remember her saying, 'We want you to be our Luna.'

I gave my mum and sister the thumbs up, stuttered thank you repeatedly and hung up. It was too much to process at once though. I mean, I was the most ecstatic I've ever been. But I could not wrap my head around the enormity of it.

All I knew was that I wasn't allowed to tell anyone outside my family for ten days, that I had a lot of homework to do and that teachers and friends would think it suspicious if I didn't do it. So I did my homework. I think my family and I had a little cake and got excited but it was very much a matter of taking it one step at a time.

By the time it came to filming, I had wrapped my head around the whole thing a little better. All I can remember is pure excitement! It didn't feel like work at all. I couldn't relate to the crew complaining about exhaustion or wondering what they were serving for lunch today. I just wanted to *live* the stories. You could say I was method acting but I was just being a kid. I also wanted everyone to stay in character, which they did not. I think at that time I was in denial of the fact that these were normal people. I would turn my head away when I saw Dan and Tom Felton laughing and joking together. I remember being flabbergasted by crew members who said they hadn't read the books and realising that this was just work for them.

And when the day came to an end and we hadn't made the shot list required but had to stop because of child labour laws I would go up to the first assistant director and tell him I didn't mind working overtime and I absolutely swear I won't tell the lawyers.

I was just incredibly naive about the business and process of film-making but I was having a fabulous time. I definitely felt like a fraud and tried to be perfect every time. Eventually I realised that the perfectionism was holding me back. The first few scenes we did were the ones in the 'Room of Requirement' where Harry is teaching us spells and it was a great place to start because they were big crowd scenes and having so many young actors there made it fun and easier to forget the cameras. The entire filming process was a whirlwind and I was in my element. But little was I prepared for just how much my life would change. I suppose I was lucky because it was a bit different back then. Social media wasn't so prevalent. I wasn't comfortable with the fame part at all as I still identified way more with being a fan. I knew how to act but I didn't know how to be a celebrity and was very awkward with it at times.

I've grown up a lot since my Harry Potter days and I've learned a lot too. For one, I realise now that I can only work on projects I love. I have to go with my heart. I made a decision a while ago to not audition for things that don't fascinate me or that I wouldn't watch. I kind of have the same rule with dating; the guy has to be utterly fascinating; otherwise he is not worth the time.

I have no time for being lukewarm or apathy. I can only take characters I respect, that elevate my spirit and make me a better person. I know now that unless the story or character really move me, I am better off turning it down and continuing to follow my passion elsewhere.

I've also learned that you can't let your happiness depend on your work. You have to find something more concrete and deeper. This will sound like a platitude but you have to go within and find the source of love there. Work will come and go but your love for your self must not disappear when the work does. You're so much more than what you do. And you can't let your happiness ride on something so fickle as your work.

You have to go back to that young child you were who did what she did purely because she loved it, not because she loved the feeling of being loved. It's an industry of great highs and crushing lows and you simply cannot lose yourself amidst the chaos.

I've learned that you need to be assertive and bold about expressing your goals and intentions. Waiting for life to happen to you is a childish attitude that you must grow out of. Nobody will come knocking on your door and offer you your dream job. They don't know the unique essence you have to offer. They haven't seen it before and it's up to you to show that to them. You have to blow their minds with it. You have to be the thing they couldn't possibly have imagined.

People are all so busy chasing their own dreams and doing their own thing so you have to make them stop and pay attention. And they will because no matter how busy everyone us, we want to be inspired. We all want something to catch us off guard and make us see the world differently.

I like that acting gives you total permission to explore sides of yourself you otherwise wouldn't. I've had so much more access to life through acting. But you just can't plan those moments of real life happening and all you can so is try stay open as much as possible.

Of course people have perceptions of me from my work on the Potter films. I don't resent that because it has opened way more doors than are shut. It is a name that carries so much weight and usually means people will at least consider me. I know that there are perceptions I have still not broken down but I don't mind because I know it rests completely in my hands to change them or not.

My proudest moment was getting the role of Emily in My Name Is Emily. I was getting to the point where I was beginning to worry if the *Harry Potter* thing was a fluke and should I resume my abandoned dream of being a 'cat lady'.

The script was the best thing I'd read in ages so for the creator of that thing which so inspired me to trust me with his work was a huge honour. And it was a role I pursued avidly. You feel a greater sense of triumph when you win something you've fought hard for. I think the biggest 'pinch me' moment was when J. K. Rowling said in an interview that I had influenced how she wrote the character of Luna in the seventh book. That's just one I'll never quite get my head around.

For anyone hoping to enter the wonderful world of acting, what are you waiting for? Join an acting class and get to work! Do it as much as you can, try on as many different characters so you can learn about yourself and what you love.

Put yourself out of your comfort zone often, that's the quickest way to have brand new experiences. Read lots too! Reading gives you experiences and feelings you may not otherwise uncover. Basically, get your buttons pushed.

Also, don't worry about getting 'there'. Acting is one of those beautiful jobs at which you only get better with age. With most jobs the deterioration of youth, beauty and all those attractive facilities, spells less work or early retirement. As an actor you never have to worry about that. Your work will only get stronger. The more life experience you have, the more loves, the more heartbreak, the more mistakes, the richer and more textured your work becomes.

After all, it is your real life that feeds your acting life so don't wait to be 'successful' to start enjoying your real life. So don't get bent on purely 'being an actor'. In many cases actors who started young, child actors get derailed by the pressure to live up to their early success because they got it before they had fully developed a strong sense of self.

All the best actors I know have side-passions, hobbies and even lifetimes of experience before they turned to acting. So stop being in such a rush. You can't really control how 'successful' you will be or which jobs you'll land. You just have to keep showing up and if you're brave enough, putting all of your heart and soul into your work and detaching from the result. And in the meantime keep living your life to the max.

How to Nail an Audition

Learn your lines!

Inside out and back to front! Learn them while doing an activity like bouncing a tennis ball so that you *really* know them. Knowing your lines will give you the ease and freedom to focus on the important stuff and let that flow.

Don't be late.

I still struggle with this one but oh, what a difference it makes when I'm ten minutes early. Auditions are already plenty stressful. You want to do everything you can to eliminate nerves. Showing up late is disrespectful of the casting agent's time. They already have so many actors to see so it makes their job easier if they can just cross you off the list. Don't give them any reason to cross you off, especially not such a silly one as bad time-keeping. If you show up late you automatically put yourself at a disadvantage. You are apologetic and indebted to them for waiting for you. You probably won't feel the confidence and freedom to totally own your role and will be wondering if the casting director actually hates you now. Save yourself this anxiety and just show up on time, and be on time, by that I of course mean be early.

Imagine that the casting agent and director are your dear friends and treat them as such.

I've heard people say, 'Pretend it's your callback,' and it's the same idea. You have to walk in there knowing these people already love you because that way they will get the best version of you. They'll get the real, warm, relaxed and confident version of you. Think of how you are with strangers, versus how you are with your closest friends. You know your best friends love you no matter what so you trust them with every piece of you. With strangers you don't trust them so you hold back, you are not so forthcoming and friendly, and you're probably a lot cagier and less likeable. And basically all the casting people want to see is your true self and all your beautiful colours. So walking in there acting like they already love you, tricks you into opening up to them. It brings forth charisma and that is what will catch their attention.

The alternative is going into the room worrying about what they think and trying to read them. Your focus is on your inadequacies, not the work. The casting director will spot your desperate need to please from a mile off and be repelled by it. They want you to inspire them, not pander to them. The thing is they'll find out eventually and it's better you work with the people whose weirdness matches your own, trust me.

Andreas Petrides

Hollywood stuntman Andreas is one of the UK's leading stunt performers, coordinators, fight arrangers and action directors. With an impressive career spanning twenty-three years and over five hundred productions, Petrides has worked with both acting and directing royalty. His impressive credits include blockbusters such as Star Wars, Gladiator, James Bond *and even* Batman.

As a child I was extremely hyperactive and always doing crazy things that drove my parents up the wall. Looking back, I really made it an interesting time for them. For as long as I can remember I used to watch classic black and white silent films on my dad's old projector and I would copy the slapstick gags they performed.

I witnessed Buster Keaton perform a run-up-the-wall somersault which I thought was amazing and decided to attempt this in my back garden using the back wall and an old mattress.

The first attempt was unsuccessful, with me landing upside down, however I persisted and by attempt three I had cracked it! I've always loved stunts and action in the movies but I never knew how I would go about doing it professionally.

Personally, I have never been one for dreams, I have always believed dreams are for dreamers and goals are for grafters. I remember at secondary school, my careers teacher asked us students what we wanted to be when we left school. I put my hand up and said, 'I want to be a stuntman in the movies.' I remember my teacher laughing and saying I required a degree in Physics and

Mathematics to become a professional stunt performer and I thought, 'Well that's the end of that!'

As a child growing up I have always loved many sports and could never pick just one to stick to. I didn't know it then but this helped me in becoming a versatile and adaptable stunt performer. Because of my love for martial arts, Bruce Lee was an inspiration to me, however my father Thalis was an amazing man and was always my idol, his guidance and belief have always driven me to be the best I can.

I've had many interesting career choices, from being in the circus to a breakdancer and even the army. My time with the circus was tough as I was always under the pressure of performing to large audiences and to the same high standard every time. It was also very rewarding and gave me live performance confidence and some great new skills that have helped me in my stunt career.

My breakdancing career started when a friend of mine came back from a trip to L.A. and brought back with him videotapes with some clips of this new form of dance called 'street dance'. I thought it was amazing and started to pick up the moves pretty quickly. I then got together with my brother and a few friends and formed a team.

We started performing at a few small venues and luckily were approached by an agent. Before we knew it we were on a tour in Europe and then performing on numerous TV shows and commercials. I had numerous special moments, including my team making a pictorial book called *Street Dance*. I also performed solo on major TV commercial around that time.

As a child I always had a fascination with the army and always had soldiers and Action Men. It was due to circumstances with my first application to register as a stuntman being declined that I made the decision to join the army. I served with both the parachute regiment and army commando units which gave me numerous skills which have all been a great aid in my career.

I remember my first paid stunt job was on an industrial safety video about why harnesses must be worn. I played a worker on a steel girder sixty foot up and had to lean too far and fall from the girder about eight foot and hang as it becomes clear that, luckily for me, I had a safety harness on.

I've since progressed since that first gig. Today I work in fifteen different areas of stunts, including sword and weapon work, high falls, wire and rope work, fire work, vehicle work, explosions, animals and computer-generated imagery work. The variety is huge and it's what keeps me from getting bored. It's just not possible! Generic stunt work, fighting and sword work are the primary and most used skills of any good working stunt performer, it's our 'bread and butter.' I have worked substantially in all the those areas and have no particular favourite as I love to work in all of them. Being versatile keeps the work fresh and non-repetitive. The big advantage with working on big movies apart from having a big action budget is rehearsal time.

With both *Star Wars* and *Gladiator* I had months to work with the artists. I break the training into three phases. The first phase is about teaching the fight techniques , the second about teaching the routine and the third about teaching the style, becoming the warrior/character. On *Star Wars*, both Liam and Ewan had already had previous fight experience prior to filming. Russell Crowe, on *Gladiator*, however, had not had any previous experience whatsoever. You wouldn't think it but sometimes the artists having previous experience can be negative as they may have bad habits from a particular fight style or martial arts background and it can sometimes be difficult to change. Generally the more time I can get to work one on one with them, the better they become and the quicker we can banish the bad habits.

I have so many favourite projects that I have worked on for various reasons. Some may be because of the particular stunt I performed; some because of the fun with the stunt guys on the job; some for the amazing locations all over the world. As a child, the *Bond* and *Star Wars* movies were a huge inspiration to me and to be working on them many years later was very cool.

I have always been loved the rush of adrenalin, however we as stunt professionals are not daredevils, anyone can do a job once and smash themselves up! We may be required to do jobs, multiple times, each time as good as the last, so we have to calculate everything. If you are required to fall down a flight of metal stairs or to be hit by and roll over a car, technique is essential and I always have used a saying, 'If you can get away with it use it' – that includes body padding and crash mats.

The job as stunt professionals is to make sure each stunt can be achieved both safely and correctly to what is required from the director and the script. I have had a few jobs go wrong due to certain things, but I have learnt from them and make sure it can never happen again. I would say this career is not a hobby and it becomes your life, you must be dedicated to your craft, both physically and mentally. Many believe they have what it takes but find out that they do not. If you really want to do it, don't let anyone stop you! I have always followed the words of the late great American stuntman Dar Robinson –'Why grow up when you can make movies?'

I love passing on my skills to keep the next generation of stuntmen safe and confident. I set up the British Action Academy. Along with my stunt colleagues we are training the younger generation of action performers and we are passionate about passing on the essential skills and training needed to become good stunt performers.

For anyone thinking of stunt work as a career, good, quality training is essential. Remember to look after your body, follow your goals and go and fulfill your destiny.

On Line

'Don't let the noise
of others' opinions,
drown out your
own inner voice'
-Steve Jobs

Since its inception, the Internet has become a phenomenon bigger than anyone could possibly have predicted. This whole new digital world at our fingertips has made the planet a smaller place, connecting generations across the globe, and unifying them in a unique sphere where anything is possible and indeed anything goes.

Nobody 'gets' social media better than the young generation. Teens can make millions from the comfort of their own homes using apps and sites like Youtube as both soapbox and office space.

Over the next few pages, some of Ireland's biggest young influencers open up their hearts and digital worlds for a unique insight into the wonders of the word wide web.

Riyadh Khalaf

Radio host and producer, Riyadh Khalaf loves YouTube, but it hasn't always been this way. Running a successful channel on the mega site had been a dream for years but persistent trolls had him signing off for over seven years. To subscriber's delight Riyadh's back with a bang, making noise, going viral and amassing an army of loyal fans.

I remember being around sixteen-years-old and using crappy dial-up Internet to check out this new website called YouTube. It had loads of random videos on it and I came across a guy, about my age, in his bedroom just chatting to the camera and I was absolutely mesmerised. Within two minutes this complete stranger felt like my best friend and I found myself searching for more and more of his videos. It was the first 'YouTuber' I had ever seen.

Within an hour I took what money I had, bought a webcam and taught myself how to do basic editing. From watching this guy online I knew I would love to be part of it and give it a go myself. This 'guy' was Tyler Oakley. At the time he had only a few hundred subscribers. Today he has over seven million. In a bizarre yet beautiful full circle-moment I got to meet Tyler two years ago and since then we have become friends and chat online from time to time. I will always thank him for inspiring me to start!

I ventured into YouTube by uploading short comedy videos of about two-to-three minutes in length. They were unbelievably low quality and I cringe watching back now. They are set to private on my channel, so I can only see them. While I cringe, I also feel a huge sense of pride in how far I've come and that I was one of Ireland's first ever YouTubers.

They are somewhat of a digital time capsule allowing me to look back on that part of my life when I was going through a lot of difficult changes. These videos were an outlet for the creativity that I had bursting in me day and night and a place that I could be myself and a place that I could be happy amongst so many fears about coming out and my sexuality.

After time, I began to get a barrage of hateful comments on my videos – many coming from the same three or four people, who would daily attack my character, my voice, the fact that I was a little effeminate and often tell me to kill myself. They would call me 'queer', 'fag', 'sick' even before I had come out and that really scared me.

Those persistent comments and the fear that these faceless profiles were people in my school or circle of friends affected my self-confidence hugely. There were few support structures in place on YouTube in the early days and so I went to the police who essentially told me they could not do nothing. As a result I left YouTube for seven years. Something I wish I had never done. My heart breaks for that young boy who was so scared that he had to quit the one thing that made him happy.

Last year I had a light-bulb moment. I realised I didn't care about other people's opinions anymore. I still had a burning desire to make great content and my dormant channel still existed on YouTube so I made a return to my online home and have never been happier.

Having a successful YouTube channel is a full time job. Juggling it with a 'real' job is something that almost kills me from exhaustion week in, week out but I keep making content because the joy I get from it outweighs the late nights and missed family dinners.

I upload once a week at the moment. From Tuesday to Friday I am thinking of ideas and making sure I have everything I need to film a video including props, lighting, microphones, camera and people who I might need to appear in the video or film for me.

Saturday is my shoot day. I will wake up early, shower and set up the room before filming for an hour or two. Sunday is edit day. I am a perfectionist so an edit usually takes me six to eight hours. On Monday I tease the video on social media, upload it at 6PM and then promote it on all my social media channels. By Monday night after an upload I spend hours replying to comments and drinking wine, usually.

To be noticed and have your channel rise above the masses you have to have a good idea. Once that is there then everything else usually falls into place. The idea must be emotive. It should shock, enrage, evoke pity or fits of laughter. A video that does none of that will never reach millions of people.

Every YouTuber dreams of going viral and if they say they don't, then they're lying! The whole concept of creating content and uploading it for public consumption around the world means that naturally your goal is to have your hard work seen and appreciated by as many people as possible.

When it happens, it's the most insane experience you could ever go through. You make a video and put it out into the world and for one reason or another, individuals and massive media outlets latch onto this piece of footage that you made in your spare time and before you know it you are being featured on the homepage of Buzzfeed, Daily Mail, E! News, Cosmopolitan, Huffington Post and BBC News – to name a few. Things get so insane that your phone simply does not stop buzzing with emails, tweets, texts and calls.

My biggest video is 'Mom Reads Son's Grindr Messages' and

it currently has three million views. The idea came to me one day when I was driving. I was trying to think of something creative, entertaining and full of shock value and then in that moment it came to me. It took me three months to convince my mom to film the video but once she did, I had a feeling I was on to a winner.

Within hours it was shared all over the globe and we still get stopped in the street because of it. I've been shopping in New York, clubbing in London or at a garden centre in Dublin and people still recognise mom and I from the video. It was the turning point for my channel. I was nervous about the reaction to it considering I was potentially putting my own mother into the public firing line but thankfully she shone like a star and is now dying to make an appearance in another video!

It got so hectic that I was awake for two days with just three hours in between because I was doing phone interviews with radio stations and websites as far afield as Sydney. While all of this is happening your channel can double or triple in size in a matter of hours.

I was so sleep deprived at one point that I actually had to place my phone on airplane mode in order to get some uninterrupted sleep! It's only after things calm down in the weeks following a viral upload that you realise this video or videos have changed your life forever.

Although I've had two virals, I now focus just as much on small-scale videos that are directly aimed at a small number of super loyal viewers. Videos where I answer questions about myself go through my memory box or vlog a big family occasion will never go viral but that's the point, they're not supposed to.

People always ask me what my channel is all about, how I would describe it in three words and those words would be 'I don't know'. It's impossible for me to boil it down to that because I cover so many genres and topics. Being so broad might be damaging but the reason is because I get so bloody bored doing one thing. I can literally go from LGBT rights to satire to life advice from the elderly to skin care and then back to comedy and satire in the space of a month.

My mind has always been a bit all over the place. If you look at the uploads on my channel you're essentially getting a peak into the madness of my thoughts and interests. I often listen to classical music and Oprah after work and then switch over to dubstep and rave music in the same session.

I live for shows like *Air Crash Investigation* and David Attenborough documentaries but I love *Big Brother* and *X Factor* just as much. Life is about variety and mixing things up. Otherwise one might go insane!

The only single consistent thread running through all my videos is that I am in all of them. It is my voice, my idea and my passion that I make sure people see. The joy of YouTube is that I can use it to paint a picture of who I am as a person – my light, my shade, my annoyances and my happiness. I have explored the idea of just doing comedy but I'm afraid that I'm not funny enough to be perfectly honest. Overall my aim is to have a super-varied channel of funny, heartfelt, inspiring and divisive videos while building a loyal and entertained fan-base and reaching milestones in the numbers of subscribers I have and other creators that I want to work with.

Once upon a time, negative comments were my biggest fear. Today they simply entertain me. I read them and almost thank the writer for giving me the time and effort to spew such nonsense under my work. What these 'Keyboard Terrorists' don't realise is that they are promoting me and my videos by engaging with them at all!

How I deal with their nastiness is by remembering it was awful people like these who drove me off YouTube in the first place and

I will never give another person or group of people that control over my life ever again. I focus on the positive comments, which are about ninety-five percent of all feedback. I laugh at how bizarre some of the comments are and finally I use these comments for content! My 'Reading Mean Comments' video with Panti Bliss got over one hundred thousand views for example. Not too shabby.

YouTube has opened doors for me in one year that I have been trying to open by myself in traditional media for seven years to no avail. It has changed my life and I am shocked daily by the opportunities I'm being offered. This shock very quickly transforms into deep appreciation and pride for the journey I've been on so far.

I was invited by Google to speak at their European HQ to three hundred brand executives about my YouTube story and how we as creators collaborate with brands and charities. This was one of the most nerve-racking things I've done but gave me such a confidence boost when it comes to public speaking. Through this I have built a strong relationship with Google and YouTube and we are working on a very exciting secret project right now!

I've met so many amazing young people who told me that my videos have helped them through tough times and that I inspired them to chase their dreams. It's simple why teenagers and young adults prefer YouTube to traditional media like TV and radio. Online the viewer feels like they can really connect with the person they choose to follow and watch.

They can comment on a video and expect to get a response, they can tweet and expect an exchange from that YouTuber, they can meet them at events and they can really see past the 'lights, camera, action' of television and truly see the real human behind the camera. On YouTube creators like me try to be one hundred percent authentic and true to ourselves, flaws and all. This way we not only accept what we may have once felt insecure about but we also empower the young people who view us to accept their perceived flaws and dislikes.

Being super-interactive and full of two-way communication is not the only thing that sets online video apart. It's the fact that a viewer can, over time, watch and enjoy seeing their favourite creator grow, age and reach their dreams. On YouTube we are not handed pre-manufactured 'stars', we are there from their birth and feel proud to watch them grow for it is the genuine ones who receive the greatest success over time.

YouTube in its nature is on demand and that's another reason it appeals so much to so many people. You can share it with your friends on virtually any online platform.

Money is always the big question on everyone's lips when it comes to YouTube. I actually find it quite rude when complete strangers essentially ask you what your yearly salary is – as if they have a free pass to ask because you make the money through YouTube videos?

Saying that, instead of divulging amounts I always find it interesting to talk about the ways in which a creator can make money for him or herself and eventually make it their full-time job. For me, I see it as a very well paying hobby but not quite a full-time job just yet. I don't think I will ever have it as my only form of work because I would miss the idea of being part of a team, something social and bigger than me . . . who knows, that might change!

YouTube aside, for years I've been working successfully in radio. Radio was one of my first loves. I began by doing a work-experience placement in a local station and then, at the age of fifteen set up my own pirate radio station from my bedroom, totally illegal, but I didn't care, I loved it! From there I went to college to study broadcasting for five years while also working in temporary and internet stations. After a while I managed to break into commercial radio as a researcher, then contributor, producer, presenter and finally a full time entertainment news anchor.

Radio may not be the most glamorous medium but it is one of the most hands-on and exhilarating. When there is an on-air technical emergency or some breaking news, you are thrust on air, with a moment's notice and given no choice but to perform and that certainly wakes you up!

In the new year I will leave radio and Ireland for a new adventure in London taking up a new video-led position at one of the world's biggest news and entertainment websites and I cannot wait. I feel as though my entire career has led to this moment and I am so ready for it. Moving to London is also a strategic move for the growth and heath of my YouTube career.

My proudest moment is the time and effort I put into helping those young kids who find some sort of hope or safe place in my videos, kids who are in same position I was in years ago. I mail them back and forth privately, mention them in videos and continue to make content they enjoy. Being that digital big brother for them is the biggest achievement and happiness for me to date.

As a YouTuber I can do what I want. I don't have to pitch an idea; I don't have to curtail my swearing, my on-camera drinking, my on-camera campness or anything for that matter. Being a YouTuber allows me to travel, to make friends all over the planet and it gives me a voice. Being a YouTuber has increased my anxieties but has also increased my love for life and my passion for the things I already loved. Being a YouTuber applies no limits or boundaries on the dreams and experiences I want to achieve. I want to act, make music, make documentaries, give a TED talk, invent something and leave a legacy. I plan to do all of these things via this wonderful website.

Riyadh's Tips to YouTube Success:

Make a few videos and just watch them yourself in private.

Don't upload them, just get used to watching yourself on screen, to the sound of your own voice and how you move. Don't change a thing about yourself; just do this to become comfortable in your own skin. Once you feel a little more confident begin uploading.

Never upload a video without first asking

If I didn't know me, would I watch this?' If the answer is 'No' then film something else.

Be consistent,

Be regular and make content you care about, talk about what you know and be unapologetically you!

Money is made via these means:

Ad Sense

Google own YouTube and thus give us the ability to place ads over our videos or in banners. Every time a user clicks through to one of these ads that are placed by Google, we get a cut and they get a cut. It's about a sixty/forty share and is paid once a month.

Sponsored videos

A brand may ask you to promote their product in a creative way in one of your videos. For me, I will only do this if I truly love the product in question and can think of an entertaining or informative way to get it into the video.

Merchandise

As your fan base builds, they will begin to ask for branded cups, shirts, posters and wristbands. These are usually sold online or at conventions.

Event appearances/Panels

Being a speaker or specials guest can be a good way to pay the rent! This is especially good if you have an area of expertise that you can bring to said event such as sex talk, cooking skills, LGBT rights and so on.

Books/Tours/Gigs

Pretty self-explanatory.

Melanie Murphy

Irish-lass Melanie Murphy is a YouTube favourite. Her channel focusing on lifestyle and beauty has teenagers all around the world logging on and clicking subscribe. Her fresh look, relatable character and joie de vivre make her stand out from the crowd.

The first thing I ever searched for on YouTube, besides a music video or a funny cat clip, was a video about weight loss. I was very overweight and in a bad place with my health and I hoped some people may have shared tips.

To my surprise, I discovered an entire community. I had contemplated starting YouTube for years but I was terrified of putting myself out there.

Uploading footage to YouTube, you're opening yourself up to judgment. I wanted to get to a good place mentally before I posted anything, that way, any negative comments wouldn't bother me so much. I started because I felt that I had a lot to share, I wanted a new hobby and wanted to make new friends and build confidence in myself.

I started getting subscribers fairly quickly; it just took a couple of videos to take off and a few shout outs from other YouTubers. I feel like, with YouTube, if you're doing something a bit different and have a standout personality, you're going to get noticed and rise above all the noise very fast. I put in a lot of effort into my video quality and editing, and tons of time into generating traffic to my channel. I share the video everywhere, network with other content creators for hours per day and I'm forever reading up about the algorithm. Two years in and I'm constantly learning and adapting.

I'd describe my channel as a lifestyle, personality-driven channel. I cover topics ranging from beauty to body image and health; I do hobbies and hauls, collaborations, whatever I'm feeling!

To stand out the only advice that helps is to simply be you. If you are yourself, it's going to be original. Nobody else has your exact humour, your anecdotes and your life experience; share that and get that across.

My most viewed video is about acne and how I like to cover it up to boost my confidence. I filmed it when I only had two hundred subscribers, on a super cheap camera, and I hated it – I almost didn't upload it. Now it already has over fifteen million views! I'm so proud of it, it has helped so many people to feel more comfortable in the skin they're in.

Like my acne video, my videos have gradually and consistently gained views. They're what YouTube refers to as 'evergreen content;' content that is always relevant. Going viral can happen by chance and it usually means getting millions of hits in a small space of time. I don't think viral should ever be anyone's aim as it's so fleeting, but it definitely does help to give a boost at the beginning. Building followers that'll stick around, that's the hard part and that's what takes time!

I realised that my channel was worth working hard on when lots of overwhelmingly positive, supportive messages from viewers started to roll in. I felt like I needed to keep it up, for each and every person who was subscribing to me, and for myself, because it was making me feel happy; the fact that it made me feel like I had a purpose was reason enough to continue, regardless of the numbers.

In saying that, I've been trolled pretty badly by another Irish YouTuber under anonymous accounts and the case ended up with the Irish police. That experience has taught me to never feed the trolls.

Acknowledging the behaviour is the worst possible thing I could ever do. I just ignore it now, I don't let it bother me and I feel so sorry for the people who do it. They're insecure and unhappy; otherwise they wouldn't bother.

The best thing about being a YouTuber is the amazing friendships you form with other YouTubers. They're the only people who get what it is like, you have a shared passion with them and there are so many wonderful, exciting events that you can all attend together. It's like being part of a secret, special club or something!

I feel like teens connect so much more to YouTubers because we interact with them, we're just regular people like them except we have cameras in our bedrooms. It's accessible, it's relatable, and it's virtual friendship.

It's always accessible, so videos can be watched again and again, and videos are easy enough to produce so some YouTubers will have multiple new videos per week. It's always up-to-date, and of course they can follow along on social media too. There is someone for everyone on YouTube, we can all find others there that look and act in a similar way to ourselves. It's nice to be able to essentially 'see yourself' represented in the media, in a way. And it can be so niche, from guys playing video games to girls showing what clothing they bought for autumn.

It takes a lot of work to get anywhere but once you do, YouTube really opens up a huge amount of doors. I've taken part in TV documentaries. I've hosted a chat show in L.A., set to air on-line. I've partnered with some of the biggest brands and charities in the world for work on different campaigns. I've presented for TV. I'm in talks with several publishing companies about writing a non-fiction book full of advice. I've interviewed superstars and I've become friends with some of the biggest YouTubers in the world and they've all been so lovely to me. I work with Google frequently doing talks and whatnot, I get to speak on panels at YouTube events and every week there are tons of interviews for radio and magazines.

Every day, I wake up and pinch myself! It means so much to me to get involved in some of the campaigns I've been working on. I really feel like with a platform like YouTube, we can do anything that we want. It enables you to skip over the regular barriers of entry into mainstream media and it is now a standalone form of media that is just as, if not more, relevant, particularly to young people.

To anyone wanting to start making YouTube videos, I'd advise them to do it because they love it and not because they want it to become a career. The passion needs to be there, if the passion is there, the money will come. Do what you love, be yourself and educate yourself about social media and all the technical stuff, and never give up. No matter how stressful it is, no matter how much hate you may receive, stick with it. It's so worth it.

I'm so scatterbrained; I'm one of those people who wants to have it all. I want to try everything! I feel like I might as well as I get one life. I'd absolutely like to write and publish; another lifelong dream is acting. I want to keep creating online content and being involved in video production, and I want to do as much as I can to raise awareness about the issues I care most about. I also want to set up some social enterprises. When you believe in yourself and work hard, there's nothing you can't do!

Clisare

Irish Youtube sensation, Clare 'Clisare' Cullen found instant Internet fame when her video 'Shite Irish Girls Say' went viral almost immediately. Steadily growing her channel over the last few years, her passion is what drives her to continue uploading sketches that make her viewers both chuckle and giggle.

The first YouTube video that caught my attention and made me realise that there was more to the site than just music videos, was one by Jenna Marbles called 'How To Trick People Into Thinking You're Really Good Looking'. Not only was it accurate and funny, but she was a girl and she was brilliant and the more of her videos I watched, the more I wanted to follow in her footsteps.

It was so refreshing and exciting to see a girl speaking her mind, saying what she wanted and making people laugh – I hadn't seen that before.

The idea of starting my own channel came to me after a short period of unemployment where I was watching YouTube videos every single day. I was so engaged with these Youtubers and their lives; I wanted to make videos for myself.

So, one weekend, when all my employed friends were off at music festival Oxegen, I made a response video to one of Jenna Marbles' videos and I called it 'What I Would Have Done At Oxegen'. Around fifty people watched it and it felt scary but thrilling! At first I was worried about friends and family seeing my videos but eventually I had to make my peace with it so I could really get stuck in. My loved ones thought I was a little mad at first but they warmed to it very quickly and are now so keen to help me film and come up with ideas. At this point they've all featured in some way or another.

I caught the bug after that first video. I started gaining an audience very quickly and I got a huge buzz out of it. It helped that one of my very early videos went viral and the channel kept growing from there. To this day, 'Shite Irish Girls Say' is my most viewed video, followed by 'How To Curse In Irish'. The idea came to me from the meme 'Shit Girls Say' and was a result of good timing and a bit of luck. The reaction was amazing and it was shared all over the world.

Going viral was so incredibly exciting – I was getting emails and calls from TV and radio shows all around the world and I was featured in all the Irish papers that week. It was the most amazing feeling. I still get 'indicators' shouted at me on the street, four years later.

It's not all about going viral though. YouTube have changed their algorithm to favour 'watch time' so now I focus on getting people to watch more of my videos and for longer. Mind you, I wouldn't say no to another viral!

I think my channel is quite unique. First and foremost, I'm Irish and that's part of what makes me different from the hundreds of thousands of American YouTubers. I have a travel series called *The Irish Bucket List*, where I travel around Ireland doing all of the cool things there is to do. No one else has anything like it. I feel I bring a new perspective, I show my viewers something they haven't seen before – like having tea in Father Ted's house or wrestling an alligator in Kilkenny!

YouTube's popularity continues to soar. It's instant, and it's under the user's control. There's no schedule and you have total freedom. It gives you an insight into other people's lives and allows you to feel more normal, make new friends and fall in love. It helps that our attention span is getting shorter and shorter and YouTube videos are minutes rather than hours. Making friends with strangers is one of the most charming things about it. Some of the nicest and most supportive people I know, I only know online.

People can't believe how much work goes into a single video. On my channel, I create sketches where I play all the characters and those take a lot of writing, shooting and editing. My travel series takes up all my spare time and eats my diesel!

With anything you put up on social media, you have to be aware of trolls. I like to take the negative comments and ask total strangers on the street to read them out to me. It turns negativity into great content, and allows me to remember the fun I had filming the video and not the horrible feeling of when I first read the comment.

I'm not often nervous uploading content because I always want people to like it. I tend to hang around the comments section for the first few hours of a new upload to gauge the reaction. The only video I was outright scared to upload was one discussing my mother's death – a rare departure from my lighthearted content but it was for an important campaign and I felt it was important to take part. The reaction to that video was so heartening; it helped me address my feelings of grief somewhat.

YouTube has allowed me to make a living and as a result of YouTube, I've been offered opportunities in areas I've always wanted to work. I was invited to audition for a number of TV shows that I have adored for years and while I might not have gotten the gigs at the time, the fact that they knew who I was, is an achievement in itself. It has taken me to all sorts of wonderful places and I've taken on numerous challenges. Perhaps my proudest moment was raising over €1000 for the Irish Cancer Society by doing the Today FM Shave or Dye as part of my Irish Bucket List and filming the transformation. It was not that long after my mother died from cancer and it meant a lot to me.

I have many dreams outside of YouTube, but in terms of my channel? I have my eye on the silver play button and maybe even one day, the gold play button. I would love to work in TV and not have photographers at events ask, 'No, but what's your real name?'

For anyone hoping to start a channel, listen up! Don't go into it for the money; do it for the love. First and foremost, you need to build a community who love and trust you. If they don't want to follow you, then you have no attraction to brands, and if they don't trust you, then you can't promote or sell anything. Money needs to be a happy consequence of you doing what you love.

Be original. Be timely. Be you!

Alexandra Ryan

CEO of online celebrity-news website, Goss.ie and showbiz journalist Alexandra Ryan always dreamed about becoming a writer. The Limerick girl had her sights set on a career in journalism but little did she know that it would lead to a prestigious showbiz journalist of the year award that would change her career plans monumentally.

I've been writing ever since I can remember. It's always been my biggest dream. I started penning short stories when I was about five or six, writing my first mini-book when I was around seven. It was about a magical tree that granted wishes to children. I've come a long way since then. I was always a very creative and emotional person and I guess writing has always been an outlet for me. In fact, the first big Christmas present I got from my parents was a typewriter.

I was the most distracted child, doing a million things. One of them was going around interviewing people. That was an early sign that I was going to be a journalist one day. I had a little notebook that I always brought around with me and I'd spy on people, writing down what they were doing. I would interview my friends, my parents and my teachers.

One Christmas I got the Talk Girl from *Home Alone* and then I was actually recording what people were saying, I didn't know what to do with all the information but I kept doing it anyway.

My dad always thought I'd end up in music and acting as they were huge passions of mine but my mum always saw me as an author. I landed somewhere in the middle I think but I still love writing books and making music so who knows, I might end up living my childhood dreams after all. My first job ever was putting together a local farming magazine – and when I mean putting together, I mean literally stapling it together, putting it in its cover and mailing it off. I did that for twenty-five pounds a day, once a week and I loved it. There were many jobs along the way from bar work to sales and marketing and I was always studying in the meantime. By the time college came around, I was studying New Media and English.

In my second year of college, we had to do a work placement and I made it my mission to get an internship with the *Limerick Post*. I walked in the door on a soaking wet day, absolutely drenched head-to-toe and asked the editor to hire me for six months. He told me 'no' straight away, that they didn't have the resources or time to teach me. I told him that he didn't have to teach me but instead to give me one week to either sink or swim – I've always been a bit of a chancer!

I went in for a week and to cut a long story short, I swam! The *Limerick Post* was my first media job and there I did a bit of everything. There was no showbiz in that paper and a lot of what I wrote involved general news, political news, features and sport. I wrote some wedding features and even motoring pieces too. Towards the end of my time there, my main thing was one-on-one feature interviews. I interviewed a man whose parents had the longest marriage in Irish history. I interviewed him about his life and it might sound boring but it's one of the only interviews that still resonates with me today.

The same goes for an interview I did with a dying artist, I went to her house and we talked about her life and what she had achieved, I was wandering around her home looking through her paintings and she was so sick she could barely stand.

Human interest stories became my thing. It's what I loved and still love about journalism. You meet different people every day; you hear stories first hand that you would never hear if you worked a regular nine-to-five office job. Gaining people's trust and having them allow you into their lives as they share their story is magical.

I stayed at the *Limerick Post* for eight months. Once my time there was over I started working for SPIN Southwest radio as a news-reader and a broadcast assistant. I got that job simply by sending in a CV. Having the *Limerick Post* on my CV definitely helped but you needed a good on-air presence too. With my acting background, I always felt at ease talking on air or being on stage or interviewing people in public, so I passed that test pretty easily.

News reading for a radio station is interesting because you have to really understand all aspects of news, international as well as local. It was the showbiz roundup at the end of each bulletin that made me happiest and that's when I really realised showbusiness is where I wanted to be. It's around the time of Spin that I started my very first blog called 'Miss Red', focusing on celebrity news and interviews. You could say that was the start of the rest of my career.

The Herald was my first big media job in the industry. I was about to start my exams in the University of Limerick when I decided to email a few different newspaper editors with a link to 'Miss Red'. I didn't know if anything would come of it but at the very least, I wanted to get myself known and get my foot in the door. I had been living in Limerick for ten years and I knew nobody in Dublin.

One of the first replies I got back was from an editor in the *Evening Herald* asking me to come down and meet them. I arrived a week later but the editor I had originally spoken to wasn't there.

Nobody knew what to do with me. I was sat down at a desk and was told to, 'Come up with a story.' I had no idea what they meant or what they wanted but I wrote a story as instructed and emailed it to the powers that be. Half an hour later, the head editor showed me the story on an A5 sheet. He sat beside me and said, 'That's going to be on page three tomorrow. When can you start?'

My college exams were literally three days away but I said I could start straight away. If it meant driving to Limerick to do an exam and coming in to the *Herald* after wards, that was fine. I wasn't going to let the opportunity slip by me.

I was in the *Herald* about two or three months when the girl who ran the 'Dubliner's Diary' left to move to Australia. The editors were interviewing loads of different people but they hadn't found the right person to take over. They asked me to do one diary shift as a sort of trial and a week later I was writing for the diary. That changed everything for me. It was a very difficult role to take on and anyone who knows the Irish newspaper industry will tell you that once you have written for the diary in the *Herald*, you can work anywhere. I was constantly going to events and parties, staying out late, trying to get the ultimate scoop and basically having no personal life at all. I loved doing it but it was stressful too, but then again, all jobs in this industry are.

I was in the *Herald* about a year to the day when I got a text from an editor in the *Irish Mail On Sunday* saying they had a job they thought I might be interested in. The *Mail On Sunday* was honestly my favourite Sunday paper, and I had always loved their Sunday showbiz diary.

A few weeks later I accepted the job of showbiz reporter. It was a secure position with a lot more control over my content and a focus on bigger and better stories, it was a new challenge for me. This time I got to pick and choose what events I wanted to go to. I also had a full week to complete a story – this meant much heavier stories involving lots of investigation and deep one-on-one interviews. I loved it. On top of that I wrote a lot of the showbiz diary. I contributed six-or-seven showbiz snippets from the week including who was going out with who, new modelling contracts, people spotted out and about and so on. Mind you, it wasn't all plain sailing, as the youngest person on the team, I definitely had to convince everyone I belonged there at such a young age – I was only twenty-two.

One of the biggest highlights from my time working in newspapers was winning showbiz journalist of the year at the NNI Awards. I got such a shock to hear that I was even nominated – I was by far the youngest person in the category. Paddy Power did odds on each category, and in mine I was the complete outsider. I remember sharing the Paddy Power link on my Facebook saying, 'Let's prove everyone wrong,' but only as a joke, I never thought in a million years that I would win.

On the day I was an absolute bag of nerves. I felt sick. I knew my family and friends were all waiting to hear the news. They announced the winner by speaking about why they chose the person they did, before announcing their name. It was only during the very last sentence that I thought maybe they were talking about me.

They said my name and it's all a blur after that. Apparently I walked up shaking my head, putting my head in my hands. I was in such shock. That day changed a lot of things for me, I had a lot more respect in the *Mail on Sunday* and it led me to editing the London showbiz diary for the UK *Mail* a few months later. It made me realise I needed a new set of goals and targets – that's where Goss.ie was born.

In the UK office, I managed a small team and got some great exclusives. Despite being in a different country, I was still well able to do the same job. Around that time I also met with the Mail On-line team in L.A. who were looking for new showbiz reporters, and I started to realise there were bigger and better opportunities out there.

The Mail Online is such a huge success and I started thinking about how there was nothing like it in Ireland, no celebrity site dedicated to Irish news.

Leaving the Mail On Sunday to set up Goss.ie was a huge risk, but it has paid off. I had been unhappy at the newspaper for a while. I wanted more responsibility and it wasn't coming my way.

I was twenty-four at this stage and I wanted to move on to the next thing. I was always climbing the ladder and I felt kind of stuck there. I had so many fears and more than once, I thought about packing the idea in and just staying in my cushy, well-paid job with an ironclad contract, but that would have been the easy option, wouldn't it?

Money was my main worry. I got so used to being paid very well and on the same date every month. I knew starting my own business would mean getting random bits of money here and there. My family was nervous for me too. They weren't sure if leaving my job was the best idea, but I couldn't even half-start Goss.ie while still being with the *Mail*. I wanted a brand new start. Once my decision was made, there was no going back. Setting my up my own business was risky. The only bit of business studying I have ever done was for my Leaving Cert and trust me, I realise now how mad that sounds. I've always said I value my working life over my education and I have worked with some great businesses and somegreat people and I learned a lot from them. I would love to do an MBA sometime but for now I think running a business day-to-day, managing people, accounts, sales, content and planning the future of the site is the best way to really educate myself.

I've thrown myself into the deep end and I really have learned so much since Goss started. I think when entrepreneurs come up with a great idea, they believe they already have all the answers and everything will work out but that's definitely not the case. If I could do it all over again, I would plan things more carefully, and taken a few more months before launching.

I started Goss with another journalist but he left six months in and that was a huge blow and very difficult to deal with, but it was also the best thing that could have happened in many ways.

I've had to take on all aspects of the business myself but that's taught me so much.

Now I'm up to date on web design, sales, content, management, taxes and accounting. I am involved in every single part of my business and not everyone can say that. One of the main things I've learned is that a business isn't a business without sales – which is hard for a publishing company. We write and give away all of our content to readers for free. We only make money from the ads surrounding our content. The days when we have no ads, we still have to provide our readers with content and that's hard. Our competitors sell magazines and newspapers and that revenue helps them run their websites.

I've learned how important it is to have good relationships in this industry; from celebrities, to PRs, to TV and radio stations. Goss.ie has received lots of support and our articles have been shared by important people. Every day, every week, every month for us at Goss is focused on driving more traffic to the site and creating more readers and bigger and better stories.

We recently launched a news wire service – making us the first showbiz newswire in the country, which has been bought by the Irish Examiner and Breakingnews.ie. The plan is to sell the newswire to more papers, sites and radio stations and that will be another stream of income for us. We also do an event now called Goss Meets LIVE where we interview three celebrities in a venue and film it live for GOSS TV, again another revenue stream.

Everything is online now. Whether that's reading a newspaper or magazine or buying a house, watching a movie, everyone is on their phone or tablet and online is definitely the future. Going online is easy enough if you have the right tools. There are so many sites and blogs now it's important to stand out and design is very important. If you create a good product and write content that people will read and share then you're more than likely going to have more readers than most magazines, and in some cases news-papers. At the moment, we have more readers than some of the daily newspapers, so that shows how much easier it can be, plus we have a lot less overheads. It's so easy to have a business idea or a plan to write a movie, a book, an album, but it's the people that take the risks that become the most successful. So many people have asked me for tips to get started or how to become a success but it all starts with taking chances, quitting your job, taking the leap and working your butt off everyday until it pays off.

At present I employ two full-time staff, two part-time and three freelancers. There are a lot of perks to this job so motivation is easy. We get invited to the best parties in town and we get lots of lovely gifts sent to the office. In saying that gifts don't pay the bills nor do they keep people happy in their job. Motivating my staff is very important to me. Sometimes I'll randomly buy everyone pizza or bring everyone out for lunch just to show my appreciation. I also let them know how much of a great job they are doing, that's very important. The news industry can be very tough and most editors rely on screaming and giving out as their method of motivation so I've always done the complete opposite and it's worked so far.

I say to everyone trying to get into the news business that you really have to understand news worthiness to be a success – knowing what photo is going to go viral or which feature will resonate with everyone so it will be shared over and over again or which celebrity people really have an interest in. That comes with time and luckily it's something I've had since I started out in this business. I won't lie. Competition motivates me too. Every time a news site or newspaper steals my content it's aggravating but it proves how much the industry needs Goss and values our content.

There have definitely been times where I have doubted myself and I've felt really under pressure – I think every entrepreneur has been there. It can be hard when you have no one to bounce ideas off or some one else to share the pressure with. Every month there are new challenges, new issues but I think it's how you deal with them and how you deal under pressure that makes you a successful entrepreneur. A lot of people reach those hard moments and just walk away, but if I wanted the easier life, the nicer option, I would have just stayed in my last job.

Little Lizard

Since setting up their Youtube channel, Little Lizard, twin brothers,
Scott and Ryan Fitzsimons, have been running a gaming empire from the
comfort of their own home. Amassing over two-million
subscribers and over one billion views in just over three years, the future
looks bright for the former game-design students from Dublin.

We first began clicking onto Youtube in 2010, around the time when we were enjoying playing games like *Call of Duty*. Back then, it was all just a hobby. Funnily enough, we can still specifically remember an incident when in the middle of an online *Call of Duty* game. Other players over the headset began to get excited because we all were in a game with a proper 'Youtuber'. We didn't really understand it at the start. We wondered why are these guys so excited about a 'Youtuber'? What did that even mean?

Of course we went online and searched Mr YouTube's name and there were loads of videos with millions of views – we were shocked. Getting in on the action, we decided to see what all of the fuss was about and watched a few videos. Needless to say, we quickly became hooked, much like everyone else. Some videos were for pure entertainment while some were helpful with tips and tricks to help you out in the game.

It's about that time we started to realise that these YouTube channels were a bit like TV shows, except a lot more personal. You could feel like you were a part of it because it was just a normal guy making videos and interacting with everyone who watched them, unlike celebrities who you know you're never going to meet or be able to talk to. These guys would answer questions in the YouTube comments section or on Twitter and it really made you feel like you were a part of it. That's one reason YouTube channels are so successful today. We did our research and we discovered that quite a few people were making a living out of gaming.

It took a few years before we decided to give it a go ourselves. When we signed up, we simply thought it would be a lot of fun seeing some interaction from other people. We never expected it to be anything more than a little hobby while we studied games design in college. In the back of our heads, we did think that if it did somehow take off and we were successful YouTubers, it would be a perfect platform for our gaming design. We could design and make games and then release them to our audience. Having a big following would be very beneficial in something like that and a lot of YouTubers have already done it. They have created games around their content and released it, instantly getting thousands of downloads from their fans. It's a games developer's dream to have instant success like that. That was always at the back of our minds but we never really expected it to go that far, we just enjoyed uploading and having a bit of fun along the way.

Our channel Little Lizard took almost a year of daily uploads just to get to ten thousand subscribers. Today we say 'just' ten thousand subscribers, but at the time it was huge for us, a massive milestone and we were delighted with it, as any aspiring YouTuber would be. After that we saw a huge climb in views and it really gave us confidence in what we were doing, so much so, that we decided to take a year off college and keep running with it. The channel was growing so fast; we didn't want to slow it down. It was around this time we started to get close to earning a full-time wage, meaning all of our time could go into YouTube and we could start to research a bit more and really get into it as a proper job.

The next milestone was one million subscribers. This had always been the dream – the gold plaque. We had seen some of the channels we used to watch hit this milestone and we used to be in awe, imagining having one million people subscribe just to watch you. That milestone came just a few weeks before our birthday.

We threw a one-million subscriber/birthday party to celebrate and invited other YouTubers we knew from all corners of the globe. YouTube allows you to meet a lot of great people and travel to a lot of cool places, all from playing some video games!

We tease our mam a lot these days about how she used to restrict our time playing video games when we were smaller, saying imagine where we would be now if she hadn't!

Our mam was always very supportive and that's one of the main reasons we are doing this today, not too many parents would be too happy with their sons dropping out of college to play games on the internet. She always trusted us and believed in us and in what we were doing; as clichéd as it sounds, we wouldn't be where we are without her.

To an outsider it might sound like child's play but we work really hard. Little Lizard usually uploads one-to-two videos every-day. It's changed a lot over time, we figured out a good balance. Our goal was for fans, who enjoy the videos, not to miss out because of too many videos were being uploaded. At the same time, we didn't want to put out too little content and have people waiting either. Through trial and error, we found that one to two videos a day for a channel like ours is perfect.A lot of people ask us why Minecraft. And the answer is simple. Minecraft is an open source game, meaning anyone can mod it, change it, and add something to it. We kept hearing the name Minecraft pop up when we had just started our college course and decided to check it out.

The game was in the very early stages then and nowhere near as big or sophisticated as it is now. Of course to check it out, we took to YouTube to see if anyone was playing it. We didn't bother looking up reviews. This sort of became the norm for a lot of games design students – just go to YouTube. We found a handful of people playing Minecraft and quickly became hooked on watching it. There was so much you could do in the game; it was like jumping into someone's imagination. Every single play-through was different, based off what the player was like and what interests they had. Some were really technical and would build futuristic cities, others were old fashioned and tried to re-create the 'Wild West'. It meant that no matter what, even if there were one hundred people doing the same thing on one hundred different channels, they were all different and unique and interesting in their own way. Everyone had their own take on the game and it was a lot of fun to watch.

In the beginning, we started recording ourselves doing a 'let's play' –in pretty bad quality as we didn't have any clue what we were doing on that side of things– and it slowly gained followers. People began giving their ideas in the comments and we would respond. It kept people coming back to check out if we had done what they suggested and in general to see how the world was progressing.

These days we're focused mainly on role-play. It takes on average of three-six hours per video between set up, scripting, editing to put up a video and it really does show in the views. In summer 2015, we went from twenty or thirty-million views a month to over one-hundred-million views a month. It was a crazy jump in such a short time. Of course it helped that kids were all off school, but it was mainly due to doing the role-play videos that numbers spiked. Role play appeals to an audience a little younger than when we started and they treat it like a TV show.

We have parents tell us sometimes that they ask their kids, 'Are you actually going to play Minecraft or just watch these guys all day?' – their response is that they just want to watch. Because our audience is young, we try wherever we can to provide some educational information in our content. For example, if we take a trip to the zoo in the game, we have info and facts on all the animals and little things like that.

Scripting storylines is fun. We try to get into the minds of our audience and think what would make us go 'wow' if we were children again? Some of our storylines are based on popular kid's movies too like *Frozen* or *SpongeBob*. It can be difficult sometimes to try and come up with new ideas everyday but usually a good brainstorming session can hammer out ten-plus ideas to run with.

From the start we always kept everything one hundred percent child friendly. We really wanted our characters to have their own personalities. We wanted our viewers to follow them and not us. That can be hard to balance when you get into doing live events but for the most part we keep the mystery there and our viewers fall in love with the characters we create rather than the ones we are ourselves. It makes it a bit more magical for the kids to see the characters in their own world rather than seeing us with a facecam in the corner of the screen.

The video-making process starts with coming up with an idea, once we have an idea we are happy with, it's onto the script. We tend to use a basic brief of what is going to happen, what characters will be involved, what maps to use etc. and then get any lines we need voiced by either friends or a few guys we have met along the way that are voice actors. Next up is the setup, which takes the longest. We have to find a map, mods that suit the script then build any parts we need. This can take a good two to three hours.

Next up, it's recording the video, taking any camera clips we need of swooping shots etc. The person who writes the script is usually the 'director' for the video and tells everyone what to do and what way it's going. We never script what we say; we let that come naturally.

After recording is done, usually an hour or two, it's on to the editing which takes maybe another hour. Then, while the video renders, thirty minutes, one of us will make a thumbnail, another thirty-ish minutes, and we're good to go.

The awesome thing is that YouTube is getting bigger and bigger every year and more and more companies are starting to take it seriously. Recently we have been approached to do movie promotions. One of our first promos was for *Kung Fu Panda 3*, where we started in the main village based off the movie and had to do some tasks for the pandas. At the end of the video, we had the movie trailer and a link to it.

Today there a thousands of people making a full-time wage from YouTube, ranging from all different types of videos. Some channels are all about vlogging, others about gaming, some are dedicated to beauty or showing off gadgets etc. How much you earn comes down to views; the more views you get, the more dollars you make. The average for gaming is three dollars per thousand views.

Gaming is one of if the highest ways to earn as it has the audience most advertisers are looking for – kids. Until recently, no one really knew if YouTubers made good money. There was always speculation but no one would clarify it. In recent times, YouTubers have begun flaunting their earnings and people have quickly realised that there is a lot of money to make from it. It's extremely difficult to get into YouTube now, purely because of the sheer number of people starting up channels.

The idea that you could make millions from your bedroom is attractive to a lot of people and that in turn makes it harder to actually do.

To say it's come naturally to us would be a lie. There were a lot of headaches along the way trying to learn how to do everything. There are no guidebooks that tell you how to use the programs, how best to set up your audio quality, what time to upload and how many videos to upload. We had to learn a lot along the way. Studying game design for a year did help but only minimal parts of that could actually be applied to YouTube.

We've been extremely lucky but we've also worked extremely hard to get where we are. Our proudest moment has been being able to support our family with this venture. We have our sister on board doing her own YouTube channel and its flying, she's doing really great. We've got our mam working with us full-time too, helping out with the business side of things and we've got a good few other friends doing YouTube too. It's great to see everyone doing well. Here at Little Lizard we employ about fifteen people, and have plenty of others contracted to do work here and there.

It has given us more motivation to make this work and not slack off because we employ people. It has helped us grow because we have a responsibility to these people. For them to keep their jobs we've got to make sure we're doing ours and that works well.

It's important to dream big. And that's exactly what we're doing. We're forever more expanding and growing and we're in the midst of building offices for everyone to work from. That's our next big step. From there, we have tons of ideas.

For anyone hoping to get into the exciting, mad world of YouTube, it's important to be original. Try to come up with an idea that thousands of others haven't done before you. Once you do that, then one of the most important things on YouTube is to stay consistent to your upload schedule. Also, make sure you enjoy whatever you are doing, because it can take a long time to start getting decent views and if you don't enjoy it you'll more than likely quit well before you hit the mark of making some revenue. Oh, and good luck . . . everyone needs a bit of luck on YouTube!

Cian Twomey

There are very few people who haven't seen at least one of Cian Twomey's hilarious skits. The Cork comedian and YouTuber found online success via video sketches based on him and his girlfriend Emily. Going viral and amassing over four-million followers, this young man has been enjoying his success and allowing his dreams to stretch beyond Facebook.

A lot of people ask me, 'Cian, can you make money with what you do?' And the answer is yes, absolutely; crazy amounts of money in fact. There are people that do what I do and are multi-millionaires. There is a YouTuber called PewDiePie who has a yearly salary of $7,400,000! Isn't that tasty? I'm not quite in his level yet, but I'm getting there.

Life online for me began to get a little bonkers when my girl-friend Emily came into my life. I had been making videos previous to her existence, mostly based around my mother Liz and my grandmother Emily. When girlfriend Emily suggested I made a video about her, I thought why not? And I'm glad I did. That one video spiralled into a series of clips that millions of people began to enjoy. My followers went from 190,000 in March, to one million in May and to three million in October and so on. You'd think I'd be used to it but I still find it pretty strange. I remember I had a very old YouTube channel and it took me two years to get 1,000 subscribers. I remember when I hit that goal; I cried with joy and hugged my mother. Looking back, it makes me laugh to think that I was hyperventilating over 1,000 subscribers, not knowing that four years on, I would be getting millions.

I should point out that the real Emily is a very nice and calm and an extremely happy woman. The character Emily is a bit more irrational and temperamental and goes out of her way to make Cian's life absolutely miserable. The videos have kind of turned into the chapters to a long and weird book of over emphasised events that I've actually experienced with Emily. When it comes to inspiration, it's the relationship itself that inspires me to create more videos. It's quite an advantage because normal day-to-day life provides video concepts for me every day!

It's kind of the luck of the draw when it comes to being popular online. It took me two years to get my page to where it is now. Being from Ireland, my advantage is that every Irish person can relate to me in some way. What I did was create small-fifteen-second Facebook videos that would relate to the majority of Ireland.

I remember I had a goal for myself, kind of a quality control method – if I uploaded a video and it didn't get one hundred likes in the first hour, I would delete it. My new method is, if I don't get a tousand likes in the first minute, I'm close to taking it down. These days, most of my videos get at least one hundred thousand likes and I plan to keep it that way!

My highest rated video to date is 'When you find out who A is in Pretty Little Liars'. The video currently has a total of 498,000 shares. 677,000 likes and 179,000,000 (one hundred and seventy-nine million) views.

It's a stupid amount of people to have watched one video but that's probably the best video I ever created because it was so current and trending at the time that pretty much every single person who watched *Pretty Little Liars* watched my video too.

I put a lot of work into my online world. I spend five to six hours a day, seven days a week on creating content for my Facebook page and YouTube channel, either scriptwriting, concept building, editing, uploading, monitoring and maintaining my social media sites. My Facebook videos are not tough at all. The hardest part about making them is thinking of concepts or finding a place where I can film and not being disturbed.

When it comes to making videos, I first brainstorm with concepts. I come up with five concepts and then narrow it down the one I think will do the best. Once I have the chosen idea, I then write out a detailed script, containing actions, dialogue, tone and characters. It's a lot easier to shoot the videos with a script; it prevents a lot of confusion. Once I have the script complete. It is time to film. Depending on the concept, the video can take between five and thirty minutes to shoot. I use an app that allows me to edit as I film so in reality, there's no actual editing involved. The closest I get to editing is if I want to tweak a few parts and tidy them up or if I want to add voiceovers into the videos to try and make it even more convincing that my characters are in fact different people entirely. I make between three and six Facebook videos a week.

When it comes to YouTube videos, that's a whole different ball game – thinking of concepts and writing scripts are the exact same method as the Facebook videos but when it comes to filming and editing, there's a lot more work involved.

YouTube needs a lot higher in production value and quality. When I make a YouTube video I use professional lighting, sound and cameras. Basically the higher the quality is of your content. Both visual, audio and dialogue itself; the better chance you have of getting your name out there.

It's a lot more competitive on YouTube because there are actually tens of thousands of creators posting each and every day to the site. The best way to make yourself different from the other creators depends entirely on your attitude towards the people who comment on your content. That alone can define whether you are meant to be creating content or not.

Most people find it ridiculously difficult to ignore hateful comments said to them, resulting in breakdowns and even career retirement! I on the other hand couldn't care less what is being said to me in a negative way and to be honest I think that I'm extremely lucky to be able to brush off hate with such ease. Not many can. I think of it this way, if someone is sad and low enough to take the time out of their day to deliberately post negative and pessimistic comments on your content, then why would you let yourself get upset over it?

The people who do it are bullies, and just like in real life, bullies are sad and frustrated people who sadly feel unhappy within themselves in some shape or form and have to release anger through a form of posting abuse online.

I get over trolls in a very simple way. Firstly, I don't look for negative comments. I focus on the positive comments and if I come across a negative comment, I ban the user from my page preventing them from ever commenting again! I realise that in the long run, I'll have the last laugh. Because I'm doing something pretty cool with my life, so why let them stop me? Do what you love and don't let anyone ever being you down.

Being original plays a huge role in creating content. Nobody wants to follow or subscribe to someone who just recycles someone else's material. It's plagiarism and that's not cool. Not many people really have dedicated series that show a crazy relationship between a boy and a girl played by the same person. The funny thing is, I now see a lot of people imitating my content trying to pass it off as their own! But hey, imitation is the best form of flattery right?

The easiest and most effective way to gain followers is to remain relatable, non-controversial, funny and consistent. That is my little recipe to a viral video.

For me, the freedom of speech and being able to do and create whatever you please is without a doubt the greatest part about being an online content creator. Making something visual which was transferred from your brains onto a video and have it watched by literally millions of people is without a doubt one of the most satisfying things ever!

There are so many opportunities that have come from these online videos. I've met some of the most well-known and coolest people ever. I've been offered TV shows and offered to go on TV shows and so on but I turned them down because long story short I don't like how TV shows are run. I also get to travel a lot which is really fun, one minute I can be in Dublin, then in London. The next in L.A., then straight from L.A. to Sydney, then back home to Cork to hug my mother and tell her not to worry!

The proudest moment I've had so far has either been hitting one-million-followers or the moment I realised I'm the second most followed content creator on Facebook in Europe! That's a pretty cool achievement and I aim to be number one this time next year! I have hit milestones I never once thought I could achieve and it's all happening so fast so I'm not exactly fully adjusted to the whole situation just yet!

For now, I'm just going to concentrate on my online career, and let life take its path. If I was born to do it, it'll happen eventually! Patience is the virtue.

Remember, for anyone hoping to make an income online, a big following is a must

When you have a big following you will have both positive and negative people in that following.

The first thing you will have to do is just accept that it will happen, no matter what you do it will happen.

It's just life I'm afraid, but if you're able to overcome it, you have the battle almost won already!

The second thing you need to do is do something no one else is doing.

You need your own niche to succeed and you need to grab people's attention. Make them want to come back for more. Strategise your content and think to yourself , 'What do people want to watch?' Think of what's current. For example, say I'm writing this in December, what's in December? Christmas. So I'm naturally going to make videos about Christmas because so many people are talking about it already. Just be you, enjoy what you're doing and if you enjoy what you do. In time, the money will come around. It won't happen overnight. But patience is the virtue.

'I began to realise how important
it was to be an enthusiast in life.
If you are interested in something,
no matter what it is, go at it full speed.
Embrace it with both arms,
hug it, love it and above all become
passionate about it.
Lukewarm is not good.'

-Roald Dahl

Acknowledgements

This book would never have been written without the help and support of a rather large bunch of special people. To my unbelievably supportive family, from the bottom of my heart, thank you for everything. To my Dad for chauffeuring me to various interviews, meetings, and airports, Mam for instilling confidence and showering me with encouragement, Daniel for putting up with my constant line of questioning of 'What sounds better?' and for his wicked eastern european infused sense of humour.

To my brilliant friends for always reminding me that no mountain is too high to climb, for holding my hand and being there for me, for making me laugh and being incredible, even from across the Irish Sea.

To Steve for being my best friend, thank you for always making me smile, patlajica.

To my team at Liberties Press for taking a chance on me and believing in me, I'll never be truly able to express how much this means to me – thank you. To my incredible contributors who have made compiling this book such an interesting, satisfying, fulfilling and inspiring experience. I am forevermore grateful for your time, patience and passion. You are all immensely talented, beautiful souls with golden hearts.

Thank you to Derek Landy, Will Sliney, Paige Toon, Cecelia Ahern, Ryan Tubridy, Laura Whitmore, Martin Dougan, Eoghan McDermott, Miriam O'Callaghan, Darren Kennedy, Steve Garrigan, Emin, Ruthann Cunningham, Markus Feehily, Philip Magee, Hozier, Rory McIlroy, Padraic Moyles, Stephanie Roche, Rob Kearney, Al Mennie, Don O'Neill, Joan Bergin, Paul Costelloe, Chupi, Blanaid Hennessy, Louise McSharry, Rick O'Shea, Arian Kennedy, Tracy Clifford, Neil Corbould, Barry Navidi, Ian O'Reilly, Chris Newman, Evanna Lynch, Andreas Petrides, Melanie Murphy, Clare Cullen, Riyadh Khalaf, Alexandra Ryan,

Cian Twomey , Ryan and Scott Fitzsimons, Tony DiTerlizzi, Michael Doherty, Danny O'Donoghue and Johnny McDaid.

Thank you also to Sarah Webb who has been a huge support throughout the years. To Joanne Byrne and Andrew Thompson and the endless agents, managers and producers who despite being pestered non-stop loyally coordinated interviews with me.

And finally to my Grandparents for blindly believing in me from day one, I hope you're smiling down, beaming with pride.

The End.

Photo Credits